AN INTRODUCTION
SUSTAINABILITY AND AESTHETICS

AN INTRODUCTION TO SUSTAINABILITY AND AESTHETICS
THE ARTS AND DESIGN FOR THE ENVIRONMENT

Edited by

Christopher Crouch, Nicola Kaye, & John Crouch

BrownWalker Press
Boca Raton

An Introduction to Sustainability and Aesthetics:
The Arts and Design for the Environment

BrownWalker Press
Boca Raton, Florida
USA • 2015

ISBN-10: 1-62734-525-6
ISBN-13: 978-1-62734-525-5

www.brownwalker.com

Cover photo: Thungsarnphoto

Publisher's Cataloging-in-Publication Data

An introduction to sustainability and aesthetics : the arts and design for the environment / [edited by] Christopher Crouch, Nicola Kaye, [and] John Crouch.
    pages cm
    Includes bibliographical references.
    ISBN: 978-1-62734-525-5 (pbk.)
    1. Sustainable design. 2. Aesthetics. 3. Art—Environmental aspects. 4. Architecture—Environmental aspects.   I. Crouch, Christopher, ed. II. Kaye, Nicola, ed. III. Crouch, John, ed. IV. Title.
    TH4860 .I58 2015
    720`.47—dc23

                                                    2014960357

ACKNOWLEDGEMENTS

Thanks to Dr Julian Goddard, Head of the School of Design and Art at Curtin University for his vision and generosity of spirit in facilitating the original symposium from which this book emerged, and to Dr Brad Pettit, the enlightened Mayor of Fremantle, whose support for the symposium was essential in making it happen. I owe a debt of gratitude to Dr Nicola Kaye and John Crouch for their invaluable help in putting the manuscript together.

CONTENTS

INTRODUCTION
Culture, Nature and Praxis.. 9
Christopher Crouch

PART ONE. ART, PHILOSOPHY ART AND LITERATURE

1. Complexity as Experience: The Contribution of Aesthetics to Cultures of Sustainability............. 25
   Sacha Kagan

2. Beauty: A Powerful Force for Sustainability and Regeneration... 33
   Maria Elena Zingoni de Baro

3. Imagine: Visions for our Sustainable Future:
   A Case Study of the Creative Expression of Sustainability Visions...................................... 41
   Susie Waller

4. Artistic Practices and Ecoaesthetics in Post-sustainable Worlds....................................... 55
   Perdita Phillips

5. Elizabeth Jolley, Friedrich von Schlegel and a Garland of Fragments:
   Creative Process as a Re-enchantment of Nature... 69
   Andrea Wood

6. Reconceptualising the Hand Made Object... 81
   Jane Donlin

7. Toward a Negative Aesthetic of Sustainability in Tim Winton's Dirt Music.............................. 91
   Erin Corderoy & Michaela Baker

PART TWO. DESIGN AND THE ENVIRONMENT

8. The Aesthetics of Sustainable Well-Being... 103
   Huilin Sun

9. Natural Dynamics... 115
   John Stanislav Sadar & Gyungju Chyon

10. Picture for Illustration Purposes Only... 127
    Chrissie Smith

11. Graphic Design and Sustainability.. 133
    Johanna Niessner

12. The Importance of Aesthetics in Sustainable Interior Design for Retail Spaces 141
Eko Pam

13. The 'House of the Future' and the Toyota Prius (MkII): Perspectives on Sustainability 147
Henry Skates & Peter Wood

14. Sustainable Fashion: From Organic Form to Digitally Manmade Pattern 155
Fanke Peng & Peter Hill

15. The Ordinary as a Precedent for Sustainability in Architecture 163
Martina Novakova & Tony Lam

16. Applying Transect Method as a Catalyst to Make a Sustainable Urban Landscape 169
Maryam Izadi

17. Culture and Nature: The Language of Symbols and Nature in the
Oeuvre of the Contemporary Polish Architect, Marek Budzyński 175
Julia Sowińska-Heim

18. The Aesthetic and Sustainable Architectural Principles of Yazd 187
Hoda Shahmohammadian & Samaneh Soltanzadeh

19. Reading for Sustainability through Botanical Aesthetics:
Embodied Perceptions of Perth's Flora, 1829 to 1929 193
John Charles Ryan

20. Identifying an Aesthetic Dimension of Sustainability in the Bangladeshi Context 203
Amzad Hossain & Dora Marinova

AFTERWORD 211
John Thackara

INDEX 215

INTRODUCTION

CULTURE, NATURE AND PRAXIS

Christopher Crouch

This book grew out of a symposium on the aesthetics of sustainability organised by the School of Design and Art at Curtin University in Perth, Australia. The symposium itself developed from a series of collegial conversations after a serendipitous encounter I had while out walking. On the pavement I had seen an object, radiating colour, that wasn't immediately recognisable. There was no subsequent revelation reminiscent of William Blake for what I had found was an abandoned sticker of two pink dolphins jumping over a rainbow in a sky filled with fluffy, pale blue clouds. It lay at the foot of a lamp post, attached to which was a handmade sign advertising artificial grass and mulched car tyres (as a water saving, weed suppressing, gardening solution). It occurred to me, somewhat obviously (but that is the mundane nature of contemporary visions) that both were texts that addressed a common subject, a pleasure in and a managing of, the environment. One was embedded in a discourse of happy oceans, the other in the virtuous quest to save water in a water starved continent. Within the respective demographics for the consumption of these signs - the high school student and the local gardener – they could be read as positive and progressive. Addressed from a broader urban perspective of seemingly unending hot weather though, both were riddled with disturbing contradictions; a scrambled, fictional ocean ecology was matched with the horror of a garden stinking of recycled rubber debris at the height of summer. Both had an aesthetic dimension, no matter how tawdry, and aspirations of an ethical duty of care, no matter how tangential, could be ascribed to both. They revealed in their rhetoric the chaos in the relationship between creating and expressing happiness in the material world. These seemingly insignificant traces of a globally polluting, carbon based economy manifested a desire for order and joy. How could these aspirations for stability and beauty be framed within the bigger context of an island continent severely impacted upon by climate change?

Our collegial conversations built over a few weeks, and began to settle into a set of questions that asked whether in this time of environmental crisis there were a coherent set of aesthetic signs and dialogues to match the current scientific discourse. Could the aesthetic offer a way of analysing an ecosystem in crisis (1) where the aesthetic subsequently becomes an active agent in remodeling it? If so, what might the dialogue between the aesthetic and sustainability be like and how might it be constituted? Inherent in these questions was the idea of the aesthetic being more than just a personal response to beauty and becoming a dynamo of social change.

The chapters that follow in this book address the issue of sustainability and aesthetics framed through policy and practice, and from institutional and personal perspectives. It would be foolish to pretend that the world and our grasp of it is anything other than fluid, transitional and liminal. Thus the tenor of the book is transdisciplinary and culturally diverse, its intention is to act as an introduction to the subject and to report back on what is happening through a variety of authorial and theoretical lenses. It is inevitable that where authors seem to provide 'solutions' they will often contradicted in other chapters. This contestation is healthy and should be embraced, for as Vandana Shiva (1997) has observed, cultural and biological diversity are intimately related. Before outlining the structure of the book and its contents at the end of this chapter, I wish to establish the broader contexts in which the book's debates about sustainability and the aesthetic are embedded.

Framing cultural relationships

Sustainable aesthetics relate to the designed world and the world of the imagination as well as the environment. In thinking about the role of the aesthetic in a quest for sustainability it is necessary to embrace the dynamic relationship between nature and culture. In modelling some examples of aestheticising (the making of and philosophising about, sensory and critical judgements on art and nature) that will be explored in more detail later, I want to examine the idea that whilst there are shared physiological responses to the world, the way in which those responses are organised and understood are social and therefore mutable.

Perhaps the best way to conceive of the formation and maintenance of an aesthetic system is to borrow and adapt from Bourdieu's habitus/field model (Bourdieu, 1977). In this sociological model the individual habitus is bound up in lived and embodied experiences. Intensely personal, the formation of habitus (in the case of our discussion, the formation of an aesthetic sensibility) is framed through activity in the wider field of (aesthetic) practice and the individual's relationship with that activity. Sometimes the individual benefits from that engagement, sometimes the individual is persuaded by the practices in the field that adopting its values are beneficial to the individual despite evidence to the contrary. This is what Bourdieu calls misrecognition (1992, pp. 167 -168). If we return to the ecstatic pink dolphin sticker it is possible to model it as an example of misrecognition in the negotiation between habitus and field and to reflect on how misrecognition at an aesthetic level has profound implications beyond the aesthetic experience. The sticker's role as an object emerging from the field of mass production is to act as a signifier for an engagement with nature, both for the consumer of the sticker and to the consumer's peer group. Within the habitus of the consumer the sticker is beautiful and demonstrates, at least, an affiliation with oceans, rainbows, the sky, dolphins and pinkness. Within the field of mass production the sticker's aesthetic role is to secure monetary exchange in favour of the producer in an act of purchase. The sticker is akin to the fly fisherman's crafted lure, a (destructive) fiction created for the benefit of the fisherman rather than the fish, in which the fish is enthusiastically complicit. The uneven relationship with the natural world that is mediated by practices within consumer culture has huge implications for the formation and application of aesthetic systems, and for an aesthetic of sustainability particularly.

It could be argued that there is no single unified field of (aesthetic) practice, rather a multitude of practices existing in parallel and overlapping. This explains how multiple, sometimes contradictory, value systems can co-exist, even within an individual's habitus. Other ways in which the negotiations between culture and nature can be characterised are by framing them through Jürgen Habermas' idea of the individual's 'lifeworld' being colonised by external social systems (McAfee, 2000, p. 26) or Antonio Gramsci's notion of hegemony (Crehan, 2002, pp. 199-200). No matter what philosophical or theoretical lens one uses to describe the process, at the heart of the conversation between humankind and nature lies the fundamental issue that objective conditions are subjectively *interpreted*, and this subjective framing create values that are contingent upon the dominant discourse in the field.

This is not to deny the importance of our shared physiological responses to the natural world and the way in which we understand it through embodied experiences (2). Certain temperatures, sound and light can provoke common pleasurable or unpleasant physical and emotional responses to them but as Lakoff and Johnson (1980) proposed thirty years ago (and reaffirmed through research since (Tay, 2013, pp. 18-20; Becker, 1997) embodied knowledge is expressed through metaphor, and metaphor is culture at work (Kövecses, 2005). Consequently whilst we all share embodied experiences, our understanding and expression of them is framed by cultural circumstances, and it follows that our perception of the physical reality of the natural world can have different meanings depending on the cultural framework through which it was approached or understood. Looking at the debates around the custodianship of the Australian Great Barrier Reef can help illustrate this point. The reef is a coral growth of enormous proportions in the ocean off the east coast of Australia (Hutchings, Kingsford &

Hoegh-Guldberg, 2008). It is currently under threat of destruction caused principally by rising global temperatures and poor management (Caldicott & Halter, 2014) and is the subject of a number of overlapping fields of practice. For the purposes of this argument the fields of practice are the governmental, the aesthetic, and the economic. It is possible to trace the change in discourse within these fields that allowed the reef to abruptly transition from an Australian national treasure to an impediment to coal mining.

In 2013 the Great Barrier Reef was the focus of a governmental analysis to acknowledge and assess its aesthetic value. At this time within the field of governmental custodianship it was constructed as a community asset, and in the report was ascribed with the experiential attributes of having "a sense of beauty", "a sense of naturalness" and "a sense of remoteness" all of which contributed to its "exceptional natural beauty … associated with contrasting colours and forms of green islands, coastlines, sweeping white sands, fringing reefs and patterns of blue waters" (Defining the aesthetic value of the Great Barrier Reef, 2013). In 2014, a change of government and a change in practices re-framed the reef, not aesthetically but economically (Redfearn, 2014). In the fresh interpretation, sustaining the reef's pristine environment would have meant the curtailing and hindering of the development of coastal mining. The reef's potential destruction as a result of coal mining could now be countenanced within the field of economic practices, the aesthetic values previously ascribed to it by one government easily discarded by another. What this demonstrates is that to assert that there is a shared, universal aesthetic appreciation of the world is to adopt a position that is at odds with the evidence of how aesthetic value is ascribed and acted upon (Lanz, 1947; Crowley, 1958; McManus & Furnham, 2006).

What is sustainability?

The aesthetic is one way in which the interpretation of nature takes place. What of nature's broader relationship with culture? How might the contemporary ecological crisis and the concept of sustainability be framed culturally?

Sustainability's colloquial meaning conveys a concern and interest in maintaining the stability of the environment, and it has become synonymous with what used to be known as environmentalism, though one does not have to do much reading to enter the world of ideological struggles over the use of the terms (Guha, 2000; Pepper, Revel & Webster, 2002). In the history of modernity, as finite natural resources disappeared (Konijnendijk, 2008), many viewed the impact upon nature by industrialisation with alarm. It is true that the new carbon fuelled economies exacerbated and speeded up the degradation of the natural environment, but it is overly simplistic to reduce this process down to a binary opposition between modernity and tradition. Over grazing by herd animals and deforestation by pre-industrial societies is well documented (Kaplan et al, 2009), as is the negative impact on the environment by those pre-industrial societies with a cultural attitude that constructed nature as boundless (Duguid, 2010). Nevertheless in the 19th century the sustainable management of land became synonymous with both a nostalgia for a halcyon rural past and the adoption of socially progressive ideals; fields of practice, as always, overlapping.

As the modern nation states industrialised, so each nation built its own history and strategy in managing the natural reserves within its boundaries. The conservation movement in 19th century Britain was a pragmatic one (Evans, 2002) sitting alongside, and sometimes engaging with, the more idealistic Arts and Crafts Movement. This movement provided a new set of critical discourses and visual signs about the natural and the vernacular, well represented by the artist Walter Crane in his woodcut celebrating May Day 1895, where an unfurling banner declares that 'The plough is a better backbone than the factory' (Figure 1).

Figure 1: *A garland for Mayday*. Walter Crane. 1895. (Private collection).

Before the full onslaught of Stalinist policies promoting heavy industry, the young industrialising USSR nevertheless reaffirmed the provision of *zapovedniki*, inviolable nature reserves (Josephson et al, 2013), and Lenin argued for a new relationship between town and country as the collapse of the consumer economy changed the nature of cities as places for recreational consumerism (Wells, 2005, p.190). On the other side of the world in Australia, Arthur Streeton working within a painterly tradition of romancing the pastoralisation of the national landscape (Hoorn, 2007), increasingly painted the bleak transformation of the landscape as forests disappeared. In 1940 he painted the desolate *Sylvan Dam in Donna Buang, AD 2000*, a vision of a lifeless and eroded Australia. Similar examples can be drawn from every society experiencing the circumstances of modernity.

The historical construction of an agricultural/industrial dialectic where an untainted agriculture was seen as in opposition to industry had always been a fiction, but it wasn't until after WWII that that it was fully acknowledged by governments that the condition of modernity implied the complete industrialisation of nature itself (Tsakok, 2011, pp. 15 − 35). This often reluctant acknowledgement by industry and government of scientific insights into the condition of the natural world slowly led to the establishment of a framework for conceptualising global sustainable development, and can be marked by a number of events. The 1962 publication of Rachel Carson's book *Silent spring* and its subsequent influence can be seen as a symbolic marker of the acknowledgment that the natural world had been frighteningly damaged, and it placed an idea that had previously been considered subversive into the mainstream (Lytle, 2007). As a result of the furore caused by the book's publication, within a decade most industrial states had environmental regulations of varying degrees of rigour in place. The United Nations Environment Programme was established in 1972 and global non-governmental organisations like the World Wide Fund for Nature (1961), Friends of the Earth (1969), and Greenpeace (1971) created an institutional environment in which the social antagonisms caused by the abuse of the natural world could be articulated and acted upon.

The term 'sustainable development' became institutionalised after the publication of the United Nations World Commission on Environment and Development's (UNCED) report *Our common future*, more commonly known as the Brundtland Report. The report was undertaken to examine the critical issue of environmental erosion caused by indiscriminate industrial and consumer development, with the intention of finding pragmatic ways of dealing with it. What emerged from the commission's deliberations was a formal acknowledgement that in a globalising economy there was a need to strengthen international cooperation to instigate new patterns of behaviour. The report called for a raising of consciousness about the interrelationship between economic growth and the environment at personal, government and non-government, local and international levels (Our common future, 1987, p. 247). The report proposed that development should be designed to meet the demands of the present without compromising the needs of future generations. This theme was picked up by the UNCED Rio Summit in 1992 where the need to protect the ecosystem was asserted in the *Rio declaration on environment and development*. Principle 1 asserts that "[h]uman beings are at the centre of concerns for sustainable development. They are entitled to a healthy and productive life in harmony with nature". This was further qualified by principle 22 that proposed that Indigenous people and their communities "have a vital role in environmental management and development because of their knowledge and traditional practices" (1992). This can be interpreted in two ways; one is positive, the other is more ambivalent.

Positively, there is an acknowledgement of a human/nature relationship that is harmonious and which is mutually beneficial. This is as much an aesthetic aspiration as it is a scientific observation. By implication principle 22 further suggests that there was a pre-industrial way of knowing the natural world, and this has hugely beneficial implications for understanding the world in different aesthetic ways. However, less reassuring is the continuing elision between the differences between sustainability on one hand and development on the other. Is it realistic to assume that development is a given, and can be reconciled with a sustainable natural world? At the heart of the notion of sustainable development is the unresolved relationship the globalising economy has with consumer culture.

The philosopher Arne Naess confronts this problem by proposing a radically different relationship with nature, where its usefulness to human culture – so central to sustainable development – is put to one side and the nonhuman world is celebrated for what it is (Naess, 1989, p. 164). This 'deep ecological' perspective involves a radical curtailment of human growth, and development is limited only to what is absolutely vital in order to sustain the functionality of human societies. The mutuality of this relationship is that a secure ecosystem is better able to support a fulfilling human life. The proposal that "the flourishing of human life and cultures is compatible with a substantial decrease of the human population" (Sessions & Naess, 1989) has political ramifications that would impact upon social and cultural acticity that are beyond this introduction, but the aesthetic implications of Naesse's position imply a profound immersion into the workings of nature itself and an experiential dialogue with natural structures. Thus, living becomes an endlessly reflexive aesthetic and ethical engagement with the natural world.

Still with one foot in a critical, humanist tradition, Serge Latouche argues for *décroissance*, translatable, somewhat inelegantly, as de-growth. Décroissance is not negative growth, but rather a concept of non-growth or a-growth in which it is possible to unfold a vision of a world that might emerge after post-development politics. In this world the population works less, consumes less and lives more fully in terms of emotional and intellectual experiences because of its dis-engagement with the ideological paradigms of consumer culture (2009, p. 9). Latouche frames an intellectual, political, cultural and social position between sustainable development on one hand and ecocentrism on the other and challenges the supposition that there is an imperative to choose between "ecocentrism and anthropocentrism, humanism and antispeciesism, absolute relativism and dogmatic universalism, and modernity and tradition" (2009, p. 98). For Latouche these binaries are diversionary, and there is a need to get "away from these old debates, which are interconnected and recurrent" because, in his opinion, they can never be resolved one way or the other (2009, p. 98). At the centre of Latouche's approach is an attempt, not to reconcile, but to expose and manage the conceptual and structural contradiction of "sustainable" development. The aesthetic dimension of Latouche's ideas of frugal abundance has yet to be mapped, but backing away from current models of economic production and the reduction of consumption must imply different ways of thinking about materials, things and travel as well as the nature of the world and how we experience it. Décroissance might also be thought of in relation to the slow movement that started as a reaction to industrialised food production in the 1980s (Osbaldiston, 2013) where it challenged the concept of instant gratification. The idea of slowing the pace of life down to allow reflection has now seeped into most aspects of cultural life including urban development (Newman & Jennings, pp. 195 – 199). The slow movement provides a set of new paradigms of cultural behaviours which have huge possibilities for an aesthetic of sustainability, such as *The clock of the long now*, a project for a clock that will keep time accurately for the next millennium (Brand, 1999).

In *Farewell to growth*, Latouche argues the difference between universalist ideology and the idea of universality, suggesting the former is a type of totalitarianism and the latter ripe for recasting as a kind of 'pluriversalism' (2009, p. 102). This allows for an aesthetic approach to the world that at once is both specifically rooted in a sense of place, and yet allows for other conceptions of what that might constitute. This then permits a productive cultural relativism and the slow erosion of the divide between nature and culture instigated by modernity. It further promotes a considered reflexive relationship to nature, which has changed continuously through history and will continue to change.

The nature of the world is to change, and yet no matter how often that truism is repeated from Heraclitus to Marx, it seems beyond our collective abilities to work pragmatically with that idea. The forest was once a feared place. Its edges were a liminal space between civilisation and chaos before the romantics turned the woodland glade into a space for contemplation. The sublime nature of the ocean, which was once represented by tales of its turbulent surface, is now better expressed by its depths. It follows that the Western, Christian, and Modern ways in which the natural world was understood, and which have a powerful legacy in the contemporary global economy, now have the potential to be replaced with approaches which are not about dominion and ownership and which open up a new ethical dimension in our relationship with the natural world and its ecosystem.

Unravelling the aesthetic

I have already suggested that the aesthetic is relational and contingent. I would qualify that by saying that it also has a potential to be shared and thus it has relevance, and (temporary) stability, to those that share it. What constitutes the nature of an aesthetic relationship between the individual and the object, and how that is articulated between individuals *about* the object has as many definitions as there are philosophers, and there are as many philosophers as there are competing value systems across and within the world's cultures. By briefly marking out some mainstream paradigms and theoretical models of the aesthetic it is possible to map out the dynamic relationship between the personal and social function of the aesthetic. The main intention is to suggest that the fluid nature of the aesthetic – by which is meant the shift in notions of what beauty is, and expectations of how it impacts upon us - facilitates an understanding of what an aesthetic of the sustainable might be and do.

In using the word *kalon*, Plato made no clear distinction between what might be considered beautiful and what might be considered admirable (Lear, 2012). This elision of meaning between sensuous pleasure and worthiness isn't just a linguistic curiosity, confusion between what we would now identify as two different sets of discourse, but an indicator that the ways in which we might think of beauty contemporaneously has a very particular cultural framing. In a contemporary colloquial Australian setting, and I would hazard a guess that it is the same in the whole Anglosphere, aesthetic pleasure is about self fulfillment framed mostly within a consumer culture. What Jameson described as the 'perpetual present' of late capitalism (Jameson, 2008) precludes a sense of either personal or historical consequences for personal action, for if one exists solely in the 'now' of consumption, the past and future are conceivable only in terms of things discarded and things to be desired. Although Debord's *Society of the spectacle* which was first published in 1967 is now a venerable text, his observation about the consumerist spectacle manifesting itself as positive, inevitable and untouchable so that "[e]verything that appears is good; whatever is good will appear", still sums up the seeming impossibility of critical reflexivity within the circulatory nature of capitalism (1994, para. 12). One powerful way this mindset can be short-circuited is by posing questions about the ethical viability of consumer capitalism. Implicit in the idea of kalon is the seed of principled engagement that sits within the notion of worthiness. We can draw from Plato the sense that beauty might need to have a purpose as well as give pleasure. This does not have to be oppressively didactic, just self actualising. It isn't difficult within the context of the current environmental chaos to imagine an aesthetic of sustainability that is emancipatory as well as pleasurable, and that there is pleasure to be gained in participating together in celebrating the healthy functioning of human society within a healthy ecosystem.

The modern European journey in unravelling what the aesthetic might be, started with Alexander Baumgarten's philosophical investigation into sensual cognition and the idea of 'thinking beautifully', but it is with the publication of Kant's *Critique of judgement* in 1790 that the aesthetic began to be applied to nature as well as to art, and the ability to judge something as beautiful or artistic becomes a subject of investigation. Allow me for the sake of argument to pluck just one Kantian notion about beauty from the interlocking network of his ideas (Guyer, 1996). For Kant beauty was diminished if it possessed what he called adherent rather than free beauty. So, he explains, a flower has a pure (free) beauty that is unconnected to purpose. As such it possesses an independent beauty that is different from a building's beauty whose impure (adherent) beauty is connected to its use. What is intriguing about this definition of beauty is threefold, and I wish to return to the brief modelling of the habitus/field relationship raised earlier. Firstly, this definition splits the ancient concept of kalon; worthiness, purpose or use has been differentiated from an autonomous, pure, sensuous way of knowing. This implies that differing fields of practice engage with beauty differently. Secondly, by suggesting that there are two ways of experiencing beauty, it refutes the unity of an aesthetic response; how can there be unity if beauty exists in a form that can then be changed through subsequent knowledge of the object? Thirdly, it follows that notions of beauty are not solely constructed in relation to the objects themselves but also to the judgements made about them. If there is a dynamic power relationship between habitus and field in which 'acting' and 'acting upon' is evident in the framing and development of ideas, then notions of beauty are also subject to dialogic and material change; it makes no difference whether these notions are about artifacts or nature itself.

The debates surrounding aesthetics post Kant in the West are multitudinous (Bowie, 1990; Jamme & Cooper, 2013) but what might be of particular relevance to this book is a brief mention of the fraught historical relationship between art and nature. It took several hundred years before nature could be viewed outside the framework of its relationship with art, and to be seen as autonomously beautiful. The 18th century notion of the picturesque codified the way nature might be appreciated by constructing views of the landscape using ideas of beauty generated originally within the artistic field of practice (Robinson, 1991). By necessity these views had to be modified as the landscape was rapidly transformed by industrialisation in the 19th century (Copley & Garside, 1994) but the Western framing of nature through the lens of art wasn't really challenged until the development of an environmental aesthetics (Rolston, 1998) that encouraged an understanding of nature – nature like swamps and wetlands - that sat outside the usual models of artistic appreciation (Giblett, 1996). To free the natural world from the aesthetic expectations of European art practices is also to free us of many other assumptions about how the world should be understood.

The Western aesthetic tradition is only one of the world's cultural systems, all of which have been inevitably modified by industrialisation as the globalised economy impacts upon traditional social orders and the natural world. Modernity is both a historical period and a social condition and as different cultures industrialise at different points along the timeline of industrial development, negotiation is constantly taking place between traditional and contemporary notions of nature. These are values laden dialogues in which verdicts about how we live our lives are made. The ancient Chinese Taoist approach to nature, perhaps best exemplified in the writings of Chuang-tzu where he encourages an approach to the world that mirrors nature's "spontaneous and mindless" journeying (Watson, 2002, p. 6), was part of the suffocating "iron house" of traditional culture challenged by Chinese modernists like Lu Xun (1972, p. 5) at the start of the 20th century. Lu Xun had studied the natural sciences, briefly training as a doctor before he became a writer, and was an antagonist of bogus traditional Chinese medicinal cures (3). His understanding of the body's physiology would have led him to dismiss Chuang-tzu's medicinal advice to take monkshood, balloon flower, cockscomb and china root as "each has a time when it is the sovereign remedy" (Watson, 2002, p. 277) and yet he would have understood the metaphorical insights into the nature of medicine provided by this observation. The need to move backwards and forwards between pre and postindustrial knowledges and between individual and social bodies of practice is an example of how Latouche's pluriversal approach might work, and it is possible to model a contemporary aesthetic response to nature in this way. It is also through a critically reflexive approach to the pre-industrial that allows movement beyond the aesthetic fetishising of the indigenous and/or the appropriation of traditional practices.

Henri Lefebvre suggested that in late capitalist society "everyday life has lost a dimension: depth. Only triviality remains" (2002, p. 78). If life is to be expanded out from a "congealed form of living" (p. 217) manifest in the reduction of aesthetic experience down into individual acts of consumption, then for Lefebvre the way to achieve life's expansion from 'lived' (passive) to 'living' (active) is to embrace the aesthetic potential of embracing everyday social activity outside of acts of consumption.

The aesthetic sensibilities we perceive operating in the past, or in cultures outside of our own, are not something we can adopt other than superficially, because they are the lived experiences of others that we codify as outsiders looking in (p. 322). There is an important and enjoyable role for beautiful things in life, but to pick and choose a cultural aesthetic as one might choose clothing is to consume the surface residue of culture. Ascribing aesthetic value to the trace of action rather than to the act itself is also to deny the power relationships that are at play in either the forging of an aesthetic or the adoption of one (Young and Brunk, 2009). This has enormous implications for principle 22 of the Rio Declaration's proposal that Indigenous people and their communities have a vital role to play in deploying their knowledge and traditional practices (Rio declaration on environment and development, 1992). To whom does that information belong and who has the responsibility for the deployment of it? Aesthetics are not conjured up Prospero like, from out the empty air.

The most recent philosophising about the autonomy of nature as a realm outside of the human (Heyd, 2013) also requires a need to qualify that recognition with practices that protect nature and ensure its survival. If nature's integrity has to be has to be impinged upon by the need to live our lives, what are the ethical issues that emerge from this practical human/nature engagement? A worldview that sees maintaining the integrity of nature as a social and cultural objective will eventually create an economy that is driven by the need for environmental protection. This in turn will frame an everyday aesthetic. The aesthetics of the everyday are social aesthetics formed by patterns of consumption and behaviours. Social aesthetics emphasise and shape things and processes, creating new meanings and interpretations. They are about relationships between people, and people and things, and those relationships are also the power relationships that take place between habitus and field.

To adopt the values and logic of everyday aesthetics in order to 'think beautifully' is to reinforce the idea that the aesthetic is contingent and contested. It would appear that an aesthetic of the sustainable might emerge through social action framed by a re-negotiation of our relationship with nature. It might even be legitimate to suggest that any such action might be better described as possessing the quality of kalon rather than beauty.

Praxis

Praxis is the dynamic relationship between thinking and acting and evaluating the consequences of action, and it is at this point that I hand the book over to the contributors. The aesthetic contestation needed to instigate a new aesthetic of sustainability involves more than reflecting on the beauty of nature or on the beauty of things produced in a sustainable culture. It involves a quotidian re-thinking of materials and their origin, their processing, their design into objects, their distribution and use, their life span and final disposal. There are aesthetic ramifications in managing landscape and the urban environment, there is a need to consider how transitioning from an unsustainable culture of planned obsolescence to a sustainable one involves reconceptualising the role of making art, and thinking about art and its purposes. Those issues are best discussed by those engaged in that process.

The book has been divided into two parts, the first looks at the central question of the book through the lens of philosophy, art and literature, the second through design and the environment. The book concludes with an afterword by John Thackara, who was the keynote speaker at the original symposium in Perth and whose presence in the global debates about design and its purpose gives constant reassurance that progressive ideas can make an impact on how the world is conceived and acted upon.

The division of the book into two parts shouldn't be seen as a reason for a discipline specific reading of it however, for whilst the chapters are gathered together in subject groupings for ease of organisation, there are underlying themes and threads that run across and through the subject matter of each chapter.

Hulin Sun, Amzad Hossain and Dora Marinova, Julia Sowińska-Heim and Hoda Shahmohammadian and Samaneh Soltanzadeh's papers deal with Chinese aesthetics in suburban Australian gardens, rural life in Bangladesh, Polish post-communist architecture and the ancient Iranian desert city of Yazd. What links these disparate subjects together is not solely the issue of sustainability. What is an implicit part of their analyses (and in Huilin Sun's case explicitly so) is an engagement with the pre-industrial aesthetics that have deep roots in the social, ethical and spiritual beliefs of societies whether they are Taoist, Christian or Islamic. Part of the creation of an aesthetic of sustainability must be a sustained dialogue between the different ideological ways of understanding the world that are in existence and the body of scientific knowledge that we also possess.

The nature of embodied knowledge and how it is acquired and how it may be communicated rests at the centre of re-imagining our world and our relationship with it. Sacha Kagan's paper discusses the nature of a sustainable aesthetic from a theoretical perspective and Perdita Phillips from the perspective of a practitioner. To understand the movement of ideas and ideology between habitus and field, between lifeworld and system, is to realise the importance of how embodied personal knowledge fits into broader theoretical frameworks. This insight is in turn important in finding ways to communicate how aesthetic sensibilities are expressed, as do Erin Corderoy and Michaela Baker in their examination of Tim Winton's novel *Dirt Music;* and the ways in which we might reflect on the qualities of materials as Martina Novakova and Tony Lam do. Mariela Zingoni talks about beauty as a way of knowing and John Ryan delves into an historical understanding of the forming of aesthetic sensibilities that is focused on flora. Both these approaches argue not only for the necessity of aesthetic experience but their potential for transforming our understanding of the world. Aesthetic readings have the potential to influence multiple practices, for as Ryan says they "help the designers, planners, conservationists, ecologists, architects and educators of today create the pleasurable metropolitan landscapes of tomorrow". Thus it becomes possible to link an analysis of how the beauty of flowers is understood with the practicalities of town and landscape planning that Marayam Izadi reveals is possible through the use of transects.

To construct a cultural space that is sustainably productive and aesthetically pleasurable it is important for creative individuals to reflexively engage with their creative practices and processes whether that be through an examination of broad theoretical imperatives operating in the field as Jane Donlin does, or through the framing of habitus experiences as in the case of Andrea Wood. Equally it is important to understand the purpose of creative process, as Susie Waller shows, in terms of social dynamics from both an etic as well as an emic perspective.

The world of culture rests between the uneasy relationship between creativity and regulation (Bauman, 1999, p. xiv). This dialectic will lie at the heart of any attempt to model an aesthetic of sustainability. Culture is about the discipline of maintenance as well as the excitement of invention. It is about discovering new ways of thinking, but also ways of consolidating how new things are known and learnt to be beautiful. Fanke Peng and Peter Hill's chapter on fashion and John Sadar and Gyungju Chyon's chapter on how technology and nature can be intimately connected show that a sustainable culture does not have to be a deficit culture and that filling the gaps left by the disappearance of an old order can be done seamlessly, and importantly for the context of this book, beautifully.

The importance of regulation, of examining how things are done, the impact they have and how judgements can be made about their value is the foundation of a scientific culture. Regulation is not just about control, it is about understanding contexts and assessing them. Reporting on practices in the field through the lenses of sustainability and the aesthetic will always be important. Eko Pam's paper on retail aesthetics, Henry Skate and Peter Woods' on visions of the future, Chrissie Smith's on advertising and Johanna Neissner's on graphic design's practices demonstrate this. The examination and regulation of what we produce is not about curtailing freedoms, it is about realising how fragile any system is and how a healthy culture needs constant monitoring and interpretation. Regulation does not have to be a denial of change, or the negation of fluidity, it can be the celebration of acknowledging the social importance of change.

Zygmunt Bauman observes that culture is simultaneously the factory of identity and its shelter (1999, p. xxix) in which case an imagined community can eventually become a field of practice. Those who see the potential of a sustainable world and understand how 'thinking beautifully' and kalon are ways of forging that world are welcomed to the following pages.

Dr Christopher Crouch is Professor of Design at Curtin University. He has written widely on the history and theory of art and design. His book 'Modernism in art, design and architecture' is a standard art school text. His most recent publication is 'Doing research in design'.

Endnotes

1. It may seem strange to substantiate this point, but given the hostility of powerful media and political factions in acknowledging the current environmental crisis it is worth pointing the reader to the website of the Intergovernmental Panel of Climate Change's website as a useful resource for countering denialist arguments with scientific data. http://www.ipcc.ch/

2. I don't have space to examine the phenomenological aspects of aesthetics here but would recommend Sepp and Embree's *Handbook of phenomenological aesthetics* as a good resource.

3. As can be seen in his short story 'Medicine' where a rice roll dipped in blood is used to 'cure' TB. (Xun, 1972).

References

Bauman, Z. (1999). *Culture as praxis*. London: Sage.

Becker, G. (1997). *Disrupted lives: how people create meaning in a chaotic world*. Berkeley: University of California Press.

Bourdieu, P. (1977). *Outline of a theory of practice*. Cambridge: Cambridge University Press.

Bourdieu, P., & Wacquant, L. (1992). *An invitation to reflexive sociology*. Chicago: Chicago University Press.

Bowie, A. (1990). *Aesthetics and Subjectivity: From Kant to Nietzsche*. Manchester: Manchester University Press.

Brand, S. (1999). *Clock of the long now: Time and responsibility*. New York: Basic Books.

Caldicott, H., & Halter, R. (2014). *Great Barrier Reef on brink of devastation in relentless quest for coal*. Retrieved from http://www.smh.com.au/comment/great-barrier-reef-on-brink-of-devastation-in-relentless-quest-for-coal-20140203-31x6q.html#ixzz3EocchKUT

Copley, S. & Garside, P. (eds). (1994). *The Politics of the Picturesque*. Cambridge: Cambridge University Press.

Crehan, K. (2002). *Gramsci, culture and anthropology*. Berkeley: University of California Press.

Crowley, D. (1958). Aesthetic judgement and cultural relativism. *The journal of aesthetics and art criticism, 17* (2), 187 – 193.

Debord, G. (1994). *The society of the spectacle*. New York: Zone Books. *Defining the aesthetic value of the Great Barrier Reef*. (2013). Retrieved from http://www.environment.gov.au/system/files/resources/7524507e-37a6-4cff-9195-cb5fe19d8f52/files/gbr-aesthetic-values.pdf

Duguid, S. (2010). *Nature in Modernity: Servant, citizen, queen or comrade*. New York: Peter Lang.

Evans, D. (2002). *A history of nature conservation in Britain*. London: Routledge.

Giblett, R. J. (1996). *Postmodern wetlands: culture, history, ecology*. Edinburgh: Edinburgh University Press.

Guha, R. (2000). *Environmentalism: A global history*. London: Longman.

Guyer, G. (1996). *Kant and the experience of freedom: Essays on aesthetics and morality.*Cambridge: Cambridge University Press.

Heyd, T. (2013). *Recognizing the Autonomy of Nature: Theory and Practice.* New York: Columbia University Press.

Hoorn, J. (2007). *Australian Pastoral: The Making of a White Landscape.* Fremantle: Fremantle Press.

Hutchings, P., Kingsford, M., & Hoegh-Guldberg, O. (2008). *The great barrier reef: Biology, environment and management.* Canberra: Csiro Publishing.

Jameson, F. (2008). *Postmodernism, or, the cultural logic of late capitalism.* London: Verso.

Jamme, C., & Cooper, I. (2013). *The Impact of Idealism: Volume 3, Aesthetics and literature: The legacy of post-kantian German thought.* Cambridge: Cambridge University Press.

Josephson, P., et al. (eds) (2013). *An environmental history of Russia.* Cambridge: Cambridge University Press.

Kaplan, J., Krumhardt, K. M. &Zimmerman, N. (2009).The prehistoric and preindustrial deforestation of Europe. *Quaternary Science reviews. 28*(27-28), 3016 – 3034.

Konijnendijk, C. C. (2008). The forest and the city: The cultural landscape of urban woodland. New York: Springer.

Kövecses, Z. (2005). *Metaphor in culture.* Cambridge: Cambridge University Press.

Lear, G. R. (2012). Beauty (Kalon). In G. A. Press (ed), *The Continuum Companion to Plato.* A&C Black.

Lakoff, G., & Johnson, M. (2008). *Metaphors we live by.* Chicago: University of Chicago Press.

Lanz, H. (1947). *Aesthetic relativity.* Palo Alto: Stanford University Press.

Lefebvre, H. (2002). *Critique of everyday life. Volume 2.* London: Verso.

Lytle, M. H. (2007). *The gentle subversive. Rachel Carson, Silent Spring, and the rise of the environmental movement.* Oxford: Oxford University Press.

Latouche, S. (2010). *Farewell to growth.* Oxford: Polity.

Redfearn, G. (2014). *Death by sludge, coal and climate change for Great Barrier Reef?* Retrieved from http://www.theguardian.com/environment/planet-oz/2014/jan/31/great-barrier-reef-australia-dredging-abbott-point-coal-export

Sepp, H. R., & Embree, L. E. (2010). *Handbook of phenomenological aesthetics.* New York: Springer.

McAfee, N. (2000). *Habermas, Kristeva, and citizenship.* New York: Cornell University Press.

McManus, I. & Furnham, A. (2006). Aesthetic activities and aesthetic attitudes: Influences of education, background and personality on interest and involvement in the arts. *British Journal of Psychology, 97* (4), 555 – 587.

Næss, A. (1989). *Ecology, community and lifestyle.* Cambridge: Cambridge University Press.

Newman, P. & Jennings, I. (2012). *Cities as Sustainable Ecosystems: Principles and Practices.* Washington: Island Press.

Osbaldiston, N. (2013). *Culture of the Slow: Social Deceleration in an Accelerated World.* New York: Palgrave Macmillan.

Pepper, D., Revill, G., & Webster, F. (eds) (2002). *Environmentalism: Critical Concepts in the Environment.* London: Routledge.

Report of the United Nations Conference on environment and development.(1992). Retrieved from http://www.un.org/documents/ga/conf151/aconf15126-1annex1.htm

Rio Declaration on Environment and Development. (1992). Retrieved from http://www.unep.org/Documents.Multilingual/Default.asp?DocumentID=78&ArticleID=1163

Rolston, H., 1988, *Environmental Ethics: Duties to and values in the natural world.* Philadelphia: Temple University Press.

Siva, V. (1997). *Monocultures of the Mind: Perspectives on Biodiversity and Biotechnology.*New York: Zed Books.

Tay, D. (2013). *Metaphor in psychotherapy.* Amsterdam: John Benjamins Publishing.

Tsakok, I. (2011). *Success in agricultural transformation.* Cambridge: Cambridge University Press.

Tzu, C. (trans. Burton Waston). (2002). *The Complete Works of Chuang Tzu*. New York: Columbia University Press.

Wells, H. G. (2005). The Kremlin dreamer in: *They knew Lenin. Reminiscences of foreign correspondents*. Honolulu: University of Hawaii Press, 190 – 194.

World Commission on Environment and Development. (1987). *Our common future*. Oxford: Oxford University Press.

Xun, L. (1972). *Diary of a madman*. New York: Norton

Young, J., & Brunk, C. (2009). *The ethics of cultural appropriation*. Hoboken: Wiley –Blackwell.

Robinson, S. K. (1991). I*nquiry into the picturesque.*Chicago: University of Chicago Press.

PART ONE. PHILOSOPHY, ART AND LITERATURE

CHAPTER ONE

COMPLEXITY AS EXPERIENCE:
THE CONTRIBUTION OF AESTHETICS TO CULTURES OF SUSTAINABILITY

Sacha Kagan

Transduction

Rather than an introduction, I prefer to label the start of this text as a 'transduction'. A transduction is the action of conversion of matter, energy or a message into another form. More specifically in medicine, transduction refers to "the transfer of genetic material from one organism (as a bacterium) to another by a genetic vector and especially a bacteriophage" (www.merriam-webster.com). Transduction has more to do with transformation processes than does introduction, i.e. merely bringing something into play in a given context. My suggested transduction is to take some Deweyian aesthetics, as well as some complexity research (and some other material I will discuss below), and invite you to virally transfer them into the field of sustainability studies. Hence the title of this chapter: 'Complexity as Experience'.

"Art as experience", as proposed by John Dewey eighty years ago, characterises aesthetics as an intense and rich relationship with the world, which we can sometimes experience in everyday life (Dewey, 1934). According to Dewey, the aesthetic experience is an integrated experience manifesting connectedness and a "sense of the including whole". Dewey's understanding of aesthetics as experience, points at personal affectivity in everyday life and at a human being's overall interrelationship with his/her environment. "Experience is the result, the sign and the reward of that interaction of organism and environment which, when it is carried to the full, is a transformation of interaction into participation and communication" (Dewey, 1934, p. 22).

Echoing Dewey's expression, I suggest that we look into "complexity as experience". Complexity as experience, I will argue here, characterises a specific type of aesthetic experience: "aesthetics of sustainability". Here, aesthetic experience becomes a tense and complex relationship with the present world a world characterised by the evolutionary challenge of the Anthropocene. In other words, aesthetics of sustainability confront us with the challenge of finding prospects for the resilience of human communities, in an age where we cannot afford anymore to perceive nature and culture through simplified schemes.

Before I move further, let me shortly explain two terms, "resilience" and "Anthropocene". Sustainability researchers often point at the importance of fostering the resilience of communities. In other words, how best to survive serious crises with a combination of adaptation and also some degree of resistance, when faced with external and internal threats. For example, in discussions on sustainable cities, several authors stress that, "building resilience depends on nurturing diversity, self-organization, adaptive learning and constructive positive feedback loops between the economic, social and infrastructural aspects of a city as a complex system" (Dieleman 2013, p. 174). On a wider scale, resilience is about averting the extinction of the human species.

The Anthropocene is a new geological period, proposed by Paul Crutzen to have started with the industrial revolution (Crutzen & Stoermer, 2000). In the Anthropocene, humankind has become a major geological factor deeply affecting the evolving conditions for the co-evolution of humans and many other species on planet Earth. This should not be misunderstood as meaning that humans are

Gods and that the technosystem has swallowed and replaced the ecosystems, rather it means humans have always been embedded in nature's dynamic and ecological evolution. Therefore, culture is always a part of nature, rather than something apart from nature. This is no news. However, what is increasingly true in the age of the Anthropocene is that human culture has so much affected natural processes on Earth, that culture has become a "planetary copilot" of nature (I am borrowing the expression "planetary copilot" from Edgar Morin).

Our present situation calls forward a perception of our complex embeddedness in "natureculture" (my use of the compound word "natureculture" navigates in between the uses of the term in ecopsychology and its uses by cultural theorists like Donna Haraway). As I argued elsewhere: "It makes little sense to continue perceiving "nature" and "culture" as two clearly separate entities. We need to heal from modernity's habit of atomizing, fragmenting, reducing complexity by means of supposedly "clear" concepts and definitions" (Kagan, 2012).

The aesthetics of sustainability

As I did in the book *Art and sustainability* (Kagan, 2011), I propose an understanding of the aesthetics of sustainability that, acknowledging previous developments in 'ecological aesthetics' and in ecofeminism (cf. e.g. Merchant 1995), roots itself in the Deweyian tradition, and brings together the insights from Gregory Bateson's perspective on aesthetics as the sensibility to "the pattern that connects", David Abram's animistic take on phenomenology, Edgar Morin's paradigm of complexity, and Basarab Nicolescu's transdisciplinarity. I will now sketch these four elements out, and for a more detailed exposition, please refer to chapter 4 in (Kagan, 2011).

The notion of a sensibility to connectedness was central in Gregory Bateson's understanding of aesthetics. He stressed the importance of being aware of relational contexts, for our survival. To Bateson, the aesthetic is that which is responsive to "the pattern which connects" (1979, pp. 8-10). A living mind has an "aesthetic preference" which is "able to recognise characteristics similar to [its] own in other systems [it] might encounter" (p. 118). Bateson posited a meta-pattern uniting all of life, and saw aesthetics as an important epistemological access to it, which reaches beyond the limits of purposive rationality.

According to David Abram (1996) historical societies based on phonetic alphabets, and especially modern industrial societies, have numbed and suffocated a whole dimension of human sensibility, which was and is still vibrant among some indigenous peoples; the sensibility to the intelligence of the 'more-than-human' - and the capacity to bridge perceptions with the non-human – i.e., the environment's complex and dynamic webs of life. We need to re-discover this numbed reflexive sensibility, which the arts and culture may play a role in re-awakening.

However, aesthetics of sustainability require even more than a mere sensibility to the pattern that connects and to the more-than-human. It requires a sensibility to complexity, as discussed by Edgar Morin, who used an excellent image:

> Th[is] sensibility will be like that of the musician's ear which perceives the competitions,symbioses, interferences, overlapping of themes in the same symphonic flow, where the brutish mind will recognise only theme surrounded by noise. (1992, p. 139)

The aesthetics of sustainability should not be merely based on a holistic sensibility, overemphasising the unity and integration of the biosphere or universe, replacing the disjunctive paradigm of modernity with a simplistic 'New Age' paradigm, but rather should be attentive to complexity, i.e., combining and contrasting unity, complementarity, competition, and antagonism. This implies firstly, a complex sensitivity that perceives as much antagonisms and competitions as complementarities and symbiosis, and that transcends the contradictions so as to reveal the complementary tension of antagonism and complementarity. Secondly, a sensitivity to wholeness and order that also perceives and values disorder, disharmony, as well as uncertainty, and that respects genesic chaos.

The aesthetics of sustainability is especially open to chaos (i.e., the chaos of chaos theories, not the chaos of Lyotard's postmodernism) as a genesic source for generativity. Life's "creative evolution" emerges not from computational capacities alone, but from the ability to deal with disorder and ambiguity as genesic forces (Morin, 1980). An aesthetic of sustainability, which is open to the generativity of chaos, then opens up a sensibility to emergence.

A transdisciplinary sensibility helps navigate through levels of reality and levels of perception, while keeping a certain direction and avoiding confusion and simplifications (cf. Kagan, 2011, pp. 240-246). NatureCulture can work as a "macro-concept" as proposed by Edgar Morin in *La method* (1980). A macro-concept harbours the dynamic tension, both contradictory and complementary, between relationships of unity, complementarity, competition, and antagonism (Morin, 1977, 1980). Across different levels of reality, we need to learn to appreciate the contradictions between different logics, and to acknowledge the great level of ambivalence, uncertainty, and indeterminacy that we have to cope with and learn from, both in our daily lives and in sustainability problems.

Such an approach to living complexity, following Morin, points at life's continuous renewal through transformations, which is driven by constant improvisations, with trial-and-error cycles, and feeds on a diversity of alternative options. "Only improvisation remains constant" (Mayer Harrison & Harrison, 1985, pp. 37, 60) and there are no fixed recipes for evolutionary success.

So we come back to resilience, or the ability to survive for the long term by transforming oneself in relationship to one's environments. Such an understanding of resilience, informed by the aesthetics of sustainability, points us at the necessity to learn from the unexpected.

Walking as 'serendipedestrian' aesthetic practice

In my book *Art and sustainability*, I discussed, in rather abstract terms, this ability to learn from the unexpected by having a certain openness to disturbances. I called this productive openness to disturbances, "autoecopoïesis" – as a contrast to Luhmann's autopoïesis. However, in the meanwhile I have also taken up another, easier and already available word. The ability to learn from the unexpected can also be discussed with an existing, popular word in the English language: serendipity. Serendipity stands for the ability to discern opportunities for learning in accidents and surprises of life, and for the sagacity of making discoveries of things which one is not looking for (Merton & Barber, 2004; Kirchberg, 2010). The wisdom coming from serendipity is needed in order for us to relate to the emergence of the new in NatureCulture's complex dynamism (Kagan, 2012).

The occurrence of an accident is in itself not enough for someone to be serendipitous, but a specific openness and sensibility is necessary, a specific sagacity. Sagacity refers to a wisdom that is grounded in sense perceptions, and that allows keen discernment and sound judgement. The required openness also means that one should be flexible, curious and alert enough to change one's goals and interests, along the way. Serendipity also involves learning across different, apparently unrelated contexts, in a transversal, often metaphorical, way. This is also called lateral thinking, learning from unique incidents by a process of abduction.

Serendipity, as embodied learning, actualises itself in the experiential process of walking. That is why Cultura21 focused its first international summer school of arts and sciences for sustainability in social transformation, in August 2010 in Gabrovo, Bulgaria, on walking as a potentially transdisciplinary method (Kagan, 2010b). And that is why I made up a derivative word, "The Serendipedestrian", at the occasion of "Sideways", a festival/long-distance-walk/conference in the summer of 2012 in Belgium.

Serendipity is a walker's wisdom. The fairy tale entitled *The Three Princes of Serendip*, published in Italy in 1557 (from Persian or Indian sources), was the inspiration for the creation of the English word serendipity by Horace Walpole in the 18th century. In this fairytale the three princes from the island of Serendip gain wisdom while walking in a foreign kingdom. They are learning, while walking and attentively observing, smelling, touching their surroundings to interpret the most subtle and nearly unnoticeable signs on the road sides. They are readily discovering what they were not looking for.

Walking-based practices put learned things in contexts, locally and ecologically, embedded in a real geography and not only conveniently virtual. Thanks to the slower rhythm, the walker heightens his or her attention. Walking across places involves moving, exchanging, comparing. Walking is transversal. The transversal is that which cuts across, walks across, different levels of reality, not only bridging them, but also travelling beyond them. Walking can even become a genuinely transversal method for knowing, sensing (in a multi-sensorial way as discussed by Tim Ingold (2008) and sometimes eventually a basis for changing the realities of local communities.

Walking is sometimes a social and political practice, reshaping the realities of shared spaces and the fiction of public space, accompanying political expressions and the articulation of democracies, as with Gandhi's famous salt march to Dandi. Walking allows both exchanges with multiple others and personal introspection for oneself. And, as an ordinary activity, low-tech rather than high-tech, it is accessible to all, and open to mixing all sorts of non elite-wisdoms from all human groups (Ingold & Lee Vergunst, 2008; Kagan, 2010a).

Serendipedestrianism is, however, of course not the only embodied way toward an aesthetic sensibility to NatureCulture's complexity. Other interesting practices, which are complementary to serendipedestrian practices, include for example certain approaches to gardening and also certain sexual experiences that can open our eyes to queer ecologies that I will discuss below. They include certain artistic practices, such as for example the practice of ecological art, to which I will turn in the last section.

First short excursus: gardening

An embodied attention to NatureCulture's complex vitality can be practiced through certain ways of gardening. One very good example of this is the internationally acclaimed gardener Gilles Clément, who understands gardens, nature and life in general, as constant transformation. His way of gardening also conveys a view of nature that is neither the dominated and alien nature of modernity, nor a sublime and virgin nature that humanity would not touch. The aesthetic experience of nature that comes out of his approach to gardening is pointing to a great diversity of species and interactions that includes humanity's peculiar responsibilities, and seeks partnerships.

With Clément, the gardener's role is not to control the plant species and constrain them into geometric patterns conceptualised a priori. The gardener's role is rather to observe the evolutionary interactions between species, learn from them, interpret them, and then intervene with the goals of fostering dynamic balance between species and of increasing biological diversity. This kind of gardener carefully observes, before acting. He or she allows and accompanies the plants' displacements through the garden, and does not try to constrain this evolution. If a plant grows in the middle of a pathway, it will not be cut. Rather, the visitor's paths will change every year, adapting to the changes brought by the movements of different plants (Clément & Jones, 2006).

With his gardens, Clément does not praise some sort of postmodern disorder, or some superficially romantic garden. Rather, he is experiencing the highly complex play of order and disorder, organisation and disorganisation and reorganisation, in his moving gardens. In this, he is very much the gardener counterpart to Edgar Morin's theoretical elaborations on the complexity of life.

Second short excursus: queer ecologies

Another embodied approach to experiencing the creative diversity in NatureCulture's dynamic complexity is through sexuality. Under the notion of queer ecology, or ecologiesas developed by Greta

Gaard and by Catriona Sandilands (Eds. Mortimer-Sandilands & Erickson, 2010), an interesting meeting of queer studies and ecofeminism occurred – ecofeminism being itself a meeting of feminism and the environmental justice movement.

Queer ecology focuses on NatureCulture's incredible sexual creativity. Indeed, sexuality in nature, whether reproductive or non-reproductive, is much more complex, polymorphic and changing than is traditionally conceived of, e.g., with the view of a functional evolution of sexuality. Nature encompasses a wide variety of sexual possibilities. A queer-ecological look at cultural history also reminds us that in the Middle Ages, Europeans were not yet constrained by hetero-normative Christian norms, and that later European colonisers repressed the more flexible sexualities of Native Americans.

Vancouver-based ecological artist Caffyn Kelley argues that, "homosexuals must bring a particular sensibility to the experience of nature. Abhorred as unnatural, and alternately as bestial, castigated as primitive, and described as the strange fruit of a civilisation grown too distant from the earth, identifying as homosexual, queer, gay or lesbian makes one attuned to the culture of nature. Nature appears not as a timeless essence, separate from human experience" (Kelley, n.d.). Kelley further sees many qualities in a queer experience of nature and of the self:

Queer is a way of choosing a radical openness instead of a fixed identity. A queer ecology might eschew the essentialising, anthropocentric tendencies of identity and identification (including taxonomies of species, gender, race), and allow us to instead choose complexity, fluidity and interconnection. (Kelley, n.d.)

Ecological art and the search for lived cultures of sustainability

I understand the notion of cultures of sustainability as part of the eco-evolutionary challenge I described above. By eco-evolutionary, I mean evolutionary in an ecological sense, with multiple levels of evolutionary and co-evolutionary processes, seeing also whole ecosystems as dynamic (Morin, 1980). The sustainability of human communities, today, depends on their capacity to co-evolve with other living systems, within rapidly changing environmental conditions (of which they are the co-pilot). It requires contextually relevant capabilities to learn, both in specific places and in a planetary context. For example, the Malaysian sustainability researcher Manickam Nadarajah proposed eight principles for a culture of sustainability in cities, which all focus on how the 'symbolic universe' of sustainable communities is closely related to a deep, spatialised knowing of ecological contexts in their local specificities, their diversities and their inter-relationships (Nadarajah & Yamamoto, 2007). In her discussion of environmentalism and cultural studies, Ursula Heise complemented such a notion of sense of place with the equally important notion of a sense of planet or eco-cosmopolitanism (Heise, 2008).

I have gained the conviction that the practice of ecological art can play a key role in training ourselves towards such cultures of sustainability, through aesthetics of sustainability. At the very least, ecological art bears an interesting potential in that respect. A working definition of ecological art can be taken from the self-understanding of ecological artists, as formulated in a statement from the 'ecoart network'. Ecological art embraces an ecological ethic in both its content and form/materials. Artists considered to be working within the genre subscribe generally to one or more of the following principles:

- Attention on the web of interrelationships in our environment – to the physical, biological, cultural, political and historical aspects of ecological systems.
- Create works that employ naturalmaterials or engage with environmental forces such as wind, water or sunlight.
- Reclaim, restore and remediate damaged environments.
- Inform the public about ecological relationships and the environmental problems we face.

- Re-envision ecological relationships, creatively proposing new possibilities for co-existence, sustainability and healing. (1)

The remaining space in this chapter does not allow a detailed discussion of the characteristics of ecological art, nor to bring concrete examples. What I do instead is to highlight seven key elements (see also Kagan, 2014), often found in ecological art practices, which bear a high potential for the aesthetics of sustainability and for experimentation towards cultures of sustainability:

1. Theirs are "connective" practices, cultivating empathy and responsible dealings with fellow humans and non-humans, rather than merely affirming an individual self in opposition to society (as discussed e.g., by Suzi Gablik (1991)); ecological artists are acting as interprets of interdependence (as discussed e.g., by Tim Collins (2004)).
2. These practices are exploring and shaping shared spaces for people and other species.
3. They are aiming to foster the non-possessive, shared authorship of a process that eventually develops a life of its own.
4. They are navigating across different scales of ecological relations at the local, regional/national, bio-regional (e.g., watersheds), and continental levels.
5. They are connecting the level of everyday activities, the level of critical reflexivity and systemic questioning, the level of envisioning and imagining of heterotopia, and sometimes also at a spiritual level.
6. The practice of ecological art is participatory, not unlike the practice of participatory action research.
7. As in the serendipitous learning process of walking, the work carried out in ecological art projects is cultivating a wisdom grounded in sense perceptions, with an iterative process of exploring and experimenting.

I am not of course claiming that all seven elements mentioned are, or have to be, present together across all forms of ecological art practice. My argument is rather that, when they are present (and especially when several of them are co-present), these elements foster the experience of the aesthetics of sustainability.

Transclusion

I do not like conclusions, and the false comfort given by the impression of "wrapping up" that they confer. Instead, please find here a few words for a suggested 'transclusion' of sorts (loosely borrowing the term from hypertext scholar Ted Nelson (1981)), i.e., I suggest some further readings pursuing the lines of reflection suggested so far. (2)

My short discussion of ecological art, above, jumped right into some key features of the practice of ecological art (discussed at some more length in Kagan, 2014), without having the space for illustrations with concrete cases of ecoart. I invite the readers to look into chapter five of *Art and sustainability* (Kagan, 2011), and into Linda Weintraub's *To life* (Weintraub 2012), where they will find descriptions and discussions of several examples of ecological art practices.

In my discussion of aesthetics of sustainability, I did not mention several relevant discussions of aesthetics. One of them is Beth Carruthers' discourse on "deep aesthetics" which bases itself on James Hillman's distinction between aisthesis and a state of anasithesis in which according to Hillman, modern individualism plunged us, (cited in Carruthers, 2013). Furthermore, Hillman and Carruthers are not the only authors and practitioners who pointed out the importance of aesthetics in order to heal a contemporary condition of anaesthesis (e.g., in the UK, the social sculpture researcher/artist Shelley Sacks, and in Germany, the philosopher Wolfgang Welsch).

Finally, I would like to refer to one author whom I mentioned at the "Aesthetics of Sustainability" conference at Curtin University of Technology, Western Australia, on October 3rd 2013, in the discussion time following my video-conferenced plenary contribution (on which this chapter is based). One colleague raised the question, whether sustainability research may be too exclusively grounded in biological discourse, and too little grounded in symbolic discourse. My response to this question was that we should explore the work that has been done in the field of biosemiotics, and then bridge cultural-scientific/humanities research with a certain kind of biological discourse that shows a great openness to an aesthetic-epistemological access to the world. In this direction of thought, I invite readers to look into the essay *Enlivenment*, by German biologist and philosopher Andreas Weber (2013).

Dr Sacha Kagan is a Research Associate at the Institute of Sociology and Cultural Organisation at Leuphana University (Lueneburg, Germany). He is Founding Coordinator at Cultura21 (an international network for cultures of sustainability) and a member of the board of the European Sociological Association's Research Network 'Sociology of the Arts'. See http://sachakagan.wordpress.com

Endnotes

1. Source: internal communication on the 'ecoart' network mailing-list, in preparation for eventual wikipedia entries (November 2011). See www.ecoartnetwork.org for more information about this network.
2. However, this bit of text does not include any real "transclusion" in Nelson's sense, requiring mutual hyperlinking, i.e. textual hyperlinks working both ways between the two hyperlinked texts (i.e. the text including the transclusions, and the source text).

References

Abram, D. (1996). *The spell of the sensuous*. New York: Random House.

Bateson, G. (1979). *Mind and nature: a necessary unity*. New York: Dutton.

Carruthers, B. (2013). Call and response: deep aesthetics and the heart of the world. In S. Bergmann, I. Blindow & K. Otts (Eds.), *Aesth/Ethics in environmental change: hiking through the arts, ecology, religion and ethics of the environment* (pp. 131-141). Zürich, Münster: LIT Verlag.

Clément, G. & Jones, L. (2006). *Gilles Clément: une écologie humaniste*. Avignon: Aubanel.

Collins, T. (2004). Reconsidering the monongahela conference. Retrieved from: http://moncon.greenmuseum.org/recap.htm

Crutzen, P. J., & Stoermer, E. F. (2000). The 'anthropocene'. *Global Change Newsletter* 41, 17-18.

Dewey, J. (1934). *Art as experience*. New York: Perigee.

Dieleman, H. (2013). Organizational learning for resilient cities, through realizing eco-cultural innovations. *Journal of Cleaner Production, 50*(1), 171-180.

Gablik, S. (1991). *The re-enchantment of art*. London: Thames and Hudson.

Heise, U. K. (2008). *Sense of place and sense of planet: the environmental imagination of the global*. New York: Oxford University Press.

Ingold, T., & Lee Vergunst, J. (2008). *Ways of walking: ethnography and practice on foot*. Farnham: Ashgate.

Kagan, S. (Ed.). (2010a). *Walking in life, art and science: a few examples*. Lueneburg: Leuphana UniversityLueneburg. Retrieved from http://www.leuphana.de/fileadmin/user_upload/Forschung seinrichtungen/isko/files/Walking_ed-Kagan_2010.pdf

Kagan, S. (2010b). Walking for social and ecological transformation. *Culture360.org*. Retrieved from http://culture360.org/magazine/walking-for-social-and-ecological-transformation/

Kagan, S. (2011). *Art and sustainability: connecting patterns for a culture of complexity*. Bielefeld: Transcript Verlag.

Kagan, S. (2012). *Toward global (environ)mental change: transformative art and cultures of sustainability*. Berlin: Heinrich Böll Stiftung.

Kagan, S. (2014). The practice of ecological art. *[Plastik]* 4. Retrieved from http://art-science.univ paris1.fr/document.php?id=866

Kelley, C. (n.d.). Environments. In *Orientation: mapping queer meanings*. Retrieved from http://islandsinstitute.pbworks.com/w/page/20166886/Queer%20Ecology

Kirchberg, V. (2010). Kreativität und stadtkultur: stadtsoziologische deutungen. In C. Hannemann, H. Glasauer, J. Pohlan, A. Pott & V. Kirchberg (Eds.), *Jahrbuch stadtregion. stadtkultur und kreativität*. Opladen, Farmington Hills: Barbara Budrich.

Mayer Harrison, H., & Harrison, N. (1985). *The lagoon cycle*. Ithaca: Herbert F. Johnson Museum of Art, Cornell University.

Merchant, C. (1995). *Earthcare: women and the environment*. London: Routledge.

Merton, R., & Barber, E. (2004). *The travels and adventures of serendipity*. Princeton, Oxford: Princeton University Press.

Morin, E. (1977). *La méthode, volume 1: La nature de la nature*. Paris: Seuil.

NB: 1992 for the English version: *Method – Towards a Study of Humankind. Volume 1: The Nature of Nature*. New York: Peter Lang.

Morin, E. (1980). *La méthode, volume 2: la vie de la vie*. Paris: Seuil.

Mortimer-Sandilands, C., & Erickson, B. (Eds.). (2010). *Queer ecologies: sex, nature, politics, desire*. Bloomington: Indiana University Press.

Nadarajah, M., & Yamamoto, A. T. (Eds.). (2007). *Urban crisis: culture and the sustainability of cities*. Tokyo: United Nations University Press.

Nelson, T. (1981). *Literary machines: the report on, and of, project xanadu concerning word processing, electronipublishing, hypertext, thinkertoys, tomorrow's intellectual revolution, and certain other topics including knowledge, education and freedom*. Sausalito: Mindful Press.

Weber, A. (2013). *Enlivenment: towards a fundamental shift in the concepts of nature, culture, and politics*. Berlin: Heinrich Böll Stiftung.

Weintraub, L. (2012). *To life! eco art in pursuit of a sustainable planet*. Berkeley: University of California Press.

CHAPTER TWO

BEAUTY: A POWERFUL FORCE FOR SUSTAINABILITY AND REGENERATION

Maria Elena Zingoni de Baro

Introduction

For thousands of years humanity's relationship to nature was both enduring and profoundly respectful. From the industrial revolution onwards, and particularly since the 1950s, a fundamental and systemic change in this relationship took place, leading to an extraordinary impact on the world's landscapes. An extractive economic model has exploited natural resources with increasing disregard for the natural world's capability to regenerate, and alongside the ecological footprint of global urban development, compromises living systems' survival.

Moving from that mechanistic worldview of fragmentation to an ecological worldview of integration, the emerging regenerative sustainability paradigm considers the world as a living, complex and dynamic whole where everything is inter-connected, and social and ecological systems are constantly in flux. Within this whole, nature and human systems are integrated and share processes of co-creation and co-evolution. This world vision recognises existential knowledge, Eastern philosophical and religious traditions and Western thinkers that share these principles, in addition to scientific discoveries in the area of quantum physics and ecology (du Plessis, 2011).

New ways of knowing are arising, and designers need to think and create buildings, cities and places in ways that reflect this philosophy. Complexity, wholeness, interrelationships and connectedness, and the value of nature and all forms of life, are the key issues of this new worldview. Mehaffy and Salingaros define the new vision for the natural and built environments in these terms:

The new paradigm is about complexity. It shapes the patterns of our use of resources and enhances the value of nature, defines the patterns of interactions between people and nature and conditions human behaviour. By considering natural and built environments a whole system, it gives meaning to the urban realm and naturally creates resilience and sustainability. Therefore, it serves more efficiently the real needs of human beings and the planet. (2011, para. 5.)

Working within the regenerative paradigm principles implies a shift in the role of practitioners and stakeholders. It is necessary to have an understanding – or "ecoliteracy" (Orr, 1992) – of how living systems work to face the challenge of designing buildings, cities, and places that enable enhanced awareness for both designers and users. Involving both practitioners and stakeholders in the design process aims to promote reflective experiences, usage and behaviours that lead to a responsible attitude of care, a feeling of belonging and co-evolution within the whole system.

This chapter outlines the importance of promoting aesthetic experiences through designed landscapes (Meyer, 2008), art and culture, and even through the "very basic and transversal practices of everyday life, such as walking" (Kagan, 2011, p. 71).

Sustainability, regeneration and the necessity of aesthetic experiences

The regenerative approach considers the Brundtland Commission's definition of sustainability as a balance line, and then incorporates greater levels of development in the process (Reed, 2007a). Restoration is the first step upwards, as seen in Figure 1, proposing that human action enables the recovering of degraded natural systems to self-organise and evolve. Regeneration then goes beyond this as it includes humans in the whole system as co-participants in the evolutionary process (Mang & Reed, 2012).

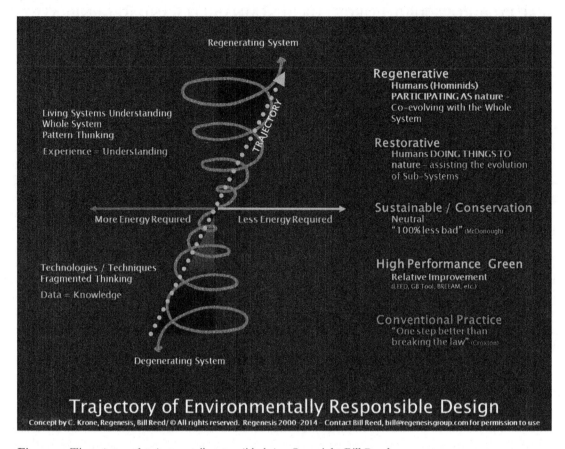

Figure 1. *The trajectory of environmentally responsible design.* Copyright Bill Reed.

Regeneration shifts from dominating nature to reflecting the constant evolution of culture and human life, integrating human aspirations and activities with the evolution of natural systems as part of essential co-evolution (Mang & Reed, cited in Zingoni de Baro, 2013). Thus, regeneration shares the tenets of systems thinking allowing for the main properties of the whole, such as ever-changing conditions, unpredictable processes, and impermanence, which are also essential qualities of life. Reed stresses this concept pointing out that "to regenerate means to give life and energy" (2007b, p. 2).

The principles of regenerative design consider communities and places as living systems, ascertaining that living systems always have a purpose, and that it is through a deep understanding of *place* as a whole, that place recuperates its core position in human life. The consideration of purpose is crucial because it expands opportunities and higher order development, allowing a system to regenerate, genuinely promoting greater resilience and complexity (Reed, 2007b). The regenerative approach to design identifies patterns and processes that have both shaped and continue to shape a place, such as natural ecology and local culture. Pattern literacy and stories help in understanding how complex systems work and evolve in a place, enabling the creation of resonant human systems to enhance those of the place and, consequently, facilitating the co-evolution of both ecological and socio-cultural systems (Mang & Reed, 2012).

In this sense, regenerative design is conducive to life because it creates new opportunities for life by working with humans and nature in rebinding social and ecological systems that lead to the real potential and vocation of a community and its place. Importantly, it involves designing with and for nature creating objects, buildings, cities and regions that work as ecosystems.

Why do we need to think about objects, buildings, cities and places in a different way? How can we design better places to live? New ways of thinking, understanding and planning for the future may bear in mind that resilience and regeneration, are essential conditions in times of climate change and population growth. Since world population is becoming increasingly urban, cities need to be re-thought within this new vision in order for them to become regenerative places for life. Hence, when considering urban design and planning, the turning point can be pioneered through projects creating green infrastructure, low-impact developments, energy efficient buildings, and environmental remediation. Many examples can be seen around the world, but in most cases have not been implemented in a systemic way.

Summarising, regenerative design, despite some differences in the various approaches is, suggests du Plessis and Cole (2011), an inherent component of the eco-centric paradigm, building on the concept of the built environment as a complex social-ecological system (Moffat & Kohler, 2008) the regenerative approach to design and development aims to foster increasing resilience. This can be achieved by reconnecting the built environment to place through relating urban life to local ecosystems, repairing degraded environments and ecosystems services, and encouraging well-being, health, and a sense of belonging (Reed, 2007; Mang & Reed, 2012; Cole et al, 2013).

The new philosophy is directly influencing the work of architects, landscape architects, urban planners and designers, and in general all practitioners engaged with design issues. That may create a more holistic and multidisciplinary conception of place and human activities, stakeholders and community involvement may lead to establishing and maintaining a symbiotic and regenerative mutual relationship that can support resilience of the whole over time (Cole et al, 2013; du Plessis & Cole, 2011).

Curiously, within the efforts of aligning human development to nature, the aesthetic dimension has been absent (Meyer, 2008). Scholars, McLennan, Meyer, Salingaros, Lubarsky and Kagan, however, have emerged claiming the need for its inclusion in the sustainability discourse.

The shifting concept of beauty: understanding beauty as a means of transformative change

Within the ecological worldview, the concept of beauty shifts from its historical conception to a new understanding that conceives of it as an essential strength of sustainability (Meyer, 2008) and regeneration. Authors from different fields of knowledge address the capabilities of beauty in promoting awareness and care for the environment and its role in education and sustainable regenerative practices.

Beauty as an essential attribute of life.
For Lubarsky (n.d.,a; n.d.,b) Western culture has dismissed the value of beauty during the past 200 years, and the decline in its appreciation is directly associated with the disregard for nature. She argues that the mechanistic conception of beauty as a subjective value considers the world's worth as a matter of human appreciation. In this vision, non-human life is considered as lacking intrinsic value, which leads to overexploitation and depletion of natural resources, biodiversity loss and environmental degradation.

Lubarsky asserts beauty is an "inherent attribute of all geo-biological systems which possess their own aesthetical worth" (2012, p. 2) and its value is independent from pleasure or displeasure. Life and beauty are closely related, relying on the multiple patterns of life and form different types of live structures. So, beauty resides in all scales of these interwoven living patterns and when life is diminished or eliminated, beauty is replaced by ugliness and the aesthetic value of the living structure is dismissed. Beauty and sustainability are consequently related because its appreciation is embedded into our daily experiences as "a part of our deep, evolutionary memory, kept alive in our daily consort with the world" (Lubarsky, 2012, p. 2). This concept is shared by Kagan (2011), and is discussed further on.

Beauty as an innately emotional affiliation of human beings.
This approach to beauty is discussed by McLennan in his book *The Philosophy of Sustainable Design* (2004), arguing that human beings have an innate biological need for beauty. Salingaros (2010; Salingaros & Masden, 2008) also shares this argument that is substantiated by the neuroscience findings regarding "the increasing evidence of the role beauty plays in stimulating the brain" (McLennan, 2004, p. 237). Since the human brain is motivated by proportion, shape and texture, this needs to be considered by designers in order to create long lasting objects, buildings and places, which is the ultimate goal of sustainable design. The importance of pleasant, attractive designs can compel people to learn and connect to buildings and places, and even to the extended surroundings including nature and community, promoting a behavioural transformation of interest and care (McLennan, 2004).

Salingaros (2010) argues that quality of life and wellbeing are related to designs that embody certain types of geometry that derive from the organisation of living organisms. Developing Wilson's definition of biophilia, as the innate emotional affinity that humans have with living systems (1984), he also states that the biophilic effect from the environment directly effects human physiological and psychological wellbeing (Salingaros, 2010). This affiliation is due to the fact that our evolution took place in living environments, where our neuro-perceptive system developed the capacity to recognise some types of geometries and structures more easily than others. Especially those structures embedded in natural and living systems like fractal structures and organised complexities (Salingaros, 2010) that suggest aesthetic experiences. It is important to note that the innate human emotional affiliation with beauty resonates deeply with biophilia and that the binomial beauty-biophilia is then a powerful strength for sustainability and regeneration.

Beauty as a catalyst in encouraging awareness and care.
In her Manifesto, *Sustaining Beauty. The Performance of Appearance*, Elizabeth Meyer raises the question that the aesthetic factor has not been addressed in the sustainability discourse. She notes the importance of aesthetic experiences in supporting sustainable communities and developing an environmental ethic stating:

I call for reinserting the aesthetic into discussions of sustainability. I will make a case for the appearance of the designed landscape as more than a visual, stylistic or ornamental issue, as more than a rear-garde interest in form. I attempt to rescue the visual, by connecting it to the body and poly-sensual experience. I will try to explain how immersive, aesthetic experience can lead to recognition, empathy, love, respect and care for the environment. (2008, p. 7)

For Kagan (2011), reconstructing the wholeness and restoring the reflexive sensibility and connection between human and non-human systems may be facilitated by the arts and culture, promoting sustainable and regenerative processes. He argues that ecological aesthetics embed the interrelation of culture and nature, interweaving the environment's webs of life or natural ecosystems and the social, political and economic aspects of society. This view also aims to re-awaken and incorporate a sensibility for the natural world that is inherent to humans and that modernist, industrial and post-industrial societies have relegated to the background, but which is still alive among indigenous peoples (Kagan, 2011).

Fostering sustainability and regeneration through aesthetic experience. Toward the recognition of the aesthetics of sustainability

Why is it important to 'experience' aesthetics? What kind of learning can be drawn from that experience? Can this learning influence individual/collective behaviour? Authors from different disciplines and approaches have written about the aesthetics of sustainability. They have produced sensitive and thoughtful work sharing the view that aesthetics and beauty are essential attributes within the sustainability discourse, notwithstanding a noted absence.

Regarding landscape architecture, of particular relevance is Elizabeth Meyer's (2008) theoretical conception of sustainable landscape architecture and the understanding of beauty as a means of transformative change, a vision shared by Kagan (2011). Meyer's (2008) manifesto aims to reinscribe the value of the visual – specifically beauty – and the prominence of aesthetic experience as promoters of transformative attitudes, intellectual and moral, toward the environment. She acknowledges the writings of Howett and Spirn in the 1980s as precursors in making the link between aesthetics and ecological design. Meyer argues that beauty and aesthetics matter in the sustainability discourse and that designed landscapes are necessary "to provoke those who experience them to become more aware of how their actions affect the environment, and to care enough to make changes" (2008, p.6). In addition, she states by "connecting the visual experience to the body and poly-sensual experience, […] immersive aesthetic experience can lead to recognition, empathy, love, respect and care for the environment" (2008, p. 7).

Considering design as a cultural ecosystem service, Meyer states that designed landscapes have the essential ability of creating memorable places where human activities and ecological processes coexist. A good example is Crissy Field Park, in San Francisco, designed by George Heargreaves & Associates, where wildlife habitats are juxtaposed with human recreational areas. The experience of beautiful designed landscapes therefore, can promote mindfulness and restorative sensations in our psyche that, in turn, can inculcate environmental values and lead to the appropriation and care of place. It should be noted that the concept of beauty in sustainable landscape design is dynamic, not generic, and is related to the landscape's resilience and capacity of regeneration (Meyer, 2008). In summarising these ideas, "Beautiful sustainable landscape design involve the design of experiences as much as the design of form and the design of ecosystems. These experiences are vehicles for connecting with, and caring for, the world around us" (p. 18).

Similarly, Kagan (2011) argues that the cultural dimension is foundational in understanding sustainability and reality because it moves from a static utopic conception to a more dynamic vision of sustainability. This is a "search process for dynamic balance", based on the comprehension of patterns that pervade and connect different aspects of reality (Kagan, 2011, p. 66). According to Kagan (2011), sustainability relies on resilience and emergence, which encompass natural and cultural diversity and the capacity of learning from the unexpected. For him, openness to uncertainties is a key issue in understanding complexity, both for nature and for human society. Understanding reality means dealing with complexity, and the literacy of complexity involves understanding how natural and human systems – comprising social, cultural, political and economic aspects – respond to unpredicted transformations in themselves and their environments, as well as their ability to create new qualities to the whole and the parts. In other words, understanding reality and sustainable processes requires knowledge about how human and non-human living systems work and evolve (Kagan, 2011; Mang & Reed, 2012).

For this author, the aesthetic of sustainability facilitates the understanding of complexity. This is possible because of the principle of "autoecopoiesis", a term coined by Kagan (2011), pointing to the intelligent and sensible response of systems to disturbance. In other words, ecological aesthetics may help in re-activating the sense of connectedness with and belonging to nature, principles that existential knowledge, Eastern philosophical and religious traditions and some Western thinkers share and celebrate. This concept, as already mentioned, is likewise explored by Salingaros (2010; Salingaros & Masden, 2008) who enhances the idea of the 'seed of conservation' that relies upon the preservation of living forms that secure the structure responsible for providing neurological nourishment to human beings, once human evolution took place in living environments.

The arts and culture, in Kagan's view, may have a central role in re-establishing wholeness, the reflexive sensibility and connection between human and non-human systems, promoting sustainable and regenerative processes. He argues that two practices are relevant to the experience of aesthetics of sustainability: ecological art and, maybe surprisingly, the practice of everyday walking. Firstly, ecological art because it relates to the web of interrelationships of our environment; it engages with natural elements like water, wind and natural materials; informs the public about ecological dynamics and reclaims, restores and remediates damaged environments. Secondly, the practice of walking allows direct contact with nature and facilitates observation, recognition and learning; moving at slow pace facilitates contextual perceptions and supports social and political values dealing with public spaces; it is accessible to most human groups whilst offering experiences that enhance attention and foster serendipity because it is open to unexpected interactions (Kagan, 2011).

Full experience with the environment therefore, can result in communication and participation. Similarly, Meyer notes in her Manifesto (2008) referring to design: "It enables social routines and spatial practices, from daily promenades to commutes to work. It translates cultural values into memorable landscape forms and spaces that often challenge, expand and alter, our conceptions of beauty" (2008, p. 1).

Conclusion

An analysis of the views of the authors from different disciplines and approaches suggests that the aesthetics of sustainability and the new understanding of beauty are essential issues in the regenerative sustainability discourse. An aesthetic of sustainability could be a common ground for the appreciation of humankind's innate affinities with beauty and nature. The perception of beauty could be a catalyst of transformative change and understanding the importance of sensory experiences through the practice of simple and daily habits lead to the appropriation and care of place.

Aesthetic experiences and reflexive sensitivity are essential in (re)-connecting us to the world around us. Given current conditions, new skills are necessary for practitioners to design environments and art works that can promote experiences to engender awareness and care for the whole system. Ecoliteracy may help in recognising patterns that connect us with non-human beings and reveal interrelationships that occur in the shared environment. This new way of thinking about communities, how they are designed within the natural environment and understanding the symbiotic relationship, presupposes sensible approaches and new skills for design practitioners to fulfil the needs of sustainable regenerative urban design practices.

Maria Elena Zingoni de Baro is an architect and urban designer from South America. Born in Argentina, she developed her professional life in Brazil as a practitioner in Architecture and Landscape architecture. In 2009 she came to Perth and since has worked at Curtin University where she is also completing her PhD at the Curtin University Sustainability Policy Institute.

References

Cole, R., Oliver, A. & Robinson, J. (2013). Regenerative design, socio-ecological systems and co-evolution. *Building Research and Information, 41*(2), 237-247. doi:10.1080/09613218.2013.747130

du Plessis, C., & Cole, R. (2011). Motivating change: shifting the paradigm. *Building Research and Information, 39*(5), 436-449.

du Plessis, C. (2012). Towards a regenerative paradigm for the built environment. *Building and Research Information 40*(1), 7-22.

Hartig, T., Bringslimark, T. & Grindal Patil, G. (2008). Restorative design: What, when, where and for whom? In S. Kellert, J. Heerwagen & M. Mador (Eds.), *Biophilic design: The theory, science and practice of bringing buildings to life* (pp. 133-152). Hoboken, NJ: John Wiley and Sons.

Kagan, S. (2011). Aesthetics of sustainability: A transdisciplinary sensibility for transformative practices. *Transdisciplinary Journal of Engineering and Science, Vol.2*, 65-73.

Kellert, S. (2008). Dimensions, elementa, and attributes of biophilic design. In S. Kellert, J. Heerwagen & M. Mador (Eds.), *Biophilic design: The theory, science and practice of bringing buildings to life* (pp. 3-19). Hoboken, NJ: John Wiley and Sons.

Landschaftspark Duisburg Nord by Latz + Partner. (n.d.). Retrieved from http://www.landezine.com/index.php/2011/08/post-industrial-landscape-architecture/

Lovins, A. (2006). Foreword. In Hargroves, K. & Smith, M. (Eds.), *The natural advantage of nations: Business opportunities, innovation and governance in the 21st century* (pp. xix-xxii). London: Earthscan/James & James.

Lubarsky, S. (2011). Reaffirming beauty: A step toward sustainability. *Tikkun, 26*(1). Retrieved from http://www.tikkun.org/nextgen/reaffirming-beauty-a-step-toward-sustainability

Lubarsky, S. (2012). Life-affirming beauty. In T. Butler, D. Lerch and G. Wuerthner (Eds.), *The energy reader: Overdevelopment and the delusion of endless growth*, (n.p.). Healdsburg, CA: Watershed Media and the Post-Carbon Institute.

Lubarsky, S. (n.d., a). On beauty and sustainability. Retrieved from http://www.rsnonline.org/index.php?option=com_content&view=article&id=1464&Itemid=122

Lubarsky, S. (n.d., b). Toward a beauty-centric education. Retrieved from http://www.ecoliteracy.org/essays/toward-beauty-centric-education

Mang, P. & Reed, B. (2012). Designing from place: a regenerative framework and methodology. *Building Research & Information, 40*(1), 23-38.

Mehaffy, M. and Salingaros, N. (2011). The pattern technology of Christopher Alexander. Retrieved from http://www.metropolismag.com/Point-of-View/October-2011/The-Pattern-Technology-of-Christopher-Alexander/

Meyer, E. (2008). Sustaining beauty. The performance of appearance: A manifesto in three parts. *Journal of Landscape Architecture*, Spring 2008.

Moffat, S. and Kohler, N. (2008). Conceptualizing the built environment as a social-ecological system. *Building Research & Information, 36*(3), 248-268.

Orr, D. (2004). Ecological design intelligence. Retrieved from www.ecoliteracy.org/essays/ecological-design-intelligence

Reed, W. (2007a). Shifting from 'sustainability' to regeneration. *Building Research and Information, 35*(6), 674-680.

Reed, W. (2007b). A living systems approach to design. *AIA National Convention May 2007- Theme Keynote Address*. Regenesis and Integrative Design Collaborative.

Salingaros, N. (2010). Life and the geometry of the environment. *The Athens Dialogues e-journal*. Retrieved from http://argos.chs.harvard.edu/cgi-bin/WebObjects/athensdialogues.woa/wa/dist?dis=19

Salingaros, N. & Masden II K. (2008). Neuroscience, the natural environment, and building design. In S. Kellert, J. Heerwagen & M. Mador (Eds.), *Biophilic design: the theory, science and practice of bringing buildings to life* (pp. 59-83). Hoboken, NJ: John Wiley and Sons.

Wilson, E.O. (1984). *Biophilia*. Cambridge, MA: Harvard University Press.

Zingoni de Baro, M. (2013). *The claisebrook story: Rediscovering the spirit of place*. Paper presented at Reading Urban Spaces, East Perth symposium at Curtin University of Technology, Perth, Australia.

CHAPTER THREE

IMAGINE: VISIONS FOR OUR SUSTAINABLE FUTURE: A CASE STUDY OF THE CREATIVE EXPRESSION OF SUSTAINABILITY VISIONS

Susie Waller

Introduction

Humanity's current way of life is unsustainable. That is, our collective lifestyle is unable to continue, as it currently exists, into the future. Not only are there not enough natural resources to sustain our current way of life, our way of life has resulted in many adverse impacts that threaten the wellbeing and survival of humanity, and that of many plant and animal species. These impacts, or global sustainability challenges, include climate change, environmental pollution and degradation, biodiversity loss and resource depletion to name but a few. As David Suzuki urges, "The crisis is real, and it is upon us" (2010, p. 36).

Visioning, a key principle and practice of sustainability, is argued to be the first step in creating a positive, sustainable future (Hopkins, 2008, p. 99). Often these visions take the orthodox form of policies, plans, strategies and reports. It is argued that the creative expression of visions through various artistic media connects us on a deeper, emotional level and can help us to imagine what a sustainable future could actually look, feel, taste, smell and sound like. (Stucker & Bozuwa, 2012). Unfortunately there are limited examples of the creative expression of positive visions for our sustainable future (Hopkins, 2008). In addressing this gap, the project *Imagine: Visions for our sustainable future*, partnering a number of sustainability practitioners with artists in Fremantle, Western Australia, was developed, to envisage a positive, sustainable future and express this creatively in written and visual form. Through a review of relevant sustainability and art literature, this chapter seeks to outline the significance of visioning to sustainability and argues for the expression of visions through various creative media. Utilising a case study and a reflective approach, it also aims to provide a concise account of the methodology, results and key learnings of the Imagine project.

Background

Human beings and the natural world are on a collision course. Human activities inflict harsh and often irreversible damage on the environment and on critical resources. If not checked, many of our current practices put at serious risk the future that we wish for human society and the plant and animal kingdoms, and may so alter the living world that it will be unable to sustain life in the manner that we know. Fundamental changes are urgent if we are to avoid the collision our present course will bring about. (Union of Concerned Scientists, 1992, para. 1)

As the 1,700 strong "senior members of the world's scientific community" above warn, humanity is at a crossroads and there are ultimately two paths to choose from (Union of Concerned Scientists, 1992, para. 14). We can continue on our current "collision course", assuming a business-as-usual approach, and risk facing -largely unprepared and reactively – the irreversible mutilation of our life-supporting planet and immense suffering. Or we can imagine a "future that we wish for human society and the animal and plant kingdoms," a positive sustainable future and subsequently determine an appropriate course of action necessary to achieve this vision; albeit within a world where we still need to confront and address the longer-term adverse impacts of contemporary sustainability challenges. The latter path allows us to be prepared and responsive, and is ultimately a radical new approach. Both paths lead to inevitable change; the situation that we are confronted with is which future and path do we choose? While the choice is ours to make, as Suzuki states, there really is no choice (2010).

The first step in creating a positive, sustainable future is visioning (Hopkins, 2008; Maine State Planning Office, 2003; Stucker & Bozuwa, 2012; Suzuki, 2010; United Nations Environment Programme, 2002). Within the context of sustainability, a vision relates to the future, an imagined and generally sought after vision of the future. A sustainability vision may relate to a determined or indeterminate future time period, though is generally long-term; a probable possible and/or preferred future; and given the anthropocentric nature and inherent hopefulness of the concept of sustainability, a sustainability vision is also generally of a positive, albeit realistic, nature.

Given the broad and interconnected nature of sustainability, a vision for our sustainable future may also incorporate many different areas or dimensions including but not limited to energy, food, transport, medicine/health, education, economy, housing, community, arts/culture, biodiversity, governance, spirituality, production and consumption. A vision aims to provide a real sense or image of what this future world would be like (Hopkins, 2008; Stucker & Bozuwa, 2012).

While used in numerous disciplines, visioning is both an important principle and practice of sustainability. For example, the first of the ten *Melbourne principles for sustainable cities* (United Nations Environment Programme, 2002), 'Vision' advocates that cities determine a long-term sustainability vision; and *The Western Australian state sustainability strategy* also recognises visioning as an integral process principle and tool in sustainability (2003). As a tool for sustainability, visioning is based on a set of sustainability principles; principles including 'intra' and 'inter' generational equity; social wellbeing and empowerment; biodiversity and ecological integrity; and economic security (Government of Western Australia, 2003, pp. 29-30; United Nations Environment Programme, 2002).

The visioning process for sustainability is founded on a sound understanding of our past (where we have been) and current situation (where we are now). This includes identifying strengths and weaknesses as well as opportunities and threats. An assessment or stocktake of these may be required. This understanding or information is then used as a basis for imagining our future sustainability vision (where we want to go). Following the creation of a vision, the process then involves the development and prioritisation of a suite of strategies and actions (how we get there) to achieve the vision (Ames, 1998; Sarkissian, Cook & Walsh, 1997).

Within the field of sustainability, the visioning process may be used by numerous sectors, including community, government, non-government, business, and on varying scales from the personal to the collective, ranging from an organisation, community, city, state, country or even globally. Regardless of the sector or scale, visioning is an engaging, bottom-up and inclusive process, and it involves each and everyone of us in imagining our vision for the future. The process of articulating one's personal vision for sustainability "is easier said than done. Before you can begin to articulate your vision, you have to understand and define just exactly what it is" (Jamir cited in, Stucker & Bozuwa, 2012, p. 56). Only by undertaking this challenging task ourselves can we contribute to the development of a collective vision; it is the joining of our visions, and the commitment to meet our shared vision, that Suzuki and others argue is fundamental to addressing our many sustainability challenges (Sustainability Leaders Network, 2011; Suzuki, 2010; United Nations Environment Programme, 2002).

Visioning is like setting a compass in that it can set the course or direction for a positive, sustainable future. This can be beneficial in a multitude of ways including: determining and prioritising an appropriate course of action (Maine Street Planning Officer, 2003, p. 3; Suzuki, 2010, p. 86); inspiring, motivating and empowering people to act (Power & Dingle, 2005; United Nations Environment Programme, 2002); and providing hope for the future, particularly during difficult times (Gibson, et al., 2005, p. 38; Government of Western Australia, 2003). Rob Hopkins, author of *The transition handbook: From oil dependency to local resilience* (2008), observes that

> It is one thing to campaign against climate change and quite another to paint a compelling and engaging vision of a post-carbon world in such a way as to enthuse others to embark on a journey towards it. We are only just beginning to scratch the surface of the power of a positive vision of an abundant future ... Being able to associate images and a clear vision with how a powered down future might be essential. (p. 94)

Many visions for sustainability, as documented in relevant policies, strategies and plans, can be very dry, uninspiring, and tend to be logical, rational and scientific (Hopkins, 2008; Stucker & Bozuwa, 2012). The language is often government, corporate, or academic-speak, and they are simply abstractions (Stucker & Bozuwa, 2012). Also, often, their outreach tends to be limited. Some visions on the other hand can be catastrophic, negative and fear-based. These grim visions for the future, as Hopkins (2008) argues, can cause "most people [to] simply switch off; they don't want to engage with them" (p. 98). People can become disempowered, unmotivated and despondent, and as Ray and Anderson warn, "(t)ransfixed by an image of our own future decline, we could actually bring it about" (Cited in, Hopkins, 2009, p. 98). Neither of these types of visions give us a real or felt sense of what a positive, sustainable future could look and feel like; nor do they engage and inspire us on a deep level to act (Stucker & Bozuwa, 2012, pp. 46-47). How can we "paint," as Hopkins deliberates, such a "compelling and engaging vision"? Art and creativity is one such way.

Just as visioning is a tool for sustainability, so creativity and the creative expression of visions are also tools. Creativity as a process can help "us learn about ourselves, gain insights about the world," (Stucker & Bozuwa, 2012, p. 51), and creative expression can allow "us to more deeply explore and articulate our visions" (Sustainability Leaders Network, 2011). The creative expression of visions can allow us to really imagine how a positive, sustainable future could be sensed (Coralie, 2008; Stucker & Bozuwa, 2012).

Creativity also engages us on a deeper, emotional and visceral level, both in exploring our personal vision and as as an observer or witness of creatively expressed visions. As Tickell notes, Professor of Sustainable Development Tim Jackson believes art and creativity have a transformative role "in relation to sustainability and our future. He suggests that it is through the artistic process itself that society will place sustainability at its heart, drawing upon art's ability to articulate a vision of the future". (British Council, 2010, p. 4). Writer Jay Griffiths echoes Jackson's sentiments:

> [W]riters and artists have a duty of care to society, musicians and poets are legislators of the soul-world. Good translators are required, not to translate from one actual language into another, but to translate between worlds, from the world of science to the world of imagination. (British Council, 2010, p. 6)

Cowling and Viner continue to argue in fact that "(a)rt and artists can help move the [sustainability] agenda from intellectual understanding to emotional engagement, and then onto action." (British Council, 2010, p.1). Transforming, as Stucker and Bozuwa state, both themselves and their audience (2012, p. 51).

In addition to engaging people on a deeper heart or spirit level, art and creativity are also valued for their ability to communicate across languages and consequently distances; arouse curiosity; inspire action; and generate debate (Gomez-Baeza as cited in De Vlieg, 2009, p. 10). Liverman argues and summarises these roles and benefits eloquently:

The arts have much to offer in catalysing understanding, dialogue and vision for a world that will live within its ecological limits. Art has global reach and can open conversations between generations, nations, and communities. Art can tell stories and give us a language through which to express our emotional experiences ... the arts can rapidly communicate their messages to global audiences in ways that erase national boundaries and create communities of common interest. Artistic endeavours can provoke us to question our humanity, create connections with others and with the natural world, and offer us a vision for alternative future. The arts spring from creativity and we need that human quality not just to produce art but also to develop the future visions for engineers, designers, businesses, technologists and scientists alike. (British Council, 2010, p. 23)

There are many artistic forms that lend themselves to the creative expression of visions including, written, visual, performance and aural forms. Hopkins (2008) advocates for interdisciplinary approaches to visioning and the creative expression of visions. In citing Atlee, Hopkins' supports "the potential power of bringing together activists, creative writers and journalists to form 'think-tanks" that create new stories [and visions] for our times. ... we should be looking to draw in the novelists, poets, artists, and storytellers." (p. 94). He gives an example of the 'Transition Tales' initiative in Totnes, England, "which aims to get people writing stories from different points during Totnes's (sic) [sustainability] transition, as newspaper articles, stories, or agony aunt columns" (p. 94).

There are limited examples of the creative expression of visions for positive, sustainable future, particularly examples that are interdisciplinary in their approach (Hopkins, 2008). Consequently I devised and implemented the Imagine Project in 2012 to respectively envisage a positive, sustainable future and express this creatively through visual art and writing.

Methodology

The Imagine project is based upon a case study and reflective practice approach, methodologies that are commonly used in practice-based research and professional settings, particularly in the social sciences and humanities. The process of reflective practice typically involves four stages: planning, acting, describing and reflecting on the process and outcomes of a relevant action (Bain et al., 2000; Schön, 1983; Waller, 2011). The Imagine project is informed by my personal, professional and academic experience in the areas of visual arts, sustainability studies, community arts, and cultural development and planning. It is also informed by sustainability and art literature previously mentioned.

While there were a multitude of local sustainability practitioners that could have been involved in the project, those selected (Table 1) were chosen for their knowledge of, and commitment to sustainability, as well as their local national and/or international prominence. They were also selected so as to represent the different sectors of the community, non-government, government, business, academia, and the dimensions of sustainability, the spiritual, Indigenous, cultural, environmental, creative, planning, policy, energy, transport, education, economic etc.

There were a large number of Fremantle artists to choose from; those selected (Table 1) were predominantly figurative artists and were chosen to represent a diversity of visual art media. Gender, age and cultural diversity were also a consideration in the selection of participants.(1)

Upon confirmation of participants and funding a project brief was written and distributed. The project brief detailed the project's background and aims, participating sustainability practitioners and artists, coordinator and contact details and process.

Sustainability Practitioners	Artists
Dr Brad Pettitt, Mayor, City of Fremantle	Susanna Castleden, Printmaking
Bruce Abbott, Founder, Replants	Lyn Mazzilli, Painting and printmaking
Josh Byrne, Director, Josh Byrne & Associates	Ian de Souza, Watercolour and inks
Professor Len Collard, Australian Research Fellow Indigenous, School of Indigenous Studies, University of Western Australia	Natalie Reid, Mixed media
Professor Peter Newman, Director, Curtin University Sustainability Policy (CUSP) Institute	Dave Wolfy, Painting/Spray-painting
Piers Verstegen, Director Conservation Council of Western Australia	Twenty Eleven, Urban art
Pilar Kasat, Managing Director Community Arts Network Western Australia	Jilalga Murray-Ranui, Indigenous art and graphic design
Sandra Krempl, Cultural Planner and PhD Candidate	Steven Christie, Illustration
Senator Scott Ludlam, Australian Greens Senator for Western Australia	Reboot, Stencil art
Shani Graham and Tim Darby, Directors Ecoburbia	Allison Snell, Sculpture/Mixed media

Table 1: Sustainability practitioners, artists and project partnerships.

Short biographies of the artists and examples of their artwork were forwarded to the sustainability practitioners, and short biographies of the sustainability practitioners detailing their roles and interests in sustainability were distributed to the artists. (2) After reviewing the material, participants were asked to nominate their top three partner preferences and forward to the coordinator for final selection. (3)

Within the project brief, sustainability practitioners were asked to prepare a written A4 page of their vision for our sustainable future. They were encouraged to draft a vision that was locally and globally considerate, to dream big, and to think about a particular focus for their vision, given the many aspects and dimensions of sustainability. No specific timeframe within which to envisage their sustainable future was set; it was however suggested within/at the end of their lifetime. The sustainability practitioners were informed that their vision was to be used by their partnered artist as the basis for their artwork. The sustainability practitioners had approximately six weeks to complete this task.

Following the receipt of the sustainability practitioners' visions, a two-hour briefing night was held. (4) The briefing night comprised an overview of the Imagine project and process, a sharing of sustainability visions, as well as a brief outline of personal and professional sustainability practice from the sustainability practitioners, and an overview from artists of their creative practice. Participants also had the opportunity to discuss with their partners their vision and artwork ideas. The development of an exhibition catalogue was suggested and unanimously supported. Following the briefing night, artists were asked to interpret and visually express their partnered sustainability practitioner's vision for our sustainable future. Artists were requested to create a two-dimensional form of any medium and size, and were encouraged to use materials of a sustainable nature in both the creation and presentation of their artwork. Artists were given just over three months to complete their artwork. (5) Final artworks were delivered and photographed for the exhibition catalogue. (6)

The resulting ten written visions and ten artworks were displayed in a six-week long exhibition at Little Creatures—a brewery and dining hall located on the Fremantle waterfront—from 28 September to 13 November 2013. The decision to exhibit in a public domain rather than an art gallery was made so as to reach a mainstream audience and maximise audience numbers—Little Creatures has a patronage of approximately 12,000 customers per week. A large board with the question 'What is your vision for our sustainable future?' inscribed across it, and large markers attached, was stationed at the exhibition to engage visitors to think about and share their own vision for the future. (7) 300 print catalogues were made freely available to visitors at the exhibition, and a further 200 were given to key funding organisations (8) for distribution through their networks. Following the completion of the exhibition, an electronic version of the catalogue was made available on the Community Arts Network WA website. (9)

Results

The written visions highlight many shared social, cultural, environmental and economic attributes of a positive, sustainable world. These included:

- The ending of the destruction of as well as the restoration and protection of ecological systems and biodiversity (e.g. through native gardens, reforestation, ecological corridors)
- Local renewable energy sources (e.g., wind, solar, hydrogen, water, geothermal), low/no-carbon footprint.
- Sustainable infrastructure (e.g., rain-water tanks, cycle paths, light rail, hydrogen buses, sustainable designed-housing and -buildings).
- Cultural diversity, including valued local Indigenous culture (e.g., through Indigenous place names, regional treaties).
- Communities of people that are aware, active, collaborative and connected, as well as connected to the environment/place and digitally connected to the international community.
- Strong arts and cultural community and activities.
- Local food production (e.g., backyard, street and rooftop vegetable gardens, composting).
- Local resource sharing (e.g., vehicle-share scheme, street office and television viewing locations) and making.
- Local employment and shorter working-hours ethic.
- A green and knowledge economy, which values social and environmental capital.
- Moderate and local consumption, and a
- Spiritual dimension, a greater consciousness, and strengthening of our senses and other ways of knowing (e.g. intuition).

Many of the visions also highlight unique attributes including: non-detainment of refugees (Kasat); education for sustainability (Kasat); new stories and storytelling (Krempl); intergenerational communities (Krempl); celebration of sustainability achievements (Graham & Darby); legalisation of gay marriage (Verstegen); and democratic and community-based models of political and corporate decision-making and management (Verstegen). Seven of the ten written visions are set within the context of Fremantle, three are non-place specific—Byrne, Krempl and Verstegen—all however are locally and globally considerate. There is not space within this chapter to highlight all of the themes of the written visions, however some of the key and noteworthy themes include:

- Significant change inevitable, planned (desirable) or unplanned (undesirable) paths to future available.
- Challenging aspects of future as a result of the adverse impact of contemporary sustainability challenges, i.e., the visions are grounded in the reality of contemporary sustainability issues e.g., climate change, peak oil etc.
- Sustainability is a journey or way of life, not necessarily a destination .
- Visions connected to the personal lives of sustainability practitioners; highlight importance of personal, present-day action.
- Critique of contemporary way of life and paradigm, including capitalism.
- Reflections/reminiscences on contemporary life and sustainability successes, seen/enhanced in future.
- Predominant focus on physical experience or sense of future sustainable world, both natural and human-made, and a
  - Link to bigger picture, i.e., "(W)hy are we here? What is our purpose?" (Abbott).

The sustainability practitioners demonstrated the use of various creative writing techniques in their visions. All of the visions were written in first-person, except Graham and Darby's, which was written in third-person. The tone of the narratives varied, ranging from the formal (Collard), sombre (Byrne), serious (Verstegen) and satirical (Abbott), to the cheerful (Graham & Darby), poetic (Ludlam) and animated (Krempl). All of the sustainability practitioners used language that was imaginative and descriptive. Two, Pettit and Kasat, also wrote their visions in narrative form, giving an account of a series of activities they undertook and features they encountered during the course of a day set in the future. Graham and Darby's vision was written in the form of a newspaper article celebrating their "20th year of monthly [community] feasts". The article includes a number of quotes from themselves and other members of the "'unintentional' community of Chesterfield, located in South Fremantle."

The artworks

The artworks were created in a variety of media, comprised of both figurative and abstract works. A brief overview is provided of three artworks from each of the three aforementioned categories.

Christie's *Everything is good and nobody minds*, (Figure 1), is a visual expression of Krempl's vision *Universal wonder*. The artwork is a hand-drawn illustration of an urban biophillic landscape in Fremantle on a re-purposed brown background. The landscape features a number of physical forms, both human-made and natural, including street-trees, street furniture, heritage buildings entwined in vegetation, roof gardens, birds flying in the sky, (10) as well as people of varying ages walking, sitting in cafes and waiting for the bus, and cycling on the road. The sky appears to be a mass of swirling of clouds.

Figure 1: Steven Christie, *Everything is good and nobody minds,* 2012, technical pen on paper and card, 255 x 370 mm. Copyright, Steven Christie.

Natalie Reid's quadriptych, *Four Ways to be Held – Being Within Wardan Lane Kodjal Kodjal Bidi Barang – Nitja Bwoora Wardan Bidi* (Figure 2) is a visual expression of Collard's vision. Each of the four panels, a silkscreen, monoprint and pencil on paper, has an English/Nyungar subtitle. Each of the panels are abstract, comprising a range of deep colours, from reds and greens to oranges and blues, as well as surface textures. The story that is represented on the four panels is based upon Wardan Lane, the first Nyungar-named street in Fremantle in 2011, *wardan* being the location of an Aboriginal dreamtime story of the local sea and land winds/spirits. The first panel depicts the male wind or *maaman mar*, the cool afternoon sea breeze or south westerly coming off the Indian Ocean to the land (also referred to colloquially as the Fremantle Doctor). The second depicts the *yorga mar* or female wind, the warm easterly wind coming off the eastern desert to meet the ocean. "Noongar dreamtime tells us that the yorga mar and maaman mar were lovers and would chase each other back and forth over the wardan [sea] and across the boodjar (land), giving Fremantle its daily easterly and south westerly breezes" (City of Fremantle, 2011).

The third panel depicts the coming together of these two winds, causing the local trees to dance and be sustained, while the fourth reflects the spirit of these winds and how when sitting under the trees and listening to the rustling leaves, "you can … hear the two lovers whispering to each other" (City of Fremantle, 2011).

Figure 2: Natalie Reid, *Four ways to be held – Being Within Wardan Lane Kodjal Kodjal Bidi Barang – Nitja Bwoora Wardan Bidi*, silkscreen monoprint and pencil on paper, quadriptych, 320 x 700mm each. Copyright, Natalie Reid.

Susanna Castleden's interpretation of Pettitt's vision, *Saturday morning*, comprises a screen print of an old map of Fremantle and the marking of Pettitt's journey from his home through the city and back again with a green line (Figures 3 and 4). On the route Castleden highlights with text his activities and sustainability features experienced throughout the day.

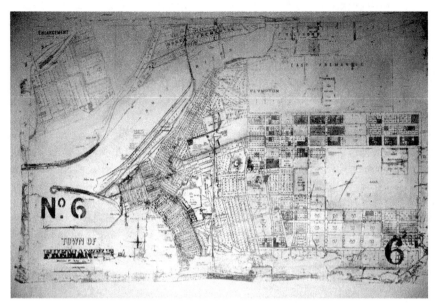

Figure 3: Susanna Castleden, *Saturday morning,* 2012, screen print and gesso on paper, 1200 x 800 mm. Copyright, Susanna Castleden.

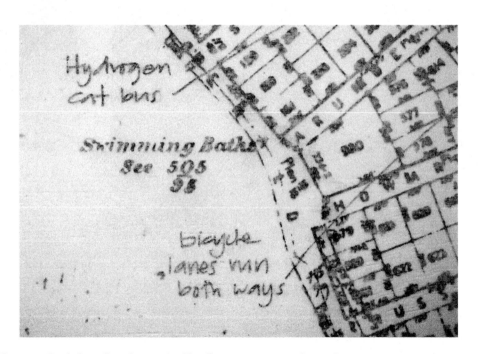

Figure 4: Susanna Castleden, *Saturday morning* (detail), 2012, screen print and gesso on paper, 1200 x 800 mm. Copyright, Susanna Castleden.

The majority of artworks capture one or a number of aspects of their partner's vision, rather than encapsulating the visions in their entirety. Twenty Eleven's is an example where the artist has honed in on one particular aspect of his partner's vision—Verstegen's concluding refrain, "Oh, and gay people can marry."

Discussion

In reflecting on the process and outcomes of the Imagine project—the fourth key stage of reflective practice—a number of key observations and recommendations for future practice were identified. The first observation relates to the varied figurative and abstract artistic expressions of the written visions. While I selected artists who were primarily figurative artists and foresaw the production of largely figurative artworks, I did not stipulate in the project brief that artists had to create figurative, representational artworks; this was left intentionally open for the artists to determine. The Imagine project was intended to give visitors a real sense of what a positive, sustainable world would be like, what it would look and feel like. As Hopkins (2008) states, it is important to "to paint a compelling and engaging vision of a [sustainable] world in such a way so as to enthuse others to embark on a journey towards it" (p. 94).

It is my opinion that the figurative or illustrative artworks, rather than abstract artworks, were more successful in giving visitors a clear and real sense of what a sustainable future could be like, as abstract artwork can be difficult to interpret. I consider the abstract expression of visions for our sustainable future can act as a further barrier to visitors engaging with and understanding sustainability and being inspired to action. One way of addressing this would have been to ask artists to provide a short written interpretation of their artworks in relation to their partners' vision that could have sat alongside the artworks in the exhibition and/or included in the catalogue. Another recommendation for future application would be to select only figurative artists and/or prescribe that the artworks are to be figurative or illustrative only.

The second observation of the Imagine project was that the written visions of the sustainability practitioners contained much 'food for thought' for the artists. While sustainability practitioners were encouraged to focus on one particular aspect or dimension of sustainability, this is problematic given the interconnected, holistic and ubiquitous nature of sustainability. Consequently it was difficult and unrealistic for the artists to encapsulate all aspects of their partner's vision for our sustainable future. While not a failure of the project, numerous possibilities for the Imagine project could have taken advantage of this. These possibilities and opportunities for similar projects include artists creating a number of artworks that express their partner's vision or artists creating a number of artworks that express each, or a number of sustainability practitioners' visions.

The third finding was that while it was not my original intention to create an exhibition catalogue detailing the written and artistic visions, the catalogue has been invaluable. Firstly the print catalogue, which was made available at the exhibition, meant that visitors could take away and digest the visions, particularly the written visions, in their own time and in further detail. And secondly, the electronic catalogue, which was uploaded to the Community Arts Network WA website following the exhibition, and where it is still located, allows for an increased and ongoing number of visitors to view the exhibition globally. In short, the print and electronic catalogue have ensured access to, and the longevity of, the project. One additional observation is that the oral recording of the written visions for both the exhibition and for inclusion in the catalogue would have been another way to improve audience accessibility for those who might be visually impaired.

The fourth observation relates to the use of various creative writing techniques by sustainability practitioners in their visions. While not necessary, perhaps the project could have been further enhanced by providing creative writing skills development to the sustainability practitioners so as to further engage the audience. This could be in the form of written information and/or a skills development workshop/s with a creative writer. This could contribute to more engaging written visions, visions that evoke strong sensory images and experiences for visitors.

Finally, the Imagine project relates to the interactive activity at the exhibition that attempted to engage visitors to think about their own vision for our sustainable future. As mentioned previously, a large board with the question 'What is your vision for our sustainable future?' inscribed across it was stationed at the exhibition, however due to inappropriate comments, had to be removed after a few days. The lack of staffing throughout the exhibition was a major reason this occurred. In my opinion, however, the large patronage of the exhibition location far outweighs the engagement aspect. One suggestion for future projects could be the development of a coinciding website where visitors can view the written and creative visions and share their own visions online.

Conclusion

Change is inevitable, it is a way of life. The truth is that the future world will be very different to what it is today, because our current way of life is unsustainable. There are simply not enough natural resources to sustain our current way of life, and our lifestyles are also threatening our existence and that of many other species, through climate change, and other adverse impacts and challenges. Our predicament necessitates us to envisage a positive, sustainable future. Visioning is a tool that can assist in imagining and creating a positive, sustainable world, and the creative expression of these visions through various artistic media can provide us with a real and felt sense of what this world could be like. The Imagine project attempts to do just this.

Susie Waller is a community cultural development and sustainability practitioner based in Fremantle, Western Australia. With a background in visual arts and sustainable development, she currently runs her own business, Enliven: Arts, Culture, Sustainability, providing a range of services, namely project conception, development and management. She is currently enrolled in PhD at Curtin University investigating the role of arts and creativity in catalysing positive sustainable change.

Endnotes

1. Many of the participants, largely the sustainability practitioners, were personally known to me prior to the project. Funding was sought and received from the City of Fremantle to pay each of the artists for their involvement in the project and the creation of the artwork. The sustainability practitioners were asked to participate in the project voluntarily or rather in their professional capacities—this however was to be compensated by the fact that they would be gifted with the resulting artwork.

2. This information was provided/approved by participants.

3. The majority of participants were partnered with their first or second preference. For the participants where this was unable to occur, I used my judgement both in terms of the sustainability practitioners' background and interest in sustainability, and the artists' creative style and previous artwork.

4. The Briefing Night was held at the Curtin University Sustainability Policy (CUSP) Institute in Fremantle.

5. It was anticipated that partners would be engaged in continued dialogue in relation to the sustainability vision and/or artwork being created following the briefing night and consequently it was recommended that one to two hours be allocated for this.

6. The catalogue was illustrated by myself and designed by Emma Fletcher, Communications and Marketing Coordinator, Community Arts Network WA.

7. The interactive message board located at the exhibition was utilised by visitors on the opening night and for a series of days of the exhibition's duration, however it had to be removed by Little Creatures staff due to inappropriate/explicit inscription. Unfortunately I was unable to locate the said

board—and consequently I was unable to view the visitor contributions—so for the remainder of the exhibition no interactive activity was available to visitors.

8. The Community Arts Network WA and the Conservation Council of Western Australia.

9. http://www.canwa.com.au/resources/LLR-Imagine-Visions-for-our-Sustainable-Future.pdf

10. The birds are not captured in the image of the artwork in the catalogue as they were added by the artist after the work had been photographed.

References

Ames, S. (ed.). (1998). *A guide to community visioning: Hands-on information for local communuities.* Oregon: American Planning Association.

Bain, J., McNaught, C., Rice, M., & Tripp, D. (2000). *Handbook for learning centred evaluation of computer-facilitated learning projects in higher education.* Perth : Murdoch University.

British Council, (2010). *Long horizons: An exploration of art + climate change.* London: British Council.

City of Fremantle. (2011) Wardan Lane unveiled. Retrieved from http://www.fremantle.wa.gov.au/home/List_of_News_and_Media/May_2012/Wardan_Lane_unveiled

Coralie, J. (2008). The oasis in the ruins: A sustaining and sustainable art. *PAN: Philosophy Activism Nature,* 5, 13-19. Retrieved from http://search.informit.com.au/fullText;dn=210322700585592; res=IELHSS

DeVlieg, M. A. (2009). Arts, culture and sustainability: Visions for the future. In A. E. Foundation (Ed.), *Arts. Environment. Sustainability. How can culture make a difference?* (pp. 9-24) Singapore: Asia-Eurpoe Foundation. Retrieved from http://www.asef.org/images/docs/Culture%20make %20a%20difference.pdf

Gerring, J. (2007). *Case study research: Principles and practices.* Cambridge: Cambridge University Press.

Gibson, R. B., Hassan, S., Holtz, S., Tansey, J., & Whitelaw, G. (2005). *Sustainability assessment: Criteria, processes and applications.* London, UK: Earthscan.

Government of Western Australia. (2003).

Hope for the future: The Western Australian state sustainability strategy: A vision for quality of life in Western Australia. Perth, Western Australia: State Government of Western Australia.

Hopkins, R. (2008). *The transition handbook: From oil dependency to local resilience.* Devon: Green Books. Maine State Planning Office. (2003). *Community visioning handbook: How to imagine – and create – a better future.* Maine: Maine State Planning Office.

Power, T., & Dingle, P. (2005). *Goal getting: The science of achieving goals.* Perth: Comet Publishing.

Sarkissian, W., Cook, A., & Walsh, K. (1997). *Community participation in practice: A practical guide.* Murdoch, Western Australia: Institute for Sustainability and Technology Policy, Murdoch University.

Schön, D. (1983). *The reflective practitioner: How professionals think in action.* New York: Basic Books.

Stucker, D., & Bozuwa, J., (2012). The art of sustainability: Creative expression as a tool for social change. *Reflections the SoL Journal on Knowledge, Learning and Change,* 12(2), 45-57. Retrieved from http://www.sustainabilityleadersnetwork.org/wp-content/uploads/2012/08/Art-of-Sustainability-Stucker-and-Bozuwa-SoL-Reflections-Journal-v12-n2.pdf

Sustainability Leaders Network. (2011). Practices. Retrieved from http://www.sustainabilityleadersnetwork.org/practices/

Suzuki, D. (2010). *The Legacy: An elder's vision for our sustainable future.* NSW, Australia: Allen & Unwin.

Tate. (2012) The Tate glossary. Retrieved from http://webarchive.nationalarchives.gov.uk/20120203094030/http://www.tate.org.uk/collections /glossary/

Union of Concerned Scientists: Citizens and Scientists for Environmental Solutions. (1992). *World scientists' warning to humanity*. Retrieved from http://www.ucsusa.org/about/1992-world-scientists.html

United Nations Environment Programme. (2002) Melbourne principles for sustainable cities. *United Nations Environment Programme: Department of Technology, Industry and Economics*. Retrieved from http://www.unep.or.jp/ietc/kms/datat/86.pdf

Waller, S. (2011). *Sustainability, sense of place and story: A case study of the Pilbara region*. (Masters dissertation). Western Australia. Murdoch, Western Australia: Murdoch University.

CHAPTER FOUR

ARTISTIC PRACTICES AND ECOAESTHETICS IN POST-SUSTAINABLE WORLDS

Perdita Phillips

Introduction

This chapter considers the question of sustainability and aesthetics from the perspective of an artist's critical reflection on contemporary environmental art practice. It adopts a specifically concretionary approach, examining the way concepts from different disciplines might be able to generate creative and speculative aesthetic possibilities. It considers scientific ecology alongside allusions to Guattari's (2000) 'three ecologies'. It argues that art and aesthetics has a role in 'unsolidifying' sustainability. Through reference to a practice-based example, it concludes with a call for an aesthetic of action in the face of the inevitable uncertainties inherent in an ecological worldview.

The dynamic field

The domain of sustainability has as many different adherents as it has variations in its applications. The very fact that interdisciplinarity is at its core, combining of the three pillars of economic, social and environmental well-being, generates a diversity of responses. It is both a strength and a weakness and to be able to reconcile these competing interests is obviously one of sustainability's greatest practical challenges. The concept of sustainability (and its frequent conflation with sustainable development), its discourse and societal application have been subject to a range of critique. Although originating from concern from the sciences about environmental issues, the vocabulary of sustainability is replete with economic terms (such as natural capital or triple bottom line). The original definition, "development that meets the needs of the present without compromising the ability of future generations to meet their own needs" (World Commission on Environment and Development, 1987, p. 37, also known as the Brundtland Report) makes explicit the centrality of an anthropocentric, progressive development mentality. Confusion arises as to whether we are developing sustainment or sustaining development (Phillips, 2007b); the word sustainability can imply maintaining stable conditions (1) and this can be interpreted as a conservative strategy and in the worst case, foster inaction rather than action (Holden, 2010).

Like many overarching concepts there is a danger that sustainability can become an empty rhetorical vessel: products (or actions) can be labelled 'sustainable' without discerning the matter of *degree* or *quality*. The more sustainability is made mainstream in government and business (2) the more it is susceptible to minor tweaking of products or systems rather than wholesale change. At the level of the individual, product greenwashing has its parallel in our rationalisation of small changes to our lives where we may be deluding ourselves about the impact we are having. Sadly there is ample evidence that environmental indicators are deteriorating (National Sustainability Council, 2013) and that we are not addressing adequately the *nature* and *scale* of the issues that are facing us. The realisation that we are living in the Anthropocene places further demands upon us to reconsider our human-centred position. The death of environmentalism has already been proclaimed (Shellenberger & Nordhaus, 2004, 2006). Mentz (2012) goes as far as to contend that we are already in a post-sustainable world.

Hector, Christensen and Petrie (2014) and others (e.g., Redclift, 2007; Weinstein & Turner, 2012; Ziegler & Ott, 2011) argue that critical reflection is required on the political and philosophical underpinnings of sustainability and sustainable development. Values and beliefs held about sustainability differ. It seems difficult to reconcile the prudentially-conservationist and environmental-preservationist positions identified by Hector, Christensen and Petrie. There are contrasting opinions as to whether unsustainability can be solved primarily by technological and economic changes or whether individual value changes are the most important element. Paradoxically, rather than relying upon the *clarification* of definitions and positions, John Robinson argues that "the power of the concept of sustainability… lies precisely in the degree to which it brings to the surface these contradictions and provides a kind of discursive playing field in which they can be debated" (2004, p. 382). Whilst remaining critical of sustainability, he goes on to argue that new configurations of sustainability can still be useful – ones that are action-oriented, go beyond technical fixes, are integrative and that incorporate "a recognition of the social construction of sustainable development, and engages local communities in new ways" (p. 369). How can a *post*-sustainability thus be made more dynamic and flexible?

Turning now to aesthetics, what are its limitations in addressing sustainability? I shall make clear at this point that I am an artist rather than a philosopher so my focus is on the practical application of aesthetics. In this chapter I am looking at aesthetics as firstly, a set of principles that underlie the work of an artist or movement and secondly, in the sense of a combination of *qualities* that pleases the visual, moral or intellectual faculties. There is a strong historico-cultural tradition of beauty being associated with harmony and balance. First I will explore how notions of aesthetics are relevant to sustainability via an examination of the concepts of complexity and resilience.

A complexity/resilience aesthetic

The systems sensibility will be like that of the musical ear which perceives the competitions, symbioses, interferences, overlaps of themes in one same symphonic stream, where the brutal mind will only recognise one single theme surrounded by noise (Edgar Morin cited in Kagan, 2010b, p. 1098).

A complex adaptive system (CAS) is a collection of elements that are interrelated by a dense network of connections. Because they are complex, cause and effect relationships are difficult to predict, but because they have self-organising elements, learning and adaptation is possible. The theoretical background for CAS comes from complexity studies, chaos and systems theory and theoretical ecology. CAS theory has been applied to ecosystems and environmental management and been used to explain various human systems. Espinosa and Walker have critically assessed the failures of sustainability and applied CAS to sustainable governance (2011) and Darnton, Elster-Jones, Lucas, & Brooks have considered the application of CAS in promoting positive environmental behaviour (2006).

Simus (2008) has investigated how a more complex ecology might affect environmental aesthetics. He argues that aesthetics should be based on appreciation of natural processes and responses should be cognisant of the effects of different spatial and temporal scales. Simus calls for an aesthetic that comes from constant, generative, dynamic and fluctuating conditions of change: 'our gaze must be adaptive, fluid and flexible according to appropriate spatiotemporal scale' (2008, p. 70). If aesthetics is to be influenced by the ecological science, it becomes critical to understand how society views, values (both positively and negatively) and responds to change. Uncertainty/complexity means that there is always an uniqueness to specific places: a fruitful area for environmental art is investigations of how we discover, value and work with local places.

Balance of nature	Nature in flux
Natural systems are closed.	Natural systems are not closed, discrete objects. They are more open with movements across boundaries.
Natural systems are self-regulating.	Natural systems are not balanced, and fluctuate.
Equilibrium comes to a point.	Natural processes have no single goal: they have no telos.
Ecological succession is fixed and its path is predictable.	Succession is not fixed but irregular.
Disturbances to natural systems are exceptional.	Disturbances are not exceptional but common and necessary.
Humans are separate and excluded from the definition of nature.	Humans make up a fundamental component of ecological systems.
Unity, harmony, order, balance.	Disunity, disharmony, disorder, imbalance.

Table 1: Balance of nature and Nature in flux. From Pickett and Ostfeld (1995), with further additions by the author.

A concept derived from CAS, is the idea of resilience in environmental systems. In the last 50 years a lot of environmental art has been concerned with seeking a balance with nature. But contrary to what the general public might like to believe, the environment is full of crises and catastrophes. It is not that disturbance doesn't happen in 'natural' ecosystems, but a question of whether systems can cope with the magnitude and speed of change. The concept of an adaptive cycle is therefore key to understanding our futures (Figure 1).

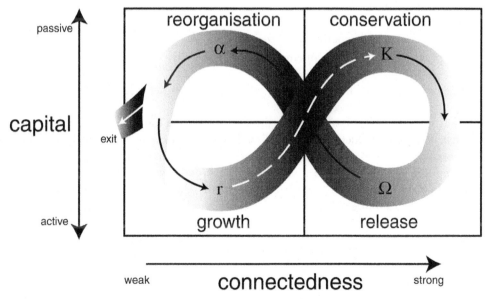

Figure 1: The Adaptive Cycle.

Imagine a coral atoll that emerges from the sea (r). Over time coral and coral sands are accumulated the island is colonised by low shrubby beach plants, then larger trees such as mangroves or coconuts. Eventually a low forest is formed (K). Then a cyclone comes along and causes a catastrophic breakdown (Ω). The coral island may slowly build up over time to form a mature community again (α). But perhaps it may not if sea levels have risen and there are no longer conditions for coral to accumulate and form a coral cay and the system *exits* to another state. Resilience is a measure of whether ecosystems are equipped to absorb disturbance and reorganise whilst undergoing change, so as to still retain essentially the same function, structure, identity, and feedbacks (Walker, Holling, Carpenter & Kinzig, 2004).

The problem western socio-ecological systems have as a whole is that they have a preference for stability and optimised conditions. A typical agricultural system hold conditions stable (K) as long as possible, favouring monocultures, which are easy to manage – to keep in the one state by pumping fossil fuels and fertilisers in to support them. Such systems 'avoid' pain, but lose out on taking advantage of adverse circumstances. With change (moving from Ω to α), the future is up for grabs. Invention, experimentation and re-sorting are the norm. Pioneer species appear seemingly from nowhere. Novelty thrives and small chance events can powerfully reshape the future (Walker & Salt, 2006). Stepping back for a moment and considering this scenario more analogically, seeing ecosystems as being-in-flux allows us to consider, do we remain (as a culture, as socio-ecological systems) stable in the same state or do we cultivate the ability to respond to change?

Part of the critical framing of an aesthetic of sustainability has already been explored by artists and thinkers such as pioneers Helen Mayer Harrison and Newton Harrison (1985) and Maja and Reuben Fowkes (Fowkes & Fowkes, 2006, 2012) and sociologist Sacha Kagan (2011). Sustainability's broad nature both mirrors the complexity of environmentalism and allows for many different aesthetic approaches. Some common characteristics I have observed in a range of contemporary environmental art include:

- a *sensibility to*, and *mindfulness of*, environments.
- *responsiveness* to and *responsibility* towards environments (Fowkes & Fowkes, 2006).
- embracing interrelatedness: *to find and make connections*: being 'sensitive to patterns that connect' (Gregory Bateson via Kagan, 2010b, p. 1098).
- valuing iterative and experimental processes.
- incorporating adaptability, ephemerality and ambiguity.

Looking more broadly I have identified eight key ecoaesthetic sensibilities of in the work of a wider range of artists (see Table 2).

No one artwork includes all of these sensibilities, but it is in these deeper qualities that new potentials in sustainability can be identified. It is possible to *create* complex adaptive systems and think and act across boundaries. A post-sustainable aesthetic asks creators/viewers/participants to decrease their consumption and also to take a transdisciplinary perspective. Transdisciplinarity goes further than interdisciplinary in that it is "the recognition of the existence of different levels of reality governed by different types of logic" (from the *Charter of Transdisciplinarity* cited in Kagan, 2010b, p. 1097).

Sensibility	Example
Making invisible processes 'visible'.	*Incompatible elements*, Josephine Starrs and Leon Cmielewski (2010 -)
Using questioning, dialogue and exchange.	*Salmoncity.net*, Kim Stringfellow (2001).
To think at different scales of time and space.	*Longplayer*, Jem Finer (1999-2999).
To explore ecological processes rather than focus on single objects (Simus, 2008).	*Das vegetative Nervensystem*, Gerda Steiner and Jörg Lenzlinger (2006).
Revisiting place as belonging-in-flux.	*Uncertainty In The City*, Snæbjörnsdóttir/Wilson (2007-2010).
To *create* complex adaptive systems.	*Peninsula Europe* projects, Newton and Helen Mayer Harrison (2003-2008).
Transdisciplinarity.	Cape Farewell Project, (founded by artist David Buckland, 2001-)
Walking on uneven ground.	*herethere* series, Perdita Phillips (2006).

Table 2. Eight Ecoaesthetic Sensibilities

Ecosystemic thinking

I have discussed elsewhere (2012) what it means to adopt a resilient style of walking as a metaphor and *tactical* position - continually adjusting your balance whilst coping with delays and picking yourself up after failure – the art of walking on uneven ground. From the range of artworks I have observed, searching for a consistent visual aesthetic of sustainability is probably missing the point. As a set of aesthetic principles underlying and guiding the work of a particular artist, they are more likely to be conceptual or intellectual in nature. The aesthetics of contemporary environmental art has moved a long way from classical or neo-Kantian notions of beauty as unity, stability and balance. What might it mean to extend the 'boundaries' of how we think? I'm arguing for an aesthetics of *thinking through* complex environmental problems – of ecosystemic thinking – of being more flexible and responsive to change and treasuring diversity (see Patchett & Phillips, 2013). Through artworks, this may be one way of *unsolidifying* the rational-economic basis of sustainability.

Zombie environmentalism

In previous work (Phillips, 2013a, 2013b) I have discussed the shift in some recent environmental art from 'nature as balance' to a darker tone. Work by artists such as Edward Burtynsky documents environmental problems and brings strong visual images of pollution and consumption to the public consciousness. But it has always troubled me as to how effective these images were in penetrating the values, opinions and actions of viewers. Connected to this is a trend in early 21st century relations with the natural world that I've defined as Zombie Environmentalism. It is:

- the behaviour of individuals or groups in society which is willingly or unconsciously *uncaring* of the natural world and the *consequences* of individual or collective behaviours.
- the apparent *attraction* to the dark side — polluted conditions make for sexy art.
- a certain tendency in some environmentalists that since disaster has come, it's time to build your survival shelter and retreat.

Sometimes the latter comes across almost as revelling in the apocalyptic. All of these are certainly coping strategies, but ultimately they are a turning away, a deadening of the senses, a deadening of materiality, a deadening of responses, a closing of perception of nonhuman worlds. Provocatively, if the world is un-beautiful, does this decouple us from ethical action? If we are already in the world of disaster then we are already post-sustainable. The question then is how to keep upright on our feet and not let the present conditions stop us from functioning.

Living beauty

The previously discussed strategy of augmenting aesthetics by borrowing from complexity and ecology is a form of scientific cognitivism that suggests environmental aesthetics can benefit from this particular method of understanding the environment. But is it a question too, of re-evaluating what might be considered beautiful with other methods of understanding and then applying this *back* to sustainability? Consider that overtly sustainable art asks of audiences to do *something* and frequently to do it differently, if not *radically* so. But these types of works can appear earnest and emit a strong sense of 'duty' that at times becomes onerous and creates 'bad art' (Anonymous Artist (who has made both good and bad environmental art), 2005). Even in the more challenging and more oblique environmental artworks, there is a tension between using art in an instrumentalist way and any notion of the autonomy of art or the independence of aesthetics. It is not the first time that art has been used to promote an ideological point of view (see Petras, 1999), but is it possible to retain a contemporary criticality with the ethical imperative implicit in any eco-aesthetics? A similar situation arises in literary ecocriticism. To explore this, instead of gleaning possibilities from the sciences as I did previously, I will pick up some threads from certain vitalist tendencies.

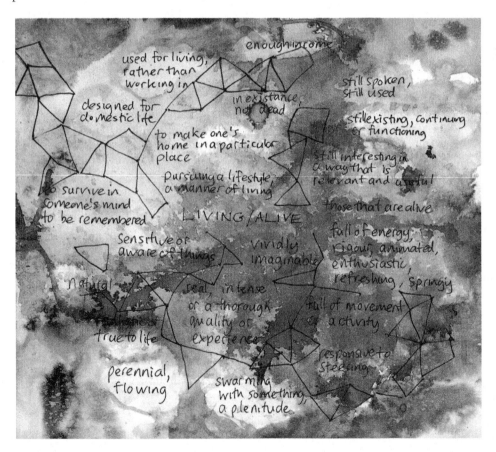

Figure 2. Living/Alive

Consider the range of values associated with 'living' and 'alive' in Figure 2. Here it can be seen that living is connected with the nonhuman other at the same time as it describes human lifestyle and place of habitation. At the same time as it is active and energetic, it is a reminder of things that are remembered and kept with us. It is vivid and imaginative but also homely and welcoming. What happens if beauty itself is seen as living, communicating and alive? Vitalism is of course something specifically rejected by today's science, but around the end of the 19th century when the limits of biological life were being explored, it was harnessed as a specific rejection of a mechanistic and atomistic biology. For these vitalists, underlying life was an invisible force that distinguished living from non-living matter (Normandin & Wolfe, 2013). More recent forms of vitalism have worked at ways of combining both process (becoming) and material:

> …objects, subjects, concepts are composed of nothing more or less than relations, reciprocal unfoldings gathered together in temporary and contingent unities… since a relation cannot exist in isolation, all entities can be understood in relation to one another. (Fraser, Kember & Lury, 2005, p. 3)

In this more modern usage the vital qualities of living things have been extended to the inorganic. The 'essence' of the vitalism is not ether-like but is in the nature of the 'becoming'. Contradictorily, at the same time as a relational framework makes 'things' appear materially insubstantial it also makes all things capable of 'movement' in the world. This of course creates an ethical imperative (3):

Rather than approach this world as a warehouse of inert things we wish to pile up for later use, we must hold ourselves accountable to a materiality that is never merely an external, blank, or inert space but the active, emergent substance of ourselves and others. (Alaimo, 2012, pp. 563-564).

Thinking about how this might be applied to aesthetics I was intrigued to discover that 167 years ago John Ruskin had written about 'vital beauty' – a definition of beauty as being capable of nourishment and therefore of change – as opposed to his more classical 'typical beauty' (Frost, 2012). The former allows us to focus upon the dynamic, creative and cooperative in nature (and art). In *Venus in Exile* (2001) Wendy Steiner notes:

> I think we must stop treating beauty as a thing or quality, and see it instead as a kind of communication… Beauty is an unstable property because it is not a property at all. It is the name of a particular interaction between two beings, a 'self' and an 'Other'.

In an interview with Arjen Mulder she describes the important role of interactivity in an artwork where in the best of cases one gives oneself up as a viewer *in a living way* so that the Other (in the artwork) may live. The idea that emerges from this milieu is to grow *generosity* into the relationships between the artist, model, artwork and audience (Steiner, 2012). Here the relationships between 'things' are treated as a living, active space.

Hope and practicalities?

> What hope is there for sustainability when conspicuous consumption holds all the cards for pleasure: self-realization, aesthetic transport, spiritual transcendence? (Steiner, 2009, p. 5)

Hope and practicalities? Can austerity be fun? Art and artists in post-sustainable times need to grapple with how we live a life that is pleasurable (and beautiful) with less consumption. Others have noted the fundamental contradiction of producing material artworks (4) (e.g., Bamford, 2011), but at this point I want to examine how consumption might otherwise be rerouted (5). This is different from creating pictures of environmental degradation. Concentrating on the top-heavy consumption by wealthy nations, which have a significant impact on global sustainability (Worldwatch Institute, 2013), it can be seen that conspicuous consumption and affluenza (see Hamilton & Denniss, 2005) are examples of zombie environmentalism. Lauren Berlant highlights the condition of cruel optimism – when something that is desired is actually an obstacle to flourishing. She deems it a double bind: "even with an image of a better good life available to sustain your optimism, it is awkward and it is threatening to detach from what is already not working" (Berlant, 2011, p. 263). She also highlights the fact that this consumer life is itself a grind.

Formulating the idea of alternative hedonism, Kate Soper points out that affluent consumption "is both compromised by its negative effects (including congestion, pollution, overwork and stress) and pre-emptive of other possible pleasures and satisfactions" (2007, p. 205). Soper's position is less ambivalent than Berlant, ascribing more agency to those who slip sideways away from the bind of consumption. She points to the dependence of globalised capitalism on consumers not connecting the consequences of consumption on environments and societies at the same time as being permanently seduced by endlessly seeking the incomplete pleasure of consuming.

By mobilising self-interest, alternative hedonism provides alternative possibilities for artists to critique consumption other than picturing the prodigious mountains of environmental waste as despair. Soper sees a role for artists in the creation and evolution of an anti-consumerist aesthetic. Aesthetic suspension and reordering is needed "whereby the commodities once perceived as enticingly glamorous come gradually instead to be seen as cumbersome and ugly in virtue of their association with unsustainable resource use, noise, toxicity or their legacy of unrecyclable waste" (Soper, 2008, p. 580). We must "detach the values of self-expressivity, excitement, and ecstasy from waste, and attach them instead to sustain-ability [sic]" (Steiner, 2009, p. 3). Such moves can highlight things that are "residual and disappearing", but it is also about "the interstitial and emerging" (Soper, 2008, p. 578).

As part of moving pleasure elsewhere, there is work to be done in making unconsumption attractive by attaching pleasure to things that cannot be consumed (e.g. surprise and wonder and Soper's diversity, change, novelty, self development). Artists are already creating experiences that highlight pleasure of gifts, giving and exchange (Purves, 2005) and highlighting sensory pleasures that consumerism denies (e.g., Slow Art Day), with the ultimate goal of permanently turning down consumption.

A second strategy for reconceptualising austerity is to rethink the quantity of happiness in life. Recognising that consumption may have given us unrealistic expectations about how much happiness the individual will encounter every day is part of this. Wanting what one has, rather than what one doesn't is related to mindfulness (Brown, Kasser, Ryan, Linley, & Orzech, 2009). But the issue is also raised when tackling the negative apocalyptic and thinking through how there can be a move on from the guilt in environmentalism. Here I take from philosopher Tim Morton's investigations into guilt, shame, melancholia and sadness:

> …normative environmentalism wants me to feel guilty or ashamed, and in doing so it scratches at the itch of human being, an itch that is already rubbed raw by the very modernity that created the current ecological emergency. (2012, p. 17)

It is a complicated argument, but for him there is a progression in intensity from guilt to shame to melancholia to sadness:

> Guilt is to shame as the sugar coating is to a chocolate. But sadness is to shame as the liquid center is to the chocolate. If we want to progress ecologically, for instance if we want to have more people accepting the reality of global warming, then we need to walk them through an experience that is phenomenologically equivalent to accepting global warming, rather than bludgeoning them

with facts or trying to 'guilt them out' or shame them, which will only breed denial. The best way to do this is to make contact with the liquid center of sadness, often frozen into melancholy, at the core of sentient being. This liquid core is the trace of coexistence, shorn of coexistents, unconditional, strange, palpable yet withdrawn, uncanny, sad. That way, no bludgeoning is required: we will have poured people into the right psychic space to accept the very large-scale, long-term issues that beset this planet. (Morton, 2012, p. 18)

Paradoxically, if the answer to any addiction to searching for happiness or fulfilment is to co-exist with sadness, this will actually bring further hope into our lives. Morton's liquid core is an acknowledgement that in the core of being, there is a sadness, a raw tenderness of absence and of resonances of coexistence with concepts like climate change or deep time that are bigger than what we can comprehend: that the *emptiness* at the centre of human existence is contradictorily full of *connections*, that although invisible, can't be denied.

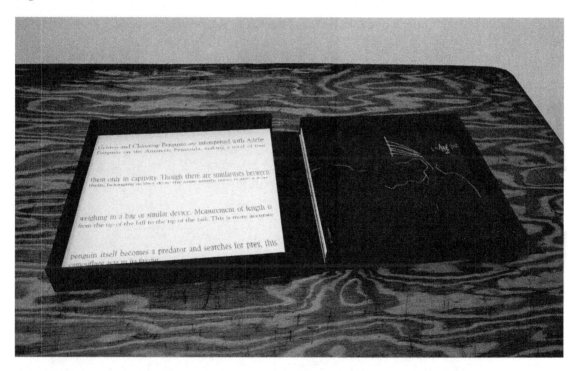

Figure 3. The .–. / .- / .- (penguin anticipatory archive)

An example: the anticipatory archive

After sustainability, we need dynamic narratives about our relation to the biosphere. (Mentz, 2012, p. 587)

In a recent project about Little Penguins (Eudyptula minor) in Sydney Harbour (following a mini-residency at The Cross Art Project) one of the artworks produced was the .–. / .- / .- (penguin anticipatory archive or P A A) (Figure 3). (6) This was a collection of images and drawings that described the breadth of issues surrounding the threatened colony at Manly. Here I attempted to draw the threads that I have discussed in this chapter together into a practical example. The Little Penguins are a cryptic and little-known inhabitant of the harbour, despite living in the middle of a global urbanised centre. I was able to see only one wild penguin at Manly Wharf, which was heavily shielded from human contact by volunteer wardens. But by collecting images, writings and thoughts about penguins my intention was to use a range of 'pasts' to craft 'futures' that we might want: "We tell stories to explore the alternative choices that might lead to feared or hoped-for futures" (Cronon, 1992, p. 1368). I was utilising anticipatory readiness: a cultivated, patient, sensory attentiveness (Bennett, 2010). It was my attempt at a project that 'stays with the trouble' (Haraway, 2013). The archive melded science, art and popular culture, with the recurrent motif of shifting the point of view (POV) of the viewer to underneath the penguin, looking up – challenging the human's position as subject.

The image shown in Figure 4 is a graphic summary of the ideas the project generated. At the same time as the content is factual, the relationship amongst elements is often wild and unruly. I wanted to turn a 'dead' document into vital possibilities by using the conceptual 'interference' between the different information sources. This kind of project is successful when invisible things come to the surface and it becomes possible to take notice of invisible matters and flows. Clearly, even this modest project looks at models of change. As the audience turned the pages of the archive in the gallery, my wider intention was to open up dialogue and debate surrounding human inaction, intervention, responses and responsibilities to the world at large.

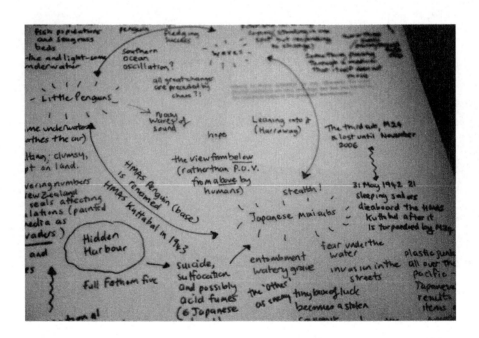

Figure 4. Relating different elements (detail of page from the .–. / .-/ .- (penguin anticipatory archive)).

An ecoaesthetic of action

Some artists make direct intervention in environmental issues, but even in the case of works such as the *P A A* the intention was an aesthetics of action. The ecoaesthetic I propose *builds* resilience, *entangles* with materiality and proposes that nonhumans, *matter*. It cultivates a prospective mind (Homer-Dixon, 2006) and coexists with sadness (Morton, 2012). It takes on the pleasure of the local and the satisfaction of the necessary, combining it with the imaginative and unruly. Engaging with uncertainty and imperfection, risk and opportunity, it allows participants to act in a contingent world: both inside the 'problem' and inside the solution. Of course no one artwork can do all of these things and that is why there are a great variety of aesthetic 'styles' in environmental art.

Why would such an ecoaesthetic be useful to sustainability? I have demonstrated that a conventional beauty, concerned with harmony and balance may not be helpful to any sustainable project. However by working with what an ecoaesthetic might consist of, we as creators/viewers/participants are in a better position to deal with the changes needed in our human/nonhuman 'societies' in the future. The post-sustainable world(s) will sound, feel and look differently, and in many cases it will not have a clear, coherent or stable aesthetics. But the fixed relations between nature-culture and the techno-economic focus of sustainability need to be unsettled. What happens if aesthetics and sustainability are made more *animated*?

At the heart of what I am talking about is responding to the zombie consumer, the user of materials and energy to no great purpose, to the turning away and confronting the sense of *in*action in zombie environmentalism. Art is not able to create the nation-wide or global change ultimately required, but it can stop us from halting or going backwards on our personal journey. Art is best when it is not purely instrumental – its greatest power can be at the level of working with 'resonances' rather than operating instructions. Is it possible to question sustainability at the same time as create a desire to act? Is it possible to undermine the conventions of top-down models at the same time as 'good' behaviour is encouraged? Is it possible to have 'goodness' in austerity at the same time as we have questioning and transformation? That is something for us to work on in the future.

Dr Perdita Phillips is an environmental artist/independent scholar based in Western Australia. She has worked with termites, bowerbirds, thrombolites, swamps, albatrosses, penguins and rubbish. Current research interests include walking, wildness and anticipatory futures. www.perditaphillips.com.

Endnotes

1. Remaining stable over time, or sustainability as the 'capacity to endure'.
2. Integrated into ISO standards and environmental reporting.
3. Even complexity theory can be linked loosely to vitalism via autopoiesis (defined as a system capable of reproducing and maintaining itself), which Kagan (2010a) uses to generate his sensibility of the 'autoecopoietic'.
4. I will not be discussing the practicalities reducing the impact of studio practice here but see Phillips (2007a).
5. Here I am specifically addressing consumption but note the much wider possibilities for artists listed in Table.
6. See www.perditaphillips.com/portfolio/16-1-1-penguin-anticipatory-archive.

References

Alaimo, S. (2012). *Sustainable this, sustainable that: New Materialisms, Posthumanism, and unknown futures.* PMLA, *127*(3), 558–564.

Anonymous Artist (who has made both good and bad environmental art). (2005). *A recipe for bad environmental art.* Artlink, *25*(3 Stirring), 27.

Bamford, R. (2011). Ecology and the aesthetics of imperfect balance. *Craft Plus Design Enquiry, 3,* Special section pp. 1-28.

Bennett, J. (2010). *Vibrant matter: a political ecology of things.* Durham: Duke University Press.

Berlant, L. (2011). *Cruel optimism*. Durham: Duke University Press.

Brown, K. W., Kasser, T., Ryan, R. M., Linley, P. A., & Orzech, K. (2009). When what one has is enough: Mindfulness, financial desire discrepancy, and subjective well-being. *Journal of Research in Personality, 43*(5), 727-736.

Cronon, W. (1992). A place for stories: nature, history and narrative. *The Journal of American History, 78* (March), 1347-1376.

Darnton, A., Elster-Jones, J., Lucas, K., & Brooks, M. (2006). *Promoting pro-environmental behaviour: existing evidence to inform better policy making. summary report. a study for the department for environment, food and rural affairs.* Retrieved from http://randd.defra.gov.uk/Document.aspx?Document =SD14002_3822_FRP.pdf

Espinosa, A., & Walker, J. (2011). *A complexity approach to sustainability: theory and application* London: Imperial College Press.

Fowkes, M., & Fowkes, R. (2006). *The principles of sustainability in contemporary art.* Retrieved from http://www.translocal.org/writings/principlesofsustainability.htm

Fowkes, M., & Fowkes, R. (2012). Art and sustainability. In J. Morray, G. Cawthorne, C. Dey & C. Andrew (Eds.), *Enough for all forever: a handbook for learning about sustainability* (pp. 215-228). Champaign, Illinois: Common Ground.

Fraser, M., Kember, S. & Lury, C. (2005). Inventive life: approaches to the new vitalism. *Theory, Culture & Society, 22*(1), 1-14.

Frost, M. (2012). Entering the "circles of vitality": beauty, sympathy and fellowship. In J. Brouwer, A. Mulder & L. Spuybroek (Eds.), *Vital beauty: reclaiming aesthetics in the tangle of technology and nature* (pp. 132-153). Rotterdam: V2_Publishing.

Guattari, F. (2000). *The three ecologies* (I. Pindar & P. Sutton, Trans.). London: Athlone Press.

Hamilton, C., & Denniss, R. (2005). *Affluenza: when too much is never enough*. Sydney: Allen and Unwin.

Haraway, D. J. (2013). Sowing worlds: a seedbag for terraforming with earth others. In M. Grebowicz & H. Merrick (Eds.), *Beyond the cyborg: adventures with Haraway*. New York: Columbia University Press.

Hector, D. C., Christensen, C. B. & Petrie, J. (2014). Sustainability and sustainable development: Philosophical distinctions and practical implications. *Environmental Values, 23*, 7-28.

Holden, M. (2010). The rhetoric of sustainability: perversity, futility, jeopardy? *Sustainability, 2*, 645 659.

Homer-Dixon, T. (2006). *The upside of down: catastrophe, creativity, and the renewal of civilisation*. Washington, D.C.: Island Press.

Kagan, S. (2010a). Aesthetics of sustainability for the ecological age: towards a literacy of complexity. *Arts. Environment. Sustainability. A Collection of Visions* (pp. 17-18). Singapore: Asia-Europe Foundation.

Kagan, S. (2010b). Cultures of sustainability and the aesthetics of the pattern that connects. *Futures, 42*(10), 1094-1101.

Kagan, S. (2011). *Art and sustainability: Connecting patterns for a culture of complexity*. Bielefeld, Germany: transcript Verlag.

Mayer Harrison, H., & Harrison, N. (1985). *The lagoon cycle*. Ithaca, New York State: Herbert F. Johnson Museum of Art, Cornell University.

Mentz, S. (2012). After sustainability. *PMLA, 127*(3), 586–592.

Morton, T. (2012). Guilt, shame, sadness: tuning to existence. *Volume, 31*(Spring), 16-18.

National Sustainability Council. (2013). *Sustainable Australia report 2013, conversations with the future*. Canberra: DSEWPaC.

Normandin, S. & Wolfe, C. T. (Eds.). (2013). *Vitalism and the scientific image in post-Enlightenment life science, 1800-2010*. London: Springer.

Patchett, M., & Phillips, P. (2013). Perdita Phillips – sounding and thinking like an ecosystem.

Antennae: The Journal of Nature in Visual Culture. 7, 114-128. Retrieved from http://www.antennae.org.uk/ANTENNAE%20ISSUE%2027.pdf

Petras, J. (1999). The CIA and the cultural cold war revisited. *Monthly Review, 51*(6), 47-56.

Phillips, P. (2007a). A friendly practice. *ArtSource Newsletter, Autumn*(Resilience: on Art and Environments), 9, 22-23.

Phillips, P. (2007b). The trouble with sustainability. *ArtSource Newsletter, Autumn*(Resilience: on Art and Environments), 6-8.

Phillips, P. (2012). Walk 'til you run out of water. *Performance Research: A Journal of the Performing Arts, 17*(4), 97-109.

Phillips, P. (2013a). *The cracks to come: notes on an urban ecoaesthetic.* Paper presented at the Institute of Australian Geographers Conference 2013, The University of Western Australia.

Phillips, P. (2013b). *Zombie environmentalism and cyclonic change.* Paper presented at the Future Nature, Future Culture[s] 2013 Balance-Unbalance Conference, Noosa, Qld.

Pickett, S. T. A. & Ostfeld, R. S. (1995). The shifting paradigm in ecology. In R. L. Knight & S. F. Bates (Eds.), *A new century for natural resources management* (pp. 65-88). Washington, D.C.: Island Press.

Purves, T. (Ed.). (2005). *What we want is free: generosity and exchange in recent art.* Albany, New York: State University of New York Press.

Redclift, M. (2007). Sustainable development (1987–2005): An oxymoron comes of age. *Sustainable Development, 13*, 212-227. doi: 10.1002/sd.281

Robinson, J. (2004). Squaring the circle? some thoughts on the idea of sustainable development. *Ecological Economics, 48*(4), 369-384.

Shellenberger, M., & Nordhaus, T. (2004). The death of environmentalism. Retrieved from http://thebreakthrough.org/PDF/Death_of_Environmentalism.pdf

Shellenberger, M., & Nordhaus, T. (2006). Post-environmentalism. In M. Andrews (Ed.), *Land, Art: A Cultural Ecology Handbook* (pp. 196-199). London: Royal Society for the Arts.

Simus, J. B. (2008). Aesthetic implications of the new paradigm in ecology. *The Journal of Aesthetic Education, 42*(1), 63-79.

Soper, K. (2007). Re-thinking the 'Good Life': The citizenship dimension of consumer disaffection with consumerism. *Journal of Consumer Culture, 7*(2), 205-229.

Soper, K. (2008). Alternative hedonism, cultural theory and the role of aesthetic revisioning. *Cultural Studies, 22*(5), 567-587. doi: 10.1080/09502380802245829

Steiner, W. (2001). *Venus in exile: the rejection of beauty in twentieth-century art.* New York: Free Press.

Steiner, W. (2009). The joy of less. *Harvard Design Magazine, Spring/Summer*(30), 1-5.

Steiner, W. (2012). Beauty as interaction. In J. Brouwer, A. Mulder & L. Spuybroek (Eds.), *Vital beauty: reclaiming aesthetics in the tangle of technology and nature* (pp. 64-80). Rotterdam: V2_Publishing.

Walker, B. H., Holling, C. S., Carpenter, S. R. & Kinzig, A. (2004). Resilience, adaptability and transformability in social–ecological systems. *Ecology and Society, 9*(2), 5. Retrieved from http://www.ecologyandsociety.org/vol9/iss2/art5/

Walker, B. H., & Salt, D. (2006). *Resilience thinking: sustaining ecosystems and people in a changing world.* Washington, D.C.: Island Press.

Weinstein, M. P., & Turner, R. E. (2012). 'Post-sustainability': The emergence of the social sciences as the hand-maidens of policy. In M. P. Weinstein & R. E. Turner (Eds.), *Sustainability science: The emerging paradigm and the urban environment* (pp. 161-176). New York: Springer.

World Commission on Environment and Development. (1987). *Our common future.* Oxford: Oxford University Press.

Worldwatch Institute. (2013, 29 October 2013). The state of consumption today Retrieved from http://www.worldwatch.org/node/810

Ziegler, R., & Ott, K. (2011). The quality of sustainability science: a philosophical perspective. *Sustainability: Science, Practice, & Policy, 7*(1), 1006-1029. Retrieved from http://sspp.proquest.com/static_content/vol7iss1/1006-029.ziegler.pdf

ELIZABETH JOLLEY, FRIEDRICH VON SCHLEGEL AND A GARLAND OF FRAGMENTS: CREATIVE PROCESS AS A RE-ENCHANTMENT OF NATURE

Andrea Wood

> Athenæum fragment 77: A dialogue is a chain or garland of fragments. An exchange of letters is a dialogue on a larger scale, and memoirs constitute a system of fragments. But as yet no genre exists that is both in form and content, simultaneously completely subjective and individual, and completely objective and like a necessary part in a system of all the sciences.
> (Friedrich von Schlegel, 1991, p. 27)

Introduction

More than 200 years ago, the philosopher Friedrich von Schlegel (1772-1829) and other *Frühromantik* writers and thinkers of the Jena School saw art and aesthetic education as central to cultural renewal and as the key to the social and political reform required for the unification or development of humankind and human self-realisation, or *Bildung* (Bieser, 2003, p. 49). Drawing on this idea, this paper reflects on aspects of my artistic practice, as well as the Romantics' concept of *naturphilosophie* —a theory about the unity of nature—and the belief that modernity has disenchanted nature by estranging humans from it. It will provide a brief outline of my residency in a chaotic archive of physical fragments of bone specimens and dust in the School of Animal Biology at the University of Western Australia, and will detail a major shift in my artistic practice: an increasing focus on Romanticism and the fragment in light of my own changing relationship to nature over time. As an outcome of the residency, questioning my own position as an artist in the increasingly depleted natural environment of Western Australia seemed not only inevitable but also necessary. The Romantic fragment, a form associated with poetic aesthetic discourse (Janowitz, 1998, p. 446; Thomas, 2008, p. 22) and a philosophical line of enquiry developed by Schlegel (1772-1829) at Jena, in the brief period (1798-1802) of the journal *Athenæum*, was employed as a tool to facilitate the production of contemporary artwork and writing as an adjunct to scientific means of understanding nature and our human connection to it. In this project, conceptual art, drawing on the fragment, and an entangled history of Romanticism and the natural sciences, attempts to re-enchant nature, to restore a sense of its mystery through art and poetry for viewers and readers in the gallery. I argue that my works *I can't tell you now what I could have told you then* and *Great Branches Fall*, components of my recent solo exhibition *Wonderfully Ordinary*, aimed to involve viewers and readers in a re-enchanting (poetic) conversation about our relationship to nature. They are an indication of the way that conceptual art—as a social model and practice of producing potentialities through creative inter-subjective exchange (Heiser, 2008, p. 3)—might participate in environmental dialogue.

The Romantic fragment

Since 2010 my work has focused on the investigation of materials (paper, ink and dust) as a means to explore the creative potential of the philosophical fragment. It linked Schlegel's conception of the fragment to aspects of creative process and invention. These included the working methods of late Western Australian author Elizabeth Jolley (1923-2007) whose teaching notes, handouts and writing reveal that she employed the fragment in various ways; and Schlegel's own daily writing practice as a method of working philosophically, as well as current writing on contemporary conceptual art. Importantly, although Romanticism has been more often associated with the poetic interpretation of aesthetic discourse in the form of fragmentary literature (Janowitz, 1998, p. 446), the conception of the Romantic fragment articulated in German Romanticism, in particular by Schlegel in the hundreds of aphorisms he wrote, differs substantially from the meanings of fragments for the English Romantic poets, and from popular Victorian cultural forms of the fragment (Thomas, 2002, p. 21). Schlegel's Romantic fragment—a philosophical conception of the fragment as an idea, concept or project existing within a chain or garland of fragments—contained a kernel of creative potential, the scope of which was much wider than the historical and literary frame typically used to approach it (Gasché, 1991, p. viii). The relevance of the Romantic fragment to my creative work and approach to nature is at this point best illustrated by Schlegel's (1991, p. 46) *Athenæum* fragment 206:

> A fragment, like a little work of art, must be quite separated from its surroundings and complete in itself—like a hedgehog.

An anecdote about an echidna

Schlegel's puzzling aphorism has been examined by a number of writers and theorists. Because the hedgehog is covered in pointy spines, or quills, and perhaps because of the revolutionary aspects of German Romanticism and the time period in which Romanticism arose, Schlegel's hedgehog has often been interpreted as uniquely and aggressively separated from the world. For example, Charles Rosen (cited in Kramer, 1997, p. 148) writes:

> Like its definition, the Romantic Fragment is complete (this oxymoron was intended to disturb, as the hedgehog's quills make its enemies uncomfortable): separate from the rest of the universe, the Fragment nevertheless suggests distant perspectives. Its separation, indeed, is aggressive: it projects into the universe precisely by the way it cuts itself off.

I argue that although Schlegel's aphorism has a number of meanings associated with his Platonism and the philosophical debate of the period, it also reflects on the early Romantics' ambition to uncover an underlying unity to nature and on the belief in the need to restore a sense of magic and mystery to it. I have thought of Schlegel's "hedgehog" a good deal. I had previously employed dust as a metaphor for interactions in the gallery between my work and viewers, and I asked myself if dust might be something like the points of a hedgehog's quills: indexes to new work, new thoughts. At the same time, I thought of Elizabeth Jolley composing stories of characters in interior domestic space, whose state of being was often illuminated by their relationship to outside elements. I was set in a landscape and was often drawn by the changing light or weather to walk and take photographs. On one of these walks in the hills in Western Australia, I discovered an echidna (a small animal, native to Australia, that has a pelt of sharp spines). Hearing me, the echidna hid under a pile of sticks, and curled up to protect the kernel of its body: spines in soft greys blending perfectly, becoming a part of the dry leaf litter and wood. As I watched and waited, camera in hand, it unfurled its spines. Each point, like the tip of Schlegel's quill dipped in ink, reached out in the many directions made by the animal's body as the little antipodean fragment transported itself through the bush. It trundled magically on its way. There was nothing separate or aggressive about it. In a process of movement and change it belonged in every way. I looked. It just *was*.

My experience with the echidna allowed me to make connections between Schlegel's thought about the fragment and my own creative practice. It was, for me, an example of the way new modes of thinking and possibilities for creative work unexpectedly arise in the process of creative research. It was as though, finally, after a long process of searching and looking, the Romantic fragment simply revealed itself to me. That is, the fragment was embodied in the echidna in multi-directional ways, but most importantly for me at that point, it revealed a space, a gap that is fundamental to the fragment, into which I could step and participate creatively.

Naturphilosophie

This meeting with the echidna led me to undertake a short residency in the School of Animal Biology at The University of Western Australia to draw and photograph the specimen collection, including the fragmentary remains of echidnas, and for my creative work and reading to take on a new direction: an exploration of the shared past of Romanticism, *naturphilosophie* and Romantic biology at Jena at a time and place when philosophy and science were not yet separated. For Beiser (2003, pp. 155-156), the post-Kantian *naturphilosophen* (Schlegel and other early Romantic thinkers) developed a metaphysics that posited an organic view of nature in which nature might be understood as one organism requiring not only observation and experiment but also a metaphysical explanation, a transcendental deduction of the 'idea' of an organism as a necessary condition of the possibility of experience. For Beiser however, the speculative aspects of *naturphilosophie* have been exaggerated, while the metaphysical concerns of others, also engaged in scientific observation and experiment at the time, have been downplayed:

> It is one of the more unfortunate aspects of the neo-Kantian legacy that, for generations, it has succeeded in portraying *naturphilosophie* as an aberration from true science, which follows the path of experiment and observation. Fortunately in recent decades it has become clear that this picture is profoundly anachronistic. It cannot come to terms with some very basic facts: that there was no clear distinction between philosophy and science in this period and that there was no such thing as a pure empirical science limited to only observation and experiment. In the late eighteenth and early nineteenth century, *naturphilosophie* was not a metaphysical perversion of, or deviation from, "normal" empirical science. Rather, it was normal science itself. From our contemporary perspective it is hard to imagine a scientist who is also a poet and a philosopher. But this is just what is so fascinating and challenging about *naturphilosophie*, which has to be understood in the context of its own time as the science of its day. (Beiser, 2003, pp. 156-157)

In contrast to Beiser, I felt it would not be hard to find scientists amongst the students and staff of the School of Animal Biology of the University of Western Australia who are also poets and philosophers. In fact, Beiser describes a history that is still in evidence and appreciated there. Although it is necessary to limit claims about the similarities between scientific and artistic research, I was struck by the way a number of chaotic and intriguing spaces of the school (hidden offices, corridors and post-graduate laboratories) resembled artists' studios: a jumble of unfinished and abandoned projects alongside projects in progress; litter, tables and benches in between papers; scientific instruments, jars and containers of materials. I was reminded of Schlegel's (1991, p. 14) critical fragment 115: "…all art should become science and all science art; poetry and philosophy should be made one".

Further, on the basis of argument and research concerning the influence of Romantic thought on Darwin's conception of nature and evolution, it is the process of evolution (revealed in the bones and adaptations of species discovered on Romantic voyages (1) in the late eighteenth and early nineteenth centuries) that unites the biological sciences with Romanticism. Indeed, Millan-Zaibert (2007, p. 10) argues that Romantic thought, including Schlegel's contribution to *naturphilosophie* and his desire to join philosophy, poetry and science, "gave shape to (nothing less than) Darwin's conceptions of nature and evolution". For many scientists and thinkers, it is the theory of evolution that comes closest to fulfilling what the early Romantics desired to discover: an underlying wholeness to nature

(Richards, 2002). Evolution shows us that nature is always in a process of change and movement. The echidna, like the hedgehog, really does know one trick, (2) and it's an evolutionary one ensuring its survival: it curls itself up like a ball to protect itself. With its skeleton showing remnant similarities to crocodiles, it contains (as we all do) within its evolutionary past the ancient beginnings of things.

Re-Enchantment

Romanticism shares a past with the complex chronology of historical developments that shaped the emergence of the modern disciplines of literature and science. Richard Holmes, in his book (2008, p. xvi) *The age of wonder: how the romantic generation discovered the beauty and terror of science*, also states:

Romanticism as a cultural force is generally regarded as intensely hostile to science, its ideal of subjectivity eternally opposed to that of scientific objectivity. But I do not believe this was always the case, or that the terms are so mutually exclusive. The notion of wonder seems to be something that once united them, and can still do so. In effect there is Romantic science in the same sense that there is Romantic poetry, and often for the same enduring reasons.

Figure 1: Andrea Wood (2011). *Echidna Skulls.* Copyright the artist.

In discussions with the School of Animal Biology, I observed that nature is seen by staff and students as a place of wonder, however learning and research is approached in material and scientifically measurable ways with an ecological focus. The specimens are used to teach students principles of biology in a material way. While the students set up microscopes and dissected frogs, I set about taking photographs and drawing. I returned to this task many times over several weeks and noticed a number of effects. I stopped consciously analysing. I became immersed in the qualities of the specimens and was emotionally moved. I felt compassion as I moved the tiny skulls and bones of the echidnas around to capture shadows, while absorbing their delicacy, the symmetries, the almost powdery surfaces and the effects of light shining on and through them. Through handling the material objects, drawing and the process of taking photographs, I experienced a sense of wonder and connectedness (see Figure 1).

Wonderfully ordinary

Recent environmental writing (Stone, 2005, p. 4) argues, just as for the writers and thinkers of the *Frühromantic* group, the natural world has become disenchanted. It asks whether a re-enchantment of nature might aid environmentalism. The Romantics' ambition to restore a sense of creative nature's beauty, mystery and magic may be seen to anticipate the concern of some contemporary environmental philosophers to develop a conception of natural things as vital and therefore worthy of respect and care (Stone, 2005, p. 5). The Romantics believed this could be achieved through cultural means by employing fragmentary Romantic art and poetry.

The drawings and photographs I made, enriched by conversations with staff and students, became the raw data on which I worked and reflected in the studio. My aim was to find a way to synthesise the residency with the principal ideas behind my research through a process of drawing and experimentation with ink on paper. I felt a need to connect my project, and what readers or viewers might experience in the gallery, to a sense of wonder and connectedness to the natural world. Returning to the studio however revealed that rather than reflecting what I had experienced looking into the spaces of the specimens and the laboratory, the drawings were literal. They perhaps resembled something like scientific illustrations. How would I translate this experience and the questions it raised in a material way?

Leafing through piles of drawings and experiments with ink on paper, I pulled the photographs out to look at them again. I started to see that the qualities of the photographs suggested an inky surface to the skulls, almost like veins and capillaries. I dropped a blot of ink onto a drawing to see if I could recreate this effect and watched as the ink dispersed, by capillary action, on the wet surface of the paper. I drew another sheet toward me on which I had drawn insects and moths, finding that if I blotted the page with another and then dropped ink on it and let it disperse, it created interesting effects. I flicked the ink with the brush and folded a sheet of fine paper and pressed. When I opened it up I found that the process had created something intriguing: a Rorschach-like inkblot suggestive of the fine symmetrical vertebrae of a tiny creature (see Figure 2).

Fragmentary studio processes led to a moment when materials combined and recombined in different ways created an unexpected outcome: the production of a way of connecting key ideas associated with the fragment with my experiences in the School of Animal Biology. In that moment, the Rorschach-like inkblot seemed something like the fragment and partly mysterious. Unlike clearly representational drawings or photographs, information confirming that it should be read as exactly one thing or another was missing. Its symmetrical form and relative incompleteness invited interpretation, an attempt to make sense of it as an image. Suggesting biological form, the blot seemed suspended midway in progress toward or away from the formation of an image, either towards completion or disintegration.

Figure 2: Andrea Wood (2012). *Ink blot*. Ink on paper. Copyright the artist.

I can't tell you now what I could have told you then

My experiences in the School of Animal Biology had caused me to re-examine the ideas of the Romantics, in part because I was in a place of research focused on understanding aspects of the Western Australian environment. Initially, my interest in ideas from a remote nineteenth century Germany had seemed confrontingly irrelevant to the current environmental concerns and research I was presented with. I wondered if I had misunderstood the Romantics' interest in science and had not, or perhaps even could not today, correctly understand their worldview. I questioned the relevance to today of what were possibly overly mystical or even religious views of nature. I also questioned my own relationship to nature from which, in my everyday life, I felt I had become increasingly estranged. In the midst of these questions, I came across a set of photographs of Grasmere, in the lake district of England, that I had taken more than twenty years ago on a small Japanese camera (see Figure 3). The photographs of the lake, rowboats and a white swan have the nostalgic quality of film and intensity of colour that stands out in this time of digital photography.

Figure 3: Andrea Wood (1989). *Grasmere*. Photograph. Andrea Wood.

Remembering that on that day I had walked first to visit Wordsworth's grave, and then on to the lake, I found a book of Wordsworth's poetry and read *Lines written a few miles above Tintern Abbey*. Perhaps it would reveal to me something of Wordsworth's view of nature. I found that Wordsworth's lines revisit a place of importance from his past and reflect on his changing relationship to nature over time. He compares a youthful, exuberant and bodily experience of nature to more internal, reverent and reflective experiences in maturity.

Wordsworth's lines led me to make a similar comparison between my own experiences. I thought of the passage of time and place between the early Romantics and today, and the distances between Romantic England and Germany and the School of Animal Biology, close to the banks of the Swan River in Perth, Western Australia. With Schlegel's aphorisms in mind, I wrote the words "I can't tell you now what I could have told you then". My intention was that these words be taken as aphoristic, nostalgic and unsure or ironic. I wanted them to raise questions. In part a meditation on a photograph, a landscape from my own past that also belongs in a time and place reminiscent of Romanticism, these words might invite viewers to meditate on them and other pasts, and to fill them with their own meanings. For example, a white swan on a European body of water might invite comparison with our Western Australian black swans and rivers. These words might speak of discussion about understandings of nature that is entangled with our present understanding and experience of it.

Dust

My studio experimentation led to decisions regarding materials that made their appearance in the exhibition. As well as reflecting on dust as a metaphor for interactions in the gallery, I also saw the poetry included in the exhibition as a conversation of dust beginning with Jolley's papers and words about poetry. Dust is contained physically within books and collects on them and exists as debris falling from seed pods and tree branches in cycles of regeneration and decay. Within my artistic practice, I see dust as metaphorical of the creative potential of the fragment on the basis of Schlegel's Platonic philosophy, which in turn, builds on Heraclitus, for whom "becoming" is circular:

> The becoming of the cosmos is explained in physical terms: fire dies and is changed into air, air dies and becomes water, water dies to become earth, and so on, an interchanging of life and death between different elements ... Heraclitus insists, in fragment after fragment, that this sequence of transformations in the cosmos goes both ways. (Nirenberg, 1996)

This is an idea of central importance to *Wonderfully Ordinary*. It was my hope that this notion of circularity, our place in the natural world, would be a metaphorical component of the exhibition. Contemporary artist and Zen Buddhist scholar Xu Bing (Wilson, 2004), exploring similar conceptions of dust and circularity, describes it as "one of the most stable of materials. It's very peaceful, it never changes. So dust is a very Zen idea". Circularity and new life may be suggested by new poetry and art works arising from an engagement with ideas, poetry and other writing and artworks of the past. It may be suggested by the employment of particular materials and processes.

Xu Bing's inventive studio processes involving the recombination of collected materials that are pregnant with symbolic meaning, in consequently unexpected ways, result in works that are intentionally open to multiple readings and therefore challenge familiar ways of thinking (Erickson, n.d.). In particular, Xu Bing's project *Background Story* (2004-2010), employing plant debris, paper, light and shadows to evoke a tradition of Chinese ink on paper, makes connections with the relationship of humankind to nature.

Great branches fall

In an interview with Ray Willibanks (1992, p. 126) Elizabeth Jolley said:

> ... the landscape in Australia can be so menacing and frightening, at the same time so beautiful and magical ... you can parallel the characters' thoughts and feelings by the external things and that makes it stronger to me ... Landscape, trees, weather, they're all a bit ordinary, but they are important.

This statement contains a number of ideas of importance for *Wonderfully Ordinary* and for my work *Great Branches Fall*, including the Romantic notion of an enchanted or 'magical' nature which may be employed in writing and the concept of creative work as a two way process in ordinary life. For Jolley, the author explores 'others' and at the same time may explore the self. (3) Jolley explains further in her tutorial handout entitled "The Art of Poetry" (n.d., p. 2):

The writer uses invention from his own heart and mind to compose characters and events found in observation. He may use events in his own life and relate these to glimpses of other people's lives. And he may use the appearance of the landscape and the changing of the seasons to show his characters and their thoughts and feelings. And of course, his own thoughts and feelings may often be revealed in the process of invention.

I thought of Jolley composing stories of characters in interior domestic space, whose state of being was often illuminated by their relationship to the landscape in which they were set. I have also often thought about the Romantic tradition of painting and writing referencing light seen through the branches and leaves of trees. Elizabeth Jolley's poem *Great branches fall* contained in her (1993) book *Diary of a weekend farmer* uses this motif. I have thought of this poem at night when the easterly wind is loud. As it blows through the branches of the trees surrounding my property it occasionally brings one down.

In Jolley's poem, words about loss are connected to the idea of transcendence in the vision of light seen through the branches and leaves of a tree. Reflecting on Jolley's words "Wonderfully Ordinary", (4) on the idea of transcendence in every day life and the loss of this vision of the *Frühromantik* period, I thought about my aim to reflect something of the early German Romantics' hope "to restore the beauty, magic and mystery of nature in the aftermath of the ravages of science and technology" (Stone, 2005, p. 4) through my creative work. Looking out from my window, I found myself focusing on a large marri tree. I had noticed it was dying some months earlier but now nearly all the leaves had fallen. The branches in the evening light stood out against the darkening sky like drawings of veins or capillaries. As I sat drawing the tree, I imagined the branches falling though space, but the drawing was contained in the rectangle of the page. It occurred to me that the branches could be installed in the gallery and that this would anchor and tie together the elements of the project.

Stone (2005, p. 4) argues that the early Romantics perceived "modernity to have estranged humanity from nature and 'disenchanted' nature by applying to it a narrowly analytic and reflective form of rationality", and that rather than representing a retreat into medievalism, the Romantics "sought to create a culture that could reconceive nature as enchanted but in a distinctly modern way". My hope was that the branches of the tree, installed as contemporary art in the gallery, might challenge familiar ways of thinking and encourage further thought.

Conclusion

As well as an idea or project in dialogue with current environmental discourse, Romantic poetry, as articulated by Schlegel—as part of a more general undertaking to establish a philosophical method for understanding the unity of all branches of knowledge and a desire to bring philosophy, poetry, art, science, and all spheres of human inquiry into contact with one another (Beiser, 2003, p. 8)—may also be seen to share something in common with current interest in interdisciplinary approaches to research (Millan-Zaibert, 2007, p. 4). My research and artistic practice provides a link to this history of ideas in a contemporary context. At its most Romantic, this project represents a striving for unity—a transformative wholeness—through artistic practice, or *Bildung*. (5)

My residency was an engagement with materials and with staff and students who study the natural history of species, with the passionate aim that such knowledge may aid their preservation. It led me to question my position as an artist. Faced with emotionally moving material evidence (a chaotic collection of physical fragments of bone specimens and dust) and equally moving discussions detailing the consequences of environmental destruction dating from the colonial settlement of Australia, I felt a desire to participate and contribute to the preservation of the natural environment.

My exhibition *Wonderfully Ordinary* consisted of fragments put together in just one of many potential new ways. It sought to create possibilities for multiple narrative readings for viewers and readers. It was hoped that *Wonderfully Ordinary* might therefore be seen as a reflection of the fragment in a particular way: as a form of participation within a chain or garland of fragments or ideas of the past, through a creative process in which ideas pass between the artist, viewer and reader. It was also intended as a meditation on the serious and sustained pursuit of creative output in the midst of an ordinary life in the present: the pursuit of a sense of wholeness through the manipulation of materials in the every day. As evidence of interactions between my practice-based research and research into the creative process, as well as my research into Elizabeth Jolley's creative process, writing and the key ideas surrounding it, the project aimed to communicate to viewers and readers something of my search and experimentation in the context of fragmentary contemporary experience over time. As an outcome of a cross-disciplinary approach to artistic research, it invited viewers and readers to become involved in a re-enchanting (poetic) conversation about ourselves and our relationship to nature (see

Figure 5). It aimed to reflect on the early German Romantics' concept of *naturphilosophie* and their desire for *bildung*, including the role of fragmentary Romantic art and poetry in the reunification of humans with nature. An 'enchanting' view of nature is one in which nature is seen as poetic, creative and partly mysterious: the fragmentary inkblot and Schlegel's enchanting and magical hedgehog (or echidna)—poetic, creative and partly mysterious—imply an appropriateness of care for natural phenomena.

Figure 4: Andrea Wood (2013). *Great Branches Fall.* Marri branch: installation view. Image copyright Heather Shaw Photography.

Artist and creative researcher Dr Andrea Wood is fascinated by fragments – of text, artworks and ideas, and by linking the history of ideas about making art with her own experience as an artist living in the hills outside Perth, Australia.

Endnotes

1. The Romanticism of Darwin's voyages is explored in Richard's (2002) book. See also (Holmes, 2008).

2. Schlegel would have surely been familiar with the ancient Greek parable about the fox (which knows many things) and the hedgehog (which knows just one big thing). See (Berlin, 1993) and (Gould, 2011).

3. Maria Suarez-Lafuente explores this idea further in her essay "Selves and others in Elizabeth Jolley's narratives' (Bird & Walker, 1991, p. 16).

4. The small collection of Jolley's creative writing teaching notes and handouts I have examined includes student writing with marginalia, including the words "wonderfully ordinary" written by Jolley. It was passed to me from a family member.

5. For further discussion relating to the importance of aesthetic education as the key to *Bildung* in the Romantic ideal see Beiser (2003, pp. 93-103).

References

Beiser, F. (2003). *The Romantic imperative: the concept of early German Romanticism.* Cambridge: Harvard University Press.

Erickson, B. (n.d.). Evolving meanings in Xu Bing's art: A case study of transference. Retrieved from http://www.xubing.com/index.php/site/texts/evolving_meanings_in_xu_bings_art_a_case_stud y_of_transrerence/

Gasché, R. (1991). Foreword. In F. von Schlegel, *Philosophical fragments* (pp. vii-xxxi). (P. Firchow, Trans.). Minneapolis: University of Minnesota Press.

Heiser, J. (2008). All of a sudden: things that matter in contemporary art. [Electronic version]. *Art & Research, 2*(1), 1-8.

Holmes, R. (2010). *The age of wonder: how the Romantic generation discovered the beauty and terror of science.* New York: Vintage Books.

Janowitz, A. (1998). The Romantic fragment. In D. Wu (Ed.), *A companion to Romanticism* (pp. 442-451). Oxford: Blackwell.

Jolley, E. & Willbanks, R. (1992). [Interview with Elizabeth Jolley]. In R. Willbanks (Ed.), *Speaking volumes: Australian writers and their work* (pp. 111-127). Melbourne: Penguin.

Jolley, E. (1993). *Diary of a weekend farmer.* Fremantle: Fremantle Arts Centre Press.

Jolley, J. (n.d). [handout].

Millan-Zaibert, E. (2007). *Friedrich Schlegel and the emergence of Romantic philosophy.* Albany, New York: State University of New York Press.

Nirenberg, R. (1996). Heraclitus and Parmenides: A supplement to Ricardo Nirenberg's fall 1996 lecture: Presocratics. The University at Albany, project renaissance. Retrieved from http://www.albany.edu/~rn774/fall96/philos3.html

Saurez-Lafuente, M. (1991). Selves and others in Elizabeth Jolley's narrative. In D. Bird & B. Walker (Eds.), *Elizabeth Jolley: new critical essays* (pp. 15-23). North Ryde, Australia: Collins Angus & Robertson.

Schlegel, F. (1991). *Philosophical fragments.* (P. Firchow, Trans.). Minneapolis: University of Minnesota Press.

Stone, A. (2005). Friedrich Schlegel, Romanticism, and the re-enchantment of nature. *Inquiry, 48*(1), 3-25.

Thomas, S. (2008). *Romanticism and visuality: Fragments, history, spectacle.* New York: Routledge.

CHAPTER 6

RECONCEPTUALISING THE HAND MADE OBJECT

Jane Donlin

Introduction

This chapter is an enquiry into the aesthetic value of the handmade object from a socio-cultural-environmental perspective, through a visual arts practice. Central to my arts practice is the question of how to address the global problem of living responsibly in a world confronted with existential threats to sustainability. Specifically, the chapter wishes to discuss how a reconceptualisation of the hand-made object may play a role in contributing to the realisation of a more sustainable future. Our under-standings of a sustainable world affects what Giddens (1991) calls 'the extensional', global dimension of the planet, as well as 'the intensional', local dimension of society. Giddens has argued that "a clear part of increased ecological concern is the recognition that reversing the degradation of the environ-ment depends upon adopting new lifestyle patterns" (1991, p. 221). Essentially, Giddens suggests that adopting new ways of life requires a fundamental shift in attitude and action, and that small changes on an intensional level can lead collectively to large changes on an extensional level.

Conditions of technical change have also affected our understandings of the handmade object. In technologically advanced societies, activities of creating and making are too frequently insufficiently appreciated, removed from an individual's everyday lifeworld experience, often resulting in a disregard or indifference for the crafts and dismissed as mere personal self-fulfilment. The premise of this chapter is that craft production, with its repertoire of skills, techniques, processes, tacit and proposi-tional understandings and its connection to communal activity, plays an important role in giving aesthetic focus and new direction to the human lifeworld. This chapter suggests that the act of making needs to be reconceptualised in terms of an aesthetic means of self-actualisation, a valuable cultural activity and a social responsibility.

I approach this project from two angles. The first is the study of literature from critical theory. I turn to theorists of philosophy and sociology, predominantly to Habermas, Adorno and Ruskin, rather than to craft theorists, because I consider social critics provide the necessary insights into the unrecognised presuppositions underlying ways of thinking, into those attitudes that have resulted in consequences of environmental threat and caused the handcrafted object to decline in importance. Luckman puts it this way: "reality is socially constructed and … the sociology of knowledge must analyze the processes in which this occurs" (quoted in Habermas, 1987, p. 139). The second is a reflection on my situation as a maker. Integral to my work is the actual experience of hand produc-tion. My work is process-based art, as I am a maker of textile objects. I engage physically with the labour-intensive practice of weaving cloth, dyeing and spinning fibre; and hand-stitching into cloth. Creating textile objects by hand as it was done traditionally for thousands of years is a painstakingly slow and repetitive process, requiring a commitment mostly unobserved by today's Western society due to its fast-paced culture of technological advance, mass production and instant gratification (Adorno, 1993), where the notion of making something by hand seems immensely outdated.

Understanding craft's historicity

Since antiquity, the practising of skilled crafts has been an intrinsic part of every society's cultural traditions and the handloom production of cloth represents one of the oldest and most complex forms of craft. By the Late Middle Ages, tapestry weavers had brought their skills to the highest level of creative competency, signifying the creative-aesthetic-expressive quality in the craft. With the rise of the Industrial Revolution, machines replaced the hand production of cloth, training in hand-production ceased and knowledge about the hand weaving of cloth fell into decline. The shift to machine production entailed a change in social attitude, involving a profound loss to humanity.

Craftsmanship played a significant role in the furthering of social knowledge throughout every stage of human development (Epstein & Prak, 2008). Historically, making was a cultural practice that informed every aspect of the human lifeworld, it entailed rituals and the passing on of social morals and values. The medieval apprenticeship, for example, was more concerned with the transmission of social values than with the learning of skill (Herzfeld, 2004, p. 50). Established cultural practices, such as making, help develop a sense of what life is, and the objects that people make represent what matters in life. Adorno (1984) puts it this way: "Life – mere life as well as the prospect of the good life – has been perpetuated by culture. And authentic art is an echo of this" (p. 357).

The desocialisation of nature and the denaturalisation of society

In technically advanced countries, science and market influences dominate its culture, but market dominance comes at a cost. Industrial progress has resulted in the exploitation of the earth's natural resources, problems of sustainability and the threat of global warming. Technical progress, Giddens (1994) proclaims, has resulted in ecology becoming almost wholly the product of human decision-making. Hence, "concern over global warming comes from the fact that the climate of the earth is no longer a naturally-given order" (p. 77). Habermas (1984) describes this shift towards science and market domination as a shift towards the rationalisation of worldviews. It is a process of social transformation that coincides with "the desocialisation of nature and the denaturalisation of society" (p. 48). Desocialisation/denaturalisation essentially entails a decline in the belief in the myths of the pre-given world of tradition and a break from the world of nature (p. 43). Habermas understands this shift from a mythological understanding of the world to a more rational outlook on life as a process of social evolution.

Social evolution is a progression of learning, leading into new levels of understandings and learning. Social evolution was set in motion when humanity began to differentiate between the natural, physical environment of nature and the socio-cultural environment of the human lifeworld. As a society's capacity to differentiate increased, the social-mythical reasoning informing one stage of development was no longer convincing and society progressed to new levels of rationalisation. In this manner a "devaluation of the explanatory and justificatory potentials of entire traditions took place in the great civilisations with the dissolution of mythological-narrative figures of thought, in the modern age with the dissolution of religious, cosmological and metaphysical figures of thought" (p. 68). Inevitably, a devaluation of the justificatory potential of the handmade object also took place. Thus the evolution towards rationality begins a process, a process that severs all magical relationships with nature and causes all relationships with traditional ways of doing things to decline in importance.

According to Habermas (1987), the lifeworld forms the core of every society and has three structural components: society, culture and socialised individuals. Society is "that structural component that determines the status – rights and duties – of group members"; culture determines societal values; whereas "socialised individuals contribute motivations that are appropriate to normed expectations" (pp. 139-140). Essentially, the lifeworld consists of rituals and traditions that serve as a kind of "interpretive mechanism through which cultural knowledge is reproduced" (p. 139). Habermas, however, retains an element of pessimism towards the notion of unproblematic tradition, for societies have attained "a level of system differentiation at which increasingly autonomous organisations are connected with one another via delinguistified media of communication" (p. 154). That is to say, the human lifeworld is subject to increasing influences of institutional hegemony. Institutional influences pose a threat to lifeworld traditions because they create systemic rules that are separate from the values of the lifeworld. Markets for example are not constrained by humanitarian values, real human needs, democratic ideals or environmental issues; markets are governed by mechanisms of supply and production (p. 154). Key to Habermas' thinking is that what binds sociated individuals to one another and secures the integration of society on an aesthetic-expressive-creative level are networks of communicative actions that flourish only in light of cultural traditions (and here I am thinking about the role of the handmade object), not in light of systemic mechanisms such as market influences (p. 137).

Adorno's aesthetic theory

Adorno (1977) posits that with our current levels of understanding there is no need to devalue a cultural tradition, or subordinate oneself to its creeds (p. 315). What is needed is reflexive tradition. Reflexive tradition, he explicates, will barely tolerate adherence to hegemonic traditionalism as a role model (p. 315). Adorno does not think that instructions from a divine revelation will provide society with direction or insight, rather, reflexivity, the re-appropriation of knowledge and the development of intellectual autonomy, suggests new understandings and redirection (p. 316). In *Minima Moralia* Adorno (1985) juxtaposes intellectual growth with economic growth. Like Habermas, he determines that modern life is mediated by dominant social structures such as the market. In a world governed by mechanisms of supply and distribution, business controls and shapes the human lifeworld. Business promotes ever-the-same products, activities and lifestyles, failing to determine real human needs, and preventing individuals from pursuing real social activities or experiencing real natural phenomena. Adorno maintains that commerce obscures what is human about us, markets create false human values, and that under the conditions of consumption lifeworld experiences lack true substance and aesthetic content (p. 15).

In his *Aesthetic Theory*, Adorno (2004) posits that the real progress of society entails a progression towards a consciousness of freedom. Real progress entails a growing understanding of real human values and needs, and real human values are synonymous with aesthetic values. Adorno found himself confronted with a history of contradiction concerning the two understandings: "The concept of progress is more refracted than in the history of technical forces of reproduction" (p. 272). Art itself is caught up in this history of antagonism and contradiction, for art is a reflection of the level of consciousness humanity has, "in art there is as much and as little progress as in society" (p. 272).

In the history of human emancipation, the mastery of a handwork technique played a significant role. Adorno maintains that technique was constitutive to art and to furthering human consciousness, "because in [technique] is condensed the fact that each artwork is a human artifact and that what is artistic in it becomes a human product" (p. 279). Adorno makes a distinction between technique and content in a work of art: technique is "the aesthetic name for mastery of material", content is the ideological abstraction of meaning, the substance of art (pp. 278 - 279). Paradoxically, technique and content are inextricably bound up together.

Adorno's extrapolations suggest that the making of art is a real human need. Creating is an authentic mode of experience; it is a way of being, of living life on more conscious levels. This is the kind of aesthetic progress that Adorno seeks. In a work of art real progress is made manifest in the 'truth content in art': "The spirit of artworks is not their meaning and not their intention but rather their truth content, or, in other words, the truth that is revealed through them" (2004, p. 365). For Adorno, art must attempt to free itself from institutional influences of dominance and become autonomous, only then can it reveal its truth content. The truth content in a work of art does not encompass the concept of beauty only; it encompasses the entire spectrum of human experience. Ultimately art represents a consciousness of needs, and if "art works have any social influence at all, it is not by haranguing, but by changing consciousness in ways that are ever so difficult to pin down" (1984, p. 344). Adorno's *Aesthetic Theory* provides the justificatory potential of the handmade object.

Ruskin's relevance to sustainability

Ruskin, a 19th century Victorian critic, is another theorist who examines the corrosive effects of denaturalisation/desocialisation on society and nature. The relevance of Ruskin, for the intent of this investigation, is in his philosophies of purposeful, creative work and in his influence on art education. Essentially, Ruskin tries to determine the intrinsic value of life itself and the human aspect of creating art was a profound way to contribute to the cultural value of social life. In *Unto This Last* Ruskin (1907c) examines the "science of the political economy of art", making a distinction between economic wealth and true wealth. Economic wealth is dominated by productivity and profits, whereas true wealth is about the making of a meaningful life. In bringing his lectures in *Unto This Last* to a close, Ruskin proclaims:

> I desire ... to leave this one great fact clearly stated. THERE IS NO WEALTH BUT LIFE. Life, including all its powers of love, of joy, and of admiration. That country is the richest which nourishes the greatest number of noble and happy human beings. [Capitals as in the original] (1907c, p. 48)

Ruskin (1907b) links the making of art to the aesthetic qualities of human experience via the powers of human intellect, imagination and creativity, "FINE ART is that in which the hand, the head, and the heart of man go together" (p. 57). The chapter in the second volume of his *Stones of Venice* entitled, *On the Nature of the Gothic* is an eloquent summary about "the true functions of the workman in art". Ruskin (2009) identifies six core 'moral' elements that characterise the Gothic, in order of importance: "1. Savageness. 2. Changefulness. 3. Naturalism. 4. Grotesqueness. 5. Rigidity. 6. Redundancy" (p. 35). These characters, when assigned to the craftsman, "would be expressed thus: 1. Savageness, or Rudeness. 2. Love of Change. 3. Love of Nature. 4. Disturbed Imagination. 5. Obstinacy. 6. Generosity. (2009, p. 35). Ruskin proceeds to examine each function in their order, but it is suffice to mention that Ruskin's *On the Nature of the Gothic* is an aesthetic, ideological-moral theorisation of medieval craftsmanship in which he insufficiently acknowledges that medieval craft guilds were driven by economic success.

The importance of *On the Nature of the Gothic* is the cultural significance of the workmanship, the nature of the work, which Morris, a key figure of the Victorian Arts and Crafts Movement, puts into words in this way: "the idea of genuine art, the expression of man's pleasure in his handiwork", without which "the hopes of the happiness of Mankind ... must inevitably cease altogether" (quoted in Faulkner, n.d.). It is the nature of the work that Ruskin tries to revive. However, his ideas of national workshops are such that they could not be realised. Mackail, quoting from Dixon's notes, states how Morris found much inspiration in the theories of Ruskin, transposing the ideas to his own line of work and to the philosophies of the Arts and Craft Movement: "It was when ... he [Morris], got to Ruskin, that strong direction was given to a true vocation – 'The Seven Lamps', 'Modern Painters'; and 'The Stones of Venice'" (quoted in Faulkner, n.d.). Central to Ruskin's beliefs is his increasing concern about the dissolving trend of art in society (Ruskin, 1907a, 1907b).

Ruskin envisions a human element in the concept of political economy, one that would enable the individual to live in a society where imaginative and creative artwork was valued. In Victorian England, where art was not an academically acknowledged subject of study, Ruskin promoted the idea that art education was a public concern, a moral obligation and a social responsibility: "no nation can neglect [art education] without endangering its intellectual existence", furthermore, art was "not the privilege of artists, connoisseurs and the educated classes, but … part of every man's inheritance and estate" (Hauser on Ruskin quoted in Landow, 2006). Ruskin pushed for an educational system that was to become integral to the arts and crafts, and indeed his philosophies spread across the European continent, eventually reaching the US, influencing movements such as the Bauhaus and Der Deutsche Werkbund, as well as the arts and crafts movements of the US. Hauser describes Ruskin's influence as "extraordinary, almost beyond description", maintaining that "the purposefulness and solidity of modern architecture and industrial art" were "very largely the result of Ruskin's endeavours and doctrines" (quoted in Landow, 2006). Hauser (1952, pp. 820-22) sums up Ruskin's influence in this way:

> [Ruskin] was indubitably the first to interpret the decline of art and taste as the sign of a general cultural crisis, and to express the basic, and even today not sufficiently appreciated, principle that conditions under which men live must first be changed, if their sense of beauty and their comprehension of art are to be awakened. (quoted in Landow, 2006)

Without doubt, Ruskin's visions are ideological, moral and utopian. For him, work and education is a moral-ethical process, but his philosophies are still relevant to discussions about sustainability, for it is about the human nature of the work, the nature of the labour.

Peter Fuller (1982), a British art critic of the 1980s and a proponent of Ruskin's theories, argues that for the crafts to be valued on a wider social level, even today, higher level craft skills must be taught at educational institutions. He suggests that classical music, dance and performance continue to persist as well-acknowledged cultural art forms, and urges that something similar needs to be achieved for the classical arts and crafts (p. 260).

Redefining what it means to make

In conclusion, if Habermas' (1984) deliberations about desocialisation/denaturalisation is a source of environmentally destructive attitudes, then the issue needs to be thought about in terms of how to re-socialise nature and re-naturalise society. Throughout the history of human development the hand-production of objects has been an influential creative force in the socio-cultural aesthetic advancement of civilisations. My research suggests that making continues to be an influential creative force in the aesthetic advancement of society, and that it is Adorno's (2004) theory of aesthetic advance that allows for the re-socialisation of nature and the re-naturalisation of society. Making is a connecting link between what individuals do on an intensional, local level and what humanity, in their full complexity and diversity, does on an extensional, global level.

Adorno's (2004) philosophies about 'real human values' and Ruskin's (1907c, 2009) insights into 'true wealth' and 'the nature of the Gothic', offer ways to put aesthetic advancement into practice. It is the nature of making that matters, not a return to old traditions. It is about the social renewal of a long-standing cultural practice, because the traditions of handcraft production are coextensive with real human values, and, as I view it, all three structural components of the human lifeworld, society, culture and the 'socialised individual', would flourish in the light of a cultural craft tradition. In my opinion, it is this that has the potential to contribute to the sustainability of the ecology.

Art practice as a cultural craft practice

I bring the chapter to a close with an overview of my art practice. As a result of my research, central to my textile-based work is the real physical experience of making, using traditional means of creating. I believe that the handloom production of cloth, spinning of fibre, dyeing with natural materials, hand stitching and using other traditional techniques, have the best potential with which to express my ideas about the connecting link between the handmade object and ecology. Textile production is a constructive-creative form of art where the basic principles of creation have remained the same for millennia; many hours of labour go into the weaving of a length of cloth. The labour incorporates thinking and manual skills on equivalent levels. Thus the work is processed-based, and experiencing the nature of the labour is for me far more important than the aim for completion. Being immersed in process is an important part of the creative-aesthetic experience.

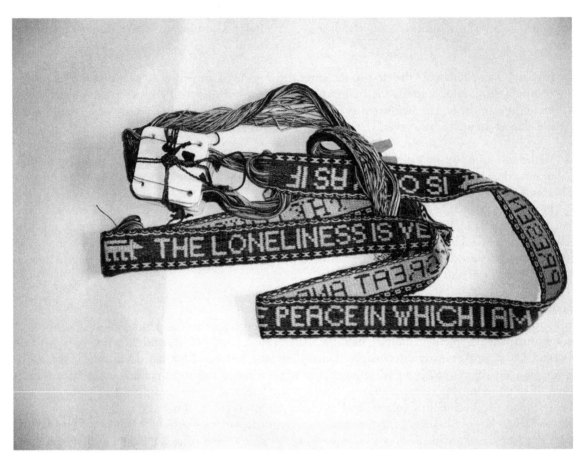

Figure 1: Continually I (2010), work in progress with weaving tablets attached.

Figure 1 depicts my tablet-woven work. Tablet weaving most likely originated in the Iron Age (Barber, 1991, p. 119) and is a technique for weaving patterned bands. Drawing on Ruskin's words, I designed the images and the letters for the work:

> The loneliness is very great, and the peace in which I am at present is only as if I had buried myself in a tuft of grass on a battlefield wet with blood – for the cry of the earth about me is in my ears continually. (1907c, p. viii)

Ruskin's words make direct reference to his despair about the effects of industrialisation on nature, which is still very relevant today. My process begins with thinking, reading, researching, designing, walks, rethinking, and playing with ideas. I tend to use raw materials such as raw wool, flax or cotton and organic, renewable matter, such as leaves for dyeing fibres.

Figure 2: Dye pot, work in progress.

Figure 2 shows a dye pot. There is an intimate relationship between the act of making and the physical experience of natural elements. For me, this is a process of reconnecting with nature, a process that is analogue to the re-socialisation of nature and the re-naturalisation of society. The dyeing of fibre takes many days to complete. Thereafter threads have to be calculated for the weave process, measured and sorted for their colours, the loom needs to be dressed, and the cloth woven, which are all slow and repetitive processes. The creative act of making is an intense and time-consuming process of self-actualisation for it involves, as Morris puts it, "pleasure in the work" (quoted in Faulkner, n.d.). Taking 'pleasure in the work' is an important part of realising the aesthetic progression towards "a consciousness of freedom" (Adorno, 2004).

Figure 3: Double weave pick-up and stitch, indigo and plant dye, linen fibre, (15 cm x 68 cm).

Figure 3 depicts a double weave pick-up cloth, meaning that two separate layers of cloth are woven at the same time, one dark, one light, allowing for imagery and pattern to be incorporated into the cloth during the weave process. Time and technique are inherent elements of this process. Into this piece I wove traditional imagery taken from my European background: the mythical tree of life, the bird of Athene and stars or snowdrops. The tree of life signifies regeneration or immortality, and "the return to the primordial state of perfection" (Cooper, 1978, p. 176), while the bird implies transcendence (Cooper, 1978, p. 20). Transcendence and immortality are important concepts. Transcendence references the significance of an experience that cannot be understood in ordinary ways – i.e., the notion of transcendence could be applied to the tacit or inexplicable experience of making – whereas immortality might reference the importance of continuous renewal; as I see it, the continuous renewal of a cultural craft practice.

The cloth is over-dyed with indigo, almost erasing the images, suggesting the dissolving trend of an important cultural tradition. I then stitched back into the cloth, simultaneously emphasising and distorting the imagery. This piece is a signifier of the traditions that have their origins in poetic-mythological understandings of the world; stories of myth are part of a society's heritage. Essentially, however, the work is about the value of human labour, about the nature of the process, about process being an important element of the creative-aesthetic experience, and about the human element of the handmade object, made manifest in the object's poetic-aesthetic content. This is the kind of aesthetic advancement I seek, and it is the work's communicative capacity that may help re-naturalise society/re-socialise nature and contribute to the realisation of a more sustainable future.

Dr Jane Donlin lives and works in Perth, Australia. She received her Master of Arts and a Doctor of Philosophy from Edith Cowan University, Perth and works in the School of Design and Art at Curtin University. She has shown her process-based textile work in numerous art exhibitions.

References

Adorno, T. (1977). Über Tradition *Kulturkritik und Gesellschaft* (pp. 310-320). Frankfurt am Main: Suhrkamp.

Adorno, T. (1984). *Aesthetic theory*. London: Routledge and Kegan Paul.

Adorno, T. (1985). *Minima Moralia: reflections from damaged life*. London: Verso.

Adorno, T. (1993). *The culture industry - selected essays on mass culture* (Vol. 3.). London: Routledge.

Adorno, T. (2004). *Aesthetic theory* (R. Hullot-Kentor, Trans.). London, New York: Continuum.

Barber, E. (1991). *Prehistoric textiles – The development of cloth in the Neolithic and Bronze ages*. Oxford: Princeton University Press.

Cooper, J. C. (1978). *An illustrated encyclopaedia of traditional symbols*. London: Thames and Hudson.

Epstein, S., & Prak, M. (2008). Guilds, innovation and the European economy, 1400-1800 (p. 362). Retrieved from http://library.ecu.edu.au/

Faulkner, P. (n.d.). Ruskin and Morris Retrieved September 16, 2013, from http://www.morris society.org/publications/JWMS/AU00.14.1.RuskinMorrisFaulkner.pdf

Fuller, P. (1982). *Beyond the crisis in art*. London: Writers and Readers Publishing.

Fuller, P. (1985). Fabric and form *Images of God, the consolations of lost illusions* (pp. 256-260). London: Chatto and Windus.

Giddens, A. (1991). *Modernity and self-identity: self and society in the late modern age*. Cambridge: Stanford University Press.

Giddens, A. (1994). Living in a post-traditional society. *Reflexive modernisation, politics, tradition and aesthetics in the modern social order* (pp. 56-197). Cambridge: Polity Press.

Giddens, A. (2000). *Runaway world*. London: Profile Books Ltd.

Habermas, J. (1984). *The theory of communicative action: reason and the rationalisation of society* (T. McCarthy, Trans.). Boston: Beacon Press.

Habermas, J. (1987). *The theory of communicative action: lifeworld and system – a critique of functionalist reason* (T. McCarthy, Trans. Vol. two). Boston: Beacon Press.

Hauser, A. (1952). *The Social History of Art*. New York: Knopf.

Herzfeld, M. (2004). *The body impolitic*. Chicago and London: The University of Chicago Press.

Landow, G. (2006). The aesthetic and critical theories of John Ruskin Retrieved September, 17, 2013, from http://www.victorianweb.org/authors/ruskin/atheories/2.2.html

Ruskin, J. (1907a). *A joy for ever (and its price in the market)*. London: George Allen.

Ruskin, J. (1907b). *The two paths*. London: George Allen and Sons.

Ruskin, J. (1907c). *Unto this last and other essays on art and political economy*. London: J. M. Dent & Sons Ltd.

Ruskin, J. (2009). *John Ruskin: selected writings*. Oxford: Oxford University Press.

CHAPTER 7

TOWARD A NEGATIVE AESTHETIC OF SUSTAINABILITY IN TIM WINTON'S *DIRT MUSIC*

Erin Corderoy & Michaela Baker

Introduction

Tim Winton's *Dirt Music* pays homage to the Romantic poets, particularly William Blake and John Keats, who were much concerned with the aesthetic relationship between human beings and the environment. This relationship signifies the movement that we now call Romanticism. Ecocriticism shares with Romanticism a recognition that "ethics and aesthetics are one" (Wittgenstein, 1999, 6.421). Given its recognition of the potential ethical and political power of aesthetic representations of the non-human natural world, ecocriticism is considered to be a descendant of Romanticism (Bate, 2000, pp. 13-14; Garrard, 1996, p. 450). However, ecocriticism is also concerned with undercutting the Romantic idealism of a "beautiful" and/or symmetrical aesthetic in non-human nature, which is an ideal that threatens non-human nature. This chapter takes an ecocritical stance and seeks to destabilise the normativity of the Romantic ideology of an aesthetic of beauty as the only source of sustainable practices and puts forward the thesis that a negative aesthetic, one in which 'beauty' or even symmetry cannot immediately be reconciled, can also lead to sustainable practices and an ethical concern for the non-human environment.

Dirt Music demonstrates the capacity of works of art to recall the experience of the "natural world" to those who exist largely removed from it and in turn to create awareness of and concern about our potentially destructive interactions with it (Lintott, 2007). Through the creation and maintenance of a negative aesthetic via the juxtaposition and trajectory of certain ethically and aesthetically charged scenarios, concern is created about sustainability for an environment that is entrenched in historical and cultural stigma. The chapter's first section outlines our conceptualisation of the negative aesthetic and its influence on an ethical response to ecosystems. The second demonstrates, through analysis of Tim Winton's *Dirt Music*, the way the negative aesthetic is applied to texts to draw readers into an ethical response toward non-humans and sustainability.

On the ethical effects of literature and the negative aesthetic

We use the term "non-human" to signify the flora and fauna that function within an ecosystem. This ecosystem is a natural phenomenon and a cultural paradigm. The former includes humans as arbiters of ecosystems, the latter includes all that is not ascribed or fixed as human in an interconnected ecosystem. Ecocriticism concerns itself with bridging this divide between disparate conceptions of ecosystems and focuses on the human as part of the natural ecosystem. This configuration seeks to eliminate the paradigmatic ecosystem, thereby encouraging a concern for sustainability. Greg Garrard sees this bridge as stemming from "direct personal experience" (2007, p. 365) with the natural ecosystem. Direct personal experience is not always possible, but can be approximated through aesthetic interaction. This interaction results in a positive of negative reaction, which leads to "awe in the presence of nature" (Garrard, 1996, p. 455).

Aesthetic effect is most frequently aligned with the sublime response (Shapshay, 2013, pp. 182-183) to natural ecosystems, rather than paradigmatic ecosystems. The foundation of the paradigmatic ecosystem is one that stems from a commitment to naming; this includes both things and places (Bate, 2000, 229). Since humans first settled or colonised lands, naming was an important way of demarcating ownership (Derrida, 2002, p. 400) and this drive to own and name has fostered an othering of "Animal" and "Plant" that essentialises categories and overshadows the subtle interactions that create and sustain an ecosystem (Buell, 2005, 84-85). An understanding of this drive to own and 'other' leads to a concern for all life existing within a natural ecosystem, even a paradigmatic ecosystem, which by extension leads to an ethic of sustainability. In this section, we demonstrate how this ethic via an examination of the way in which literature can serve as "direct personal experience" and how this connects to the development of an ethical imagination.

The relationship between readers and texts is the subject of much debate (and not a little contention) in both literary theory and philosophy (See e.g. Barthes, 1977; Macherey, 1978; Rushdie, 1990; Nussbaum, 1992; Rimmon-Kenan, 2005; Wisker, 2014). In this chapter, however, our concern is to mount an argument that literary texts are both capable of, and an ideally suited medium for, the development of an ethical imagination, and hence ethical praxis. We will then demonstrate the ways in which this is true of *Dirt Music*, and argue that the imagination it develops is an ethical one, which prompts a response to the world, and the non-human environment in particular, which is concerned with sustainability.

Dirt Music is an exploration of the enduring issues surrounding the interaction of human and non-human nature within an ecosystem, and demonstrates the need for them to be examined in a contemporary setting. Winton's novel embodies the idea of the ethical and the aesthetic as one. The portrayals of these interactions operate in a way that, "while it cannot be logically framed as a theme or propositional content, can nonetheless be witnessed: 'it shows itself' [(Wittgenstein, 1999, 6.522)]" (Stengel, 2004, p. 615). It is this 'showing' of itself that evokes both an ethical and an aesthetic response in readers. We contend that Winton evokes this response in his readers via a negative aesthetic. This is possible given that the negative aesthetic is inherently "response-dependent", as negative aesthetic values are related both to "properties in objects and to the cognitive stock, imaginative associations, emotions and biases" (Brady, 2011, p. 93) of individuals.

Readers are particularly important to our conception of the negative aesthetic; although the position of the reader has been much contested it is finding new importance in considerations of the aesthetic in texts (Armstrong, 2011, p. 89). We do not contend that reader-response is the only embodiment of the aesthetic, or the negative aesthetic, but that it is evidently central to considerations of the praxis to come from aesthetic examinations. This praxis is found in the drive to an ethical concern for natural ecosystems and is especially relevant to the sustainability project. In essence, praxis cannot begin without a reader upon whom the aesthetic, in this case, a negative aesthetic, can impact, which manifests in an ethical response.

In order to demonstrate how Winton's novel achieves the effects we suggest that it has, it is necessary first to make an argument for how literature might have ethical effects. Martha Nussbaum argues that "the aesthetic is ethical and political" (1998, p. 344). In fact, she continues, the novelist's skill in showing situations allows him/her to "make a contribution to a public victory over obtuseness and emotional deadness" (Nussbaum, 1998, p. 344). As we will discuss in more detail below, it is precisely this combatting of "emotional deadness" that the juxtapositions of events in the trajectory of Winton's novel achieves. The nineteenth century American novelist, Henry James, contended that novelists are in a position, via the ways in which they portray events, to embody a "projected morality" (Nussbaum, 1970, p. 45) in their work. It follows that novelists are in a unique position to lead "our emotions to a more honest confrontation with our own selves and the real impact our conduct has on the lives of others" (1998, p. 343). As we will demonstrate below, the portrayal of events in *Dirt Music* has the effect of extending this concern to include the lives of non-human animals, and even the ecosystem itself. The important issue to clarify at this point in the argument is *how* this might be achieved.

Following Aristotle, Nussbaum identifies four defining characteristics of novels and philosophy which take seriously James' idea of a "projected morality":

(1) an insistence on the plurality and non-commensurability of the valuable elements of a well-lived life; (2) an insistence on the importance of contextual complexity and particularized judgment in good deliberation; (3) an insistence on the cognitive role of the emotions; and (4) an insistence on human vulnerability and the vulnerability of the good (1998, p. 348).

The salient point that Nussbaum makes here is that it is novels, rather than abstract moral theorising, which are best equipped to help us realise these characteristics. A small but growing body of empirical research bears this out, demonstrating that "[r]eaders of fiction tend to have better abilities of empathy and theory of mind" (Mar et al., 2009, p. 407) than readers of non-fiction, even when researchers control for other factors, such as intelligence and language ability (Mar et al., 2006), as well as gender and tendency to be absorbed in a narrative (Mar et al., 2009).

This ability of the novel, as mentioned with reference to Wittgenstein above, is demonstrable via the ways in which novels are able to portray incidents that maintain contextual complexity and engage our emotions in such a way as to allow them to fulfill the cognitive role that Nussbaum identifies. In line with this, as we demonstrate in the following section, "negative feelings in aesthetic experience can acquaint us with a range of feelings not available with easy beauty" (Brady, 2011, p. 97). Freed from what James calls the "standing terms" of our everyday language, the novelist's use of language involves an "immense array of terms, perceptional and expressional" (1970, p. 339) that allows the portrayal of events to transcend the everyday realities and assumptions in which we usually find ourselves mired. In the following section we examine some of the 'perceptional and expressional terms' used by Winton in his portrayal of the trajectory of events in the novel, and the effects these have on the reader.

A second way in which novels achieve an ethical effect is via the cultivation of a particular type of imagination. Ihab Hassan suggests that the imagination plays a role in creating and disassembling worlds or scripts (1978, pp. 778-779). Richard Rorty conceives of literature as "world-making": the "metaphoric redescription" (Leypoldt, 2008, p. 145) of events and agents in a world. If we combine Hassan and Rorty's perspectives, we arrive at a picture of literature in which a literary work, such as a novel, engages the imagination of the reader, via metaphoric redescription, in such a way as to enable the reader to create a world. As Hassan points out, this world-making may take the form of the building of a script, which we might conceive of as an action-guiding framework, responsive to the metaphorically re-imagined world. Through interdisciplinarity, the reader (Philippon, 2012, p. 169), their imagination, and their response to the negative aesthetic, can be managed such that an ethical response is elicited, which in turn affects ingrained behaviours and attitudes (Philippon, 2012, p. 168). We contend that *Dirt Music* manages this ethical turn via a negative aesthetics of sustainability.

A negative aesthetic creates situations in which "negative feelings such as uneasiness, distaste, dislike, revulsion, but also fascination" (Brady, 2011, p. 83) are used to evoke a changing of perspective in the reader. Situations involving traumatic or otherwise unpleasant interactions between humans and non-human nature are juxtaposed throughout the novel, often rather briefly and surreptitiously, and are used to evoke sensations and emotions in readers that may lead to a changing of perspectives toward the natural world. This response is similar to that which aestheticians consider the sublime. A negative aesthetic response is a response to the human place within nature that encourages a reflective and active position (Shapshay, 2013, p. 181). This position is possible because of the cultural significa-tion of the non-human as "other" (Derrida, 2002, p. 399). The otherness of the non-human is made explicit in *Dirt Music*, but it is dealt with in such a way as to draw the reader to consider the non-human other from a subjective position. This subjective position, which stems from the negative aesthetic, creates a sublime response that triggers concern for the non-human as an entity that deserves as much concern as a fellow human. The negative aesthetic resignifies that humans are also a part of a natural ecosystem (Calkins, 2012, p. 33); the rational reflex that comes from the sublime response instigates a concern for that ecosystem. *Dirt Music* affects the sublime response to a negative aesthetic by setting up contrasts between human and non-human nature; each is positioned within an integrative ecosystem that encourages intersubjectivity between the non-human and the human participants.

These contrasts position readers as transient beings whose positional perspectives change according to the scenario to which Winton directs their attention. Winton frequently juxtaposes events in a non-linear trajectory in which trauma to humans is subsequently juxtaposed with trauma to a close proxy, such as an aesthetically pleasing or benign animal, and often to a "cypher" animal or plant, which in turn incites in readers a response that is negative. As will be discussed in detail in the following section for example, there is a movement in the novel from human trauma, to trauma to a dog (a benign animal), to trauma to blowfish (a cypher animal). This negative response is similar to that which occurs in what has come to be known as "reparative reading". "Reparative reading" is a term coined by Eve Sedgwick in relation to Queer Theory (1), but it has extensive applications in ethical responses to literary aesthetics. This reparative response stems from a position of psychic damage or trauma that bears within it the possibility of a "reparative function" (Hanson, 2011, p.102). The reparative function exposes the reader to "the process of reconstructing a sustainable life" (Hanson, 2011, p. 105) in the wake of trauma. Sedgwick suggests that "the reparative reader tries to organize the fragments and part-objects she encounters or creates" (2004, p. 146), and comes to realise an ethical response to the past as to the present and future. These fragments and part-objects can be suggested to the reader, as in *Dirt Music,* through a trajectory of events that thereby lead to the reparative response and to a realisation of an ethical role within the sustainability of ecosystems. This ethical response is then inscribed onto a non-human cypher, which bears the new script of an entity deserving ethical concern commensurate with that accorded to a fellow human.

The cypher is a nullity or "zero" entity (Gilbert and Gubar, 1984, p. 9 and OED 'cypher'), and in this formulation permits the reader to invest the ethical concerns and feelings they built up as a negative response to human-centred events upon the non-human entity. This responsiveness is two-fold and can lead to further essentialising, anthropocentrism, and a drive to the pathetic fallacy, each of which see non-humans exhibiting human responses to the environment and stimuli. This is the hazard, but the hazard is easily managed by maintaining sensitivity to non-human individuality and interdependence. The phenomenon of the cypher is that it acts as an aesthetically odd or unpleasant, but generally ideologically un-inscribed flora/fauna, which is then open to ethically-motivated inscriptions, thus destabilising the 'beauty' aesthetic that generally informs sustainable concerns.

The ideal position for the cypher is that it be invested with a need for concern and an ethical imperative to sustain life, not to invest it with characteristics and formulations that are specifically human or to carry over feelings or ideological inscription. The negative aesthetic encourages concern and an ethical impetus to exist interdependently within an ecosystem resulting in sustainable practice and a shift to a more sustainable ecosystem paradigm, one that is much closer to the natural state of an ecosystem. The trajectory and reader response delivered in *Dirt Music* and the negative aesthetic circumvents the training that humans have to "infer human agency everywhere" (Garrard, 2012, p. 155). The negative aesthetic reveals an ecosystem in which interdependence rather than human-centrality (Bate, 2000, p. 138) is an attainable and sustainable norm. The cypher is instrumental to achieving this norm as it reveals that a previously unconsidered or reviled entity holds a role within an ecosystem that is essential, and not necessarily over and above the human role. The sublime response to the negative aesthetic involves the reader in an ethical realisation of their role as an interdependent agent within an ecosystem whose impetus to sustainability is motivated by a desire to achieve better results for all entities within the system rather than results that only benefit the human, or that are derived from preconceived notions of a paradigmatic ecosystem.

Practising a Negative Aesthetic of Sustainability

The sublime response to the negative aesthetic is transcribed into a concern for non-humans upon which humans exert an influence. The trajectory of events in *Dirt Music* motivates a reconsideration of the nature of ethical interactions between humans and non-humans. It also evokes an emotional and aesthetic reaction of concern towards the natural world, which gradually extends to encompass not just those non-humans that are beautiful or purposeful to human beings, but also non-humans that are not deemed beautiful or purposeful. In particular, the structure and framing of Winton's novel invites the reader to consider the way in which aesthetic concerns influence reactions toward the natural world, particularly how the presentation of the phenomena of the natural affects the attitudes towards, and actions of, the observer.

The series of events that leads to the negative aesthetic is a trajectory. The trajectory establishes an ethical drive or connection with the events of the novel, and by extension an impetus toward maintaining sustainable natural ecosystems. The first trajectory in *Dirt Music* is initiated with a car accident in which the family of Luther Fox, one of the protagonists, are severely mutilated and ultimately killed. The trajectory is followed by events detailing the senseless destruction of animals and environment, which lead up to a second car crash that almost exactly mirrors the first.

At the first car crash, Fox finds his brother in their upside-down ute, its "beetle-like underbelly" (Winton, 2012, p.117) exciting revulsion. This revulsion is a signpost to the reader to respond in kind. And when Fox finds his brother's pulpy arm loosely affixed to a body that "feels like a kitbag full of loose tools" (Winton, 2012, p.117) the revulsion aids in triggering an ethical response. The negative aesthetic plays out here to highlight the very un-humanness and indeed the interdependence that fundamentally exists in the natural ecosystem between humans and the largely reviled beetle. The sole expression is not to feel an ethical impulse to help a beetle, but to experience intersubjectivity between the human and non-human. The human and non-human are alike frail, helpless and dependent on a system of interconnectedness for survival.

The negative aesthetic, as shown in *Dirt Music*, triggers responsiveness to humanness and non-humanness that transcends privilege and permits an ethical and integrated conception of an ecosystem, of the place of the human and non-human within an ecosystem. The interrelation of the natural and non-natural is continued when Fox burrows into the cab to search for his brother's wife, Sally. Fox is assaulted by the smell of "shit and Juicy Fruit" finding Sally with "bits of metal protruding from her trunk" (Winton, 2012, p.117). Running from the wreck, Fox discovers his nephew, Bullet, "his head rent like a cantaloupe, still smelling of soap, [his] pyjamas clean" (Winton, 2012, p.118); as if to herald the absurdity of the situation, the "chained dog barks" (Winton, 2012, p.118) and Fox finds his favourite, his niece, Bird.

Bird is "like a fallen kite" (Winton, 2012, p.118). Here there is a play on the bird and a metonym for the human endeavour to encroach upon and conquer the world beyond their natural sphere, which is to say that the human place within an ecosystem is not to fly. The scene continues, after trying to drag Bird's body to the house, Fox, "his collarbone grind[ing] like a broken joist" (p.118), relents and the scene folds back: first the moon, then the wind, which makes the wire of the fence sing and the weeds hiss. Beyond the site of the wreck "the heavy orange blossoms of the Christmas trees shiver in the night and beyond them the beetle backs of melons shine" (p.119). This world beyond Fox's world continues to thrive, to struggle through the assignations of naming "Christmas" trees and "beetle" melons. Each interdependently functions as part of the larger ecosystem, and Fox, his family and the beetle belly of the ute are out of place, and they, like nature, become unfocused – peripheral to an expansive and complex ecosystem. This negative aesthetic, the sublime folding back into a rational and ethical position is focused in this one scene, but each scene within *Dirt Music* is as interconnected as the elements of the car crash.

The trajectory of events that follow from the first car crash and lead to the second reveal a day of excessive carnage in which, attempting to impress a city girl, one of the "big kids" was seen,

> Stomping blowfish, ripping the jaws from live trumpeters [...] A live boxfish, harmless and silly-looking, about the size of a softball, was shoved beneath the back wheel of the idling depot truck. The spray of gore, the laughter. (Winton, 2012, p.121).

After this recollection, Fox approaches his dog, the same that was chained and barking during the car crash scene, which is "already panting on the step and it leaps against him for comfort, as though the whole day has been a confounding of routine" (Winton, 2012, p.121). The dog plays an important role, its presence in chains reaffirmed the negative aesthetic of the previous scene, and here it reveals the discrepancy between those animals humans covet as proxies or as near-human and those considered ugly or as non-entities, such as the blowfish. The cypher animals, the fish, are thereby inscribed with a concern for the cruelty done to them. This occurs not because one might feel the fish to be an extension of one's humanity, as one might the dog, but because the interconnectedness of the scenes, the world-making of the events, creates a trajectory toward an ethical response.

The negative aesthetic is further evidenced in the following chapter, which sees Fox 'at home' in a reef, a position later problematised by his attempt to make an island his home, the rather plain and average sea-life is described in an aesthetically pleasing way and the reader is shocked away from the pleasant scene as Fox surfaces and "begins to *see* what he is looking at" (Winton, 2012, p. 131, emphasis added). Fox sees his dog as subject to an unnatural ecosystem in which life and death are appropriated as the domain of humans rather than nature. Fox

> walks up to the dog which lies in a stain of itself on the chain's end. Fragments of hair and meat discolour the sand. There's blood underfoot but no flies yet. [...] He pops the hood [of his vehicle], sees the V8's blasted entrails (Winton, 2012, p.131).

The next witness to the carnage is Georgie, the second protagonist and Fox's double. Georgie hears a gunshot and she goes to Fox's vehicle to check it out, she sees the damage done to the car and in the same breath notes "the spray of dog on the sand" (Winton, 2012, p.132). The contrast and equal significance given to the dog and the car elicits a shame for the use we make of such proxy animals. This shame is tantamount to the reparative response, which, as noted earlier, drives an ethical commitment to undo the structures and ideologies that lead to shame. In this case shame stems from the equal position ascribed to car and animal and, as that follows, from the images of human carnage and carnage of animals that are not "considered" at all, the event is doubly imbued with an aesthetic, world-making, negative impact of the human place within ecosystems.

Fox and Georgie operate as doubles and as such their characterisation works at the same level as the interrelatedness of the novel's events. In sum, they sustain each other – they enact the natural ecosystem and this is nowhere more evident than in the double event of the car crash. Each of these events occurs at roughly the same landmark within the novel and similar aesthetic information is given at the two events. The second accident involves Georgie as the 'saviour' and it almost exactly mirrors the first. In a reversal of the first crash, Georgie sees a child along the road before she notices the car in the ditch. The language and the setting here are also opposite to those of the first crash: it is daytime, the car is upright and the significance of the pulpy arm is transcribed as being "stripped to the bone. The muscle was a snarl of meat and tendon" (Winton, 2012, p.280); everything is clear and matter of fact. The language is slightly less poetic and far more objective; it is observational rather than whimsical. Even the relation of human flesh to meat, a function that drives the negative aesthetic in this scene, is clinical. All energy is focused on the car accident as Georgie, "struggl[es] toward...bright matter-of-factness" (Winton, 2012, p. 280). It is this "matter-of-factness" that frequently clouds conceptions of the human as interconnected within an ecosystem. "I think; therefore, I am independent of, and above, nature" seems almost to be the real axiom. Both accidents demonstrate Rudolf Arnheim's contention that the negative aesthetic involves "a clash of uncoordinated orders...when each of its parts has an order of its own, but these orders do not fit together, and thus the whole is fractured" (quoted in Lorand, 1994, p. 402). This sense of orders that do not fit with each other, which result in a fracturing of wholeness, resurfaces in the deterioration of Fox on the island.

The place of humans in the ecosystem is not the only position challenged through the negative aesthetic. Georgie ministers to Avis, the victim of the accident, and the discussion moves to the murder of Fox's dog, and the Fox family in general. Avis' comment that, "Those Foxes. They were low. And thieves" foregrounds her comment that "it wasn't right about the dog" and that her "conscience is clear. Except for the dog" (Winton, 2012, p. 283). These comments interrelate; they create a picture that marries the negative aesthetic of Avis's maimed body with that of the eviscerated dog. Further, the fact that Avis refers to the Fox family as "Foxes", portrays them as a skulk of foxes, rather than a human family, and thus brings to mind one of nature's most stereotyped animals. The fox is seen as low and thieving, and is absolutely foreign to the Australian ecosystem. In many ways, so too is the domestic dog. This marrying of images builds to the realisation of the impact that human intervention has on the ecosystem. Avis regrets the death of the dog, but is still solidly against the Foxes. In discussing the Fox family as "the Foxes", an association is made that extends the negative aesthetic to become an ethical response. It motivates one to consider those animals that are positioned as outcast and also encourages consideration of the way that humans "build" ecosystems by introducing external elements that are incommensurate with sustainable or ethical practice.

This incommensurability between the marked and unmarked ecosystem is most prevalent towards the end of the novel when Fox inhabits an island that forms part of an archipelago. This island he intends to make his home, much as he ascribed "homeness" to the reef in the scene just before he sees that his dog has been eviscerated. The events that have been discussed all influence and impact on the way the events of Fox's time on the island are portrayed as well as projected – they impact on the "world-making" of the narrative. This influence of world-making as it relates to a trajectory of events that results in the negative aesthetic and an ethical response is most clear in the consideration of 'limbs' as they are dealt with symbolically and literally.

Limbs, highlighted already, feature as an aesthetic frame through which to encounter and consider the negative response. The image of the maimed arms from the two car crashes heavily influences the aesthetic information given while Fox inhabits the island. We can also conceive of the novel as something of an ecosystem in which the events are inherently interconnected and it is for this reason that we can discuss events toward the end of the novel as they connect to earlier events that continue to influence and speak to each other in a web of meaning. Fox's interactions on the island, and the island itself, are often described in fleshy terms, drawing a connection with the traumatic events that preceded them revealing a mutual deterioration of both Fox and the ecosystem. As Fox feels himself become a part of the ecosystem, he is also becoming distant from it through his position as an unnatural element, one that depletes the ecosystem without offering anything in return.

This trajectory is first set up by displaying the constancy and interconnectedness of the island ecosystem as separate from Fox, and his agitation at this position results in him "throwing stones or breaking tree limbs to no purpose" (Winton, 2012, p. 355). After a storm obliterates a giant boab tree and Fox notes "a few amputated limbs [that] lie smouldering beyond it" (Winton, 2012, p. 362) the connection with the earlier events of the novel is established and the reminder of the "limbs", first seen at the two car crashes, enforces the response to the negative aesthetic, which affects an ethical response in kind. Prior to the evisceration of the tree, an event foreshadowed by the senseless killing of the blowfish and Fox's dog, Fox recalls in detail that his father had removed some Tuart trees and "ground out the stumps vengefully" (Winton, 2012, p. 359) in response to a tree having fallen and impaled Fox's mother during a storm. This juxtaposition offers stark insight into the way the negative aesthetic operates through a trajectory of events. Storms, a natural and sustainable element of an ecosystem, might tear down trees but they do not generally cause a mass culling. The actions taken by Fox's father seem shockingly extreme compared with the death of his mother. This trajectory between life and death measured through trauma reveals the privileged position that people hold in "managing" ecosystems. The ethical consideration that the reader is lead to enforces the requirement for interdependence rather than an overt and potentially damaging governance of ecosystems.

When Fox realises that he cannot function as part of the ecosystem, after being severely maimed and injured, his deterioration signifies the possible effect his presence is having on the island ecosystem. Fox notes that "he's exhausting the food around him, the stream is shrinking" (Winton, 2012, p. 419) and he would have to move around continuously or destroy both the ecosystem and himself. With reference to himself, and by extension the force humans exert on ecosystems to suit themselves, Fox notes, "None of it lives here; it doesn't spring from here and it will neither settle nor belong" (Winton, 2012, p. 419).

Conclusion

The benefit of the negative aesthetic in effecting ethical commitment and practice has been widely overlooked, but through interdisciplinary research much can be discovered about the way it might be used to encourage sustainable practices. Tim Winton's *Dirt Music* is an example of how the negative aesthetic in literature encourages readers to respond ethically. This response is elicited through the juxtaposition of negative events that interrelate, triggering the imagination into acknowledging the ecosystem as a unified whole, one in which humans function with non-humans sustainably rather than as overseers. Utilising an interdisciplinary approach that takes account of ideological structures, the ability for aesthetics to create new links via the imagination and the sublime, the ethical effects of novels and the way non-humans are positioned as "other" suggests the negative aesthetic to be of great potential value in considering the role of aesthetics to sustainable practices. It is important in a world that is so steeped in the paradigms and ideologies of the unsustainable, that creative modes of reviewing, reassessing, and creating new practices be embraced in the move toward a sustainable future.

Erin Corderoy is a Master of Research candidate in English Literature at Macquarie University where she also works as a Research Assistant on ethics projects. Her main research areas are aesthetics, ethics and the environment. Erin's research primarily focuses on nineteenth-century English literature with an emphasis on the Gothic mode.

Dr. Michaela Baker is Academic Director for Professional and Community Engagement (PACE) in the Faculty of Arts at Macquarie University. She holds a PhD in Philosophy on Sartre from Macquarie University Her research interests include existentialism and phenomenology, philosophy and literature, ecocriticism, postcolonialism, and theatre.

Endnotes

1. Ecocriticism is in the process of integrating Queer Theory as a means to analyse the position of the non-human as other, thus it is relevant to integrate practices from queer theory into ecocritical readings. Refer to Garrard (2010) and Garrard (2011)

References

Armstrong, P. B. (2011). In Defense of Reading: Or, Why Reading Still Matters in a Contextualist Age. *New Literary History*, *42*(1), 87-113.

Barthes, R. (1977). The Death of the Author. *Image, Music, Text* (Essays selected and translated by Stephen Heath). New York: Hill & Wang.

Bate, J. (2000). *The Song of the Earth*. London: Picador.

Brady, E. (2011). The Ugly Truth: Negative Aesthetics and Environment. *Royal Institute of Philosophy Supplement*, *69*, 83-99.

Buell, L. (1999). The Ecocritical Insurgency. *New Literary History*, *30*(3), Ecocriticism, 699-712. Retrieved from http://www.jstor.org/stable/20057562

Buell, L. (2005). *The Future of Environmental Criticism: Environmental Crisis and Literary Imagination*. Oxford: Blackwell Publishing.

Calkins, J. (2012). How Is It Then With the Whale?: Using Scientific Data to Explore Textual Embodiment. *Configurations*, *18*(1-2), 31-47.

Derrida, J. (2002). The Animal That Therefore I Am (More to Follow). Trans. David Willis. *Critical Inquiry*, *28*(2), 369-418. Retrieved from http://www.jstor.org/stable/1344276

Gilbert, S. M. and Gubar, S. (1984). *The Madwoman in the Attic: The Woman Writer and the Nineteenth-Century Literary Imagination*. New Haven: Yale University Press.

Garrard, G. (1996). Radical Pastoral? *Studies in Romanticism*, *35*(3), Green Romanticism, 449-465. Retrieved from http://www.jstor.org/stable/25601184

Garrard, G. (2007). Ecocriticism and Education for Sustainability. *Pedagogy*, *7*(3), 359-383. Retrieved from http://muse.jhu.edu/journals/ped/summary/v007/7.3garrard.html

Garrard, G. (2011). *Ecocriticsm*. London: Routledge.

Hanson, E. (2011). The Future's Eve: Reparative Reading After Sedgwick. *The South Atlantic Quarterly*, *110*(1), 101-119.

Hassan, I. (1978). Toward a Transhumanized Earth: Imagination, Science, and Future. *The Georgie Review*, *32*(4), 777-795. Retrieved from http://www.jstor.org/stable/41397828

James, H. (1970). *Art of the Novel*. New York: Charles Scribner's Sons.

Leypoldt, G. (2008). Uses of Metaphor: Richard Rorty's Literary Criticism and the Poetics of World-Making. *New Literary History*, *39*, 145-163

Lintott, S. (2007). Ethically Evaluating Environmental Art: Is It Worth It? *Ethics, Place and Environment*, *10*(3), 263-277.

Lorand, R. (1994). Beauty and Its Opposites. *Journal of Aesthetics and Art Criticism*, *52*(4), 399-406.

Love, H. (2010). Truth and Consequences: On Paranoid Reading and Reparative Reading. *Criticism*, *52*(2), 235-241.

Macherey, P. (1978). *A Theory of Literary Production*. (Geoffrey Wall, trans.). London: Routledge and Kegan Paul.

Mar, R.A., Oatley, K., Hirsch, J., dela Paz, J. & Peterson, J.B. (2006). Bookworms versus nerds: Exposure to fiction versus non-fiction, divergent associations with social ability, and the simulation of fictional social worlds. *Journal of Research in Personality*, *40*(5), 694-712.

Mar, R.A., Oatley, K. & Peterson, J.B. (2009). Exploring the link between reading fiction and empathy: Ruling out individual differences and examining outcomes. *Communications: The European Journal of Communication Research*, *34*(4), 407-428.

Nussbaum, M. (1992). *Love's Knowledge: Essays on Philosophy and Literature*. Oxford: Oxford University Press.

Nussbaum, M. (1998). Exactly and Responsibly: A Defence of Ethical Criticism. *Philosophy and Literature*, *22*(2), 343-365.

Philippon, D. J. (2012). Sustainability and the Humanities: An Extensive Pleasure. *American Literary History*, *24*(1), 163-179. doi: 10.1093/alh/ajr056

Rimmon-Kenan, S. (2005). *Narrative Fiction: Contemporary Poetics (2nd edition)*. London and New York: Routledge.

Rushdie, S. (1990). *Is nothing sacred?* New York: Granta.

Sedgwick, E. K. (2004). Paranoid Reading and Reparative Reading, or, You're So Paranoid, You Probably Think This Essay Is About You. In *Touching Feeling: Affect, Pedagogy, Performativity* (123-152). Durham, USA: Duke University Press.

Shapshay, S. (2013). Contemporary Environmental Aesthetics and the Neglect of the Sublime. *British Journal of Aesthetics*, *53*(2), 181-198.

Stengel, K. (2004). Ethics as Style: Wittgenstein's Aesthetic Ethics and Ethical Aesthetics. *Poetics Today*, *25*(4), 609-625.

Winton, T. (2001). *Dirt Music*. Sydney: Pan Macmillan Australia.

Wisker, G. (2014). Nothing wasted: engaging values and the imagination. How can working with feminist speculative fictions enthuse and engage students with social justice and sustainability in an age of austerity? *Journal of Gender Studies*, *23*(1), 1-15.

Wittgenstein, L. (1999). *Tractatus Logico-Philosophicus*. Translated by C. K. Ogden. Mineola, NY: Dover.

Part Two. Design and the Environment

CHAPTER EIGHT

THE AESTHETICS OF SUSTAINABLE WELL-BEING

Huilin Sun

Much debate has surrounded the topic of sustainability in a material sense, but its link to aesthetics and emotional well-being is scarce. In this chapter I will discuss the connections between gardening, values, aesthetics and well-being. I will examine how I make decisions based on my visual, ideological and cultural sensibilities, my understanding of Chinese garden design principles, and my enquiries into sustainable gardening. This study is underpinned by my interest in the human-nature relationship and my belief in the importance of emotional well-being as paramount to social and material well-being. Some of the questions to be addressed in this paper include: How do we define a sustainable garden? What is an aesthetically pleasing garden from a mainstream Australian point of view? Can we challenge this view so that a sustainable garden is also aesthetically pleasing? What would be the benefits of this? (1)

Australian gardening gurus have been outlining what they believe to be sustainable gardening. Evers & Hodgson (2011) examined how members of community gardens engage with local Alternative Food Networks, their attitudes towards food production, and the food choices they make. Sustainable Gardening Australia (SGA) (2014) is a not-for-profit, non-government, volunteer-driven organisation dedicated to changing the way Australians garden. SGA is working towards achieving vibrant and sustainable communities and a healthy, biodiverse planet by achieving real, continually improving and easily understood environmental solutions for gardeners (ibid).

Key elements of a sustainable garden in the Perth region include water-wise, eco-friendly and multipurpose. Strategies to achieve these goals include strategic planning, soil improvement and mulching (Hahn, 2013). Plants in a sustainable garden should perform multiple purposes such as providing shade, producing fruit and attracting wildlife (Morris, 2013). Strategies such as Chop and Drop pruning, allowing natural leaf litter to enrich soil, and using green kitchen waste for composting are other effective means to maintaining a sustainable garden (Gardening Trends, 2013). The use of power tools and pesticide should also be kept to a minimum. A machine such as a lawn mower uses fossil fuel and creates noise and air pollution that is not conducive to attracting wildlife. Sustainable development meets the needs of the present without compromising the ability of future generations to meet their own needs (World Commission on Environment and Development, 1987, p. 27). A sustainable garden has wider implications in the context of sustainability studies. Unfortunately, mainstream Australian gardens are not sustainable due to their owners' lack of understanding of the importance of sustainability. Findings from Dzidic & Green's research (2011) suggest that current social norms need to be challenged to encourage homeowners to adopt more sustainable practices so that new developments present an opportunity for neighbours to compete over the 'greenest' housing design rather than the greenest lawn.

I take a critical approach to the mainstream Australian garden by analysing its historical underpinning and cultural values that follow the post-Christian philosophical view that humans should control nature (2). This reflects the values of a dominant Anglo-European culture in Australia and informs many of their everyday decisions. Aesthetics is social, cultural and ideological. All people tend to consider their own cultural beliefs as universal ones (Kalheuer, 2009, p. 30), however, I think values can be decoded through analysing their material manifestations. For example, the prevalence of manicured lawns is the result of a cultural belief in its attractiveness, which has become 'universal' in Australian mainstream aesthetics. Many Australians prefer lawns in gardens because "It looks nice and you can kick a footy on it" (Duff, 2013). This ideology is often more of a historical imagination than a reality.

Historically, many Australians played in the front yard and grew vegies in the back yard (Stella, 2014). Most 20th century houses had play areas in the back yard and rarely grow vegies in the front. My research indicates only 5% of the houses in my neighbourhood incorporate a vegie garden in the front. The right to a backyard barbecue, swimming pool and ample space for ball games is a cherished aspect of the Australian suburban dream (Kellett, 2011). The front garden, which in most cases is covered by lawns, has become a display, showing the neighbours the owner of the house is 'one of them'. We could see the lawn quite differently if we were to change our vantage point. Many modern gardeners and conservationists acknowledge that the grasses from which lawn is grown are introduced weeds. Weeds can be plants from other countries, or species from other regions of Australia (Department of Agriculture, 2001). Although Buffalo grass has been used for lawns and pastures in Australia for over 180 years (Layt, 2014), it is still an introduced species from another continent. Invasive introduced plants have major impacts on natural bushland (Urban Design, Cultural Heritage & Landscape Unit and Land for Wildlife, 2002). Ground covers such as Kikuyu and Buffalo grass, amongst other invasive plants, reduce the diversity of native plants and destroying the habitat of native animals; cause injury to native animals or harming them through toxicity; choke waterways and wetlands and destroying aquatic habitat. Seddon (2005) pointed out the Anglo-Australian's dilemma in choosing local plants, "[Australians] are a nation of gardeners … [who] suspect that lawns and many of [their] European plants are too demanding of scarce [water] supplies, but can't imagine [their] streets and gardens without them".

Government water authorities view the lawn as a water-waster. The lawn is a legacy from English aesthetics, but on a different continent; in a different climate it seems bizarre, but not if one doesn't question the social, cultural and ideological norm.

Figure 1: Aesthetics are ideological. Photo: Huilin Sun.

The aesthetics of mainstream Australian gardens project control and deeply embedded cultural values that are difficult to change. Despite some changes in attitude due to the desire to conserve water sources or save the cost of watering, the norm of an Australian garden still tends to involve mostly lawn in the front garden, which is typically decorated by trees and shrubs below the gutter line. Recent mainstream garden trends advocate less plants and more geometrical lines in their design. The garden and the house are clearly demarcated as 'one' and 'the other' physically and visually. Industrial shapes and geometrical lines dominate spaces, as do clipped hedges, pathways and garden features. Recent landscape designers choose not to follow traditional design principles of planting in groups of odd numbers to create natural-looking drifts that ebb and flow into one another:

But what if we choose not to create natural looking gardens? What if we're stricter in the ways we plant, using even-numbered groupings, creating straight edges and geometric shapes, and using strips and blocks of limited plant varieties? The use of planting in blocks and strips links beautifully with a move toward simpler and more minimalistic garden design; it gives the same crisp demarcation in the planting that is achieved through hardscape elements. (The LifeStyle Magazine, 2014)

These aesthetics project order and reflect an ideology of keeping Nature under control. From my perspective, a typical contemporary Australian garden is something to manage and to look at, not something to be inside of.

Figure 2: Jerry Evans, The Water Garden at Kiftsgate Court.

In offering an alternative to this, I contrast the Australian approach with that of the Chinese who see themselves as part of nature. The Chinese garden emanated from a human desire to make a contribution to nature. Traditional Chinese gardeners work with nature. Keswick (1988) articulated the genesis of Chinese gardens in her foreword for the translation of the seventeenth century book *The crafts of gardens:*

On finding these two elements [yin and yang, which are represented by water and rock] are pleasingly balanced in a natural site, the Chinese, at least from the time of the Seven Sages, felt an urge to embellish them with some small tokens of man. Placed in the hills or by the lakes, little roofed and open-sided pavilions transform whole landscapes into *Jardins Trouves:* views of them focus the wilderness; views from them are framed in their pillars. 'Once we have a *ting* [pavilion]', one saying goes, 'we can say we have a garden.' (p. 20)

This is why architecture harmonises with the garden, and forms a complementary visual dialogue with it. The manmade and the natural are given equal respect. The trees are more beautiful with the building as a backdrop; the building more interesting because the tree's natural forms soften the building's geometrical lines. This working partnership in Chinese garden design reflects the Daoist philosophy of living in harmony with nature or "achieving harmony through aligning human nature with the rest of nature" (Ann & Du, 2002).

The Chinese garden

A Chinese garden is a celebration of nature and art. The Chinese view their gardens as an art form and art is a medium through which humans harmonise with nature. "The supple and powerful strokes of the calligraphy in which they were written echoed the shapes of leaves and branches all around: man and nature harmonised in art" (Keswick, 1988, p. 25). In contrast to the Australian presentational garden, a Chinese garden is a space in which one enters, like a painting. When complementing scenery, a Chinese person would say: "This scenery is so beautiful, it can enter a painting"; and in turn, appraising a landscape painting: "This painting is so exquisite, one can travel in it". The appreciation of nature, romanticised and stylised, is reflected in painting, which is emulated when creating a garden. The walls of the garden act as the paper on which a painting is painted, and the garden is the painting itself. "The spaciousness and simplicity in landscape paintings are aimed at in garden design" (p. 23) (Figure 3). The human/nature harmonisation in landscape paintings is achieved through leaving space in the painting for an imaginary entrance of the viewer. The harmonisation in gardens is through celebrating craftsmanship of the manmade components and the qualities of the natural elements. The aesthetics of appreciating nature and celebrating the art are key elements of Chinese garden design.

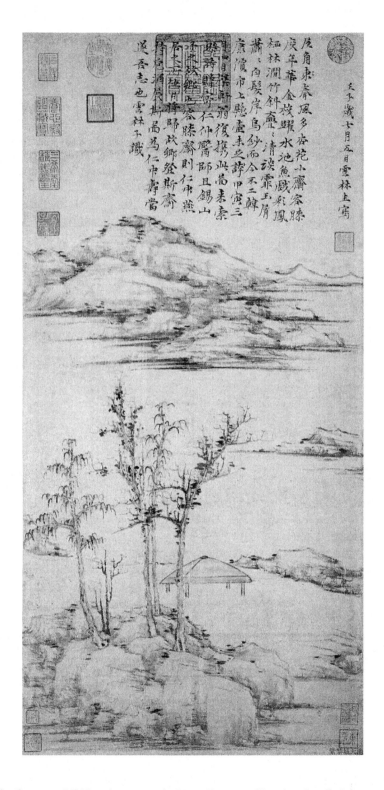

Figure 3: *Autumn Pavilion, 1339,* Ni Zan (1301–1374). Yuan Dynasty, Hanging Scroll, Ink on paper, Copyright Taiwan Museum.

Most sustainable gardens in the Perth Region have so far neglected their aesthetic dimensions. Naturalist gardens tend to look just like the local bushland. Their aesthetics tend to be flat, nondescript and at times messy. Naturalist gardeners are more interested in preserving indigenous plant species and wildlife rather than aesthetics. In criticising a native garden, one of my neighbours said: "The council wouldn't know what to collect and what to leave behind [at green waste collection]" (Adams, 2012). Productive gardens often look like farms with rows of vegetables in season. The focus of these gardens tends to be on how much food the garden produces rather than how nice it looks. The Chinese garden, however, although rather preoccupied with aesthetics, has never been concerned with sustainability. It could be considered an elitist approach to gardening. My aim in gardening is to synthesise the three and create a new approach to gardening. This requires keeping all the three aspects of gardening in mind in all decision making.

In my own garden I planned the planting and pruning from a sustainable, productive and an aesthetic viewpoint. I planted the right trees in the right place, allowing them to grow to the right height, so that they provide natural shade and solar gain. This reduces the need for artificial cooling and heating which both create greenhouse emissions. 89% of heat gain in summer in the Perth region is through the glassing in of windows and doors (Morris, 2013). By planting trees indigenous to the area I have been able to attract native birds, contributing to a more balanced eco-system. In the food productive areas, herbs and vegetables thrive. By applying the Chinese theories of garden making (Liu, 2002), I was able to consider design elements such as space, parameters, layers, depth, distance, composition, presentation, relationship, sight line, viewpoints, form, light, shade, movement, shadows, reflection and architecture.

Now I will examine the details of how I make decisions in my garden making process based on my visual, ideological and cultural sensibilities, my understanding of Chinese garden design principles, and my enquiries into sustainable gardening.

My garden-making project began with a house renovation project of my own residence. This 1968 double-brick house occupies the middle third of a 712 square metre block. My theory of renovating a house is that the garden and the house is one project. Since a garden takes time to establish, I have often prioritised working on the garden. As the garden became more established, a conflict arose. This conflict is between the aesthetics of the garden and the aesthetics of the house. The colour scheme of the house became a distraction to the garden. The manmade component and the natural elements were not harmonising.

The main disharmonising manmade element was the gutter. One of the first changes I made to the house was to paint the dark-blue roof tiles with a light warm rosy pink. This is not a conventional colour by any standard, but I had two reasons for choosing it. One is environmental, the other psychological. 'Insulpaint' is a special product that cools the house naturally in summer by reflecting the sun's heat. Buildings consume 40% of all material resources (Morris, 2013). A product such as this is essential in Perth under the scorching summer sun. In order for this product to work well, it has to have a pallid palate. The effects of colour on the human psyche have been well researched (Mahnke, 1996). A pleasant colour, such as light warm rosy pink, would uplift the moods of the residents. From feeling 'the blues' to feeling 'rosy' was a positive 'colour renovation'. However, this choice had created many challenges which led me to embark on a three-year journey of choosing the right colour for my gutter. The main problem was the gutter was fighting for visual attention with the trees. The colour of the gutter, Pale Eucalypt, is pleasant because it is derived from the leaf of a local tree. In the context of my garden design however, it is the wrong colour for my gutter because it distracts from the garden. This is against my aesthetic ideal of living in harmony with nature and celebrating nature. The Chinese approach to garden making would not draw visual attention to the gutter.

Reflecting upon my choice of the gutter colour I realised how I was swayed by others and emulated my neighbours, most of whom accentuate their gutters. I initially sought inspiration from the neighbourhood by observing how others have painted their gutters and hoped to find a good example. This method failed because there were no sufficient successful examples from which I could analyse, theorise and learn from. My data gathering and analysis however had pointed out what does not work. When 70% of Perth's residences accentuate their gutter, it creates a cultural statement; "Look at my gutter, it's important". Although there are practical and economical reasons why this is the case, many just follow what the neighbours do without thinking. Some modern houses would use a bland, insipid and lifeless colour scheme for the house, which in some cases would work if there was a garden to complement it. Unfortunately, most of these 'MacMansions' cover almost every inch of the block, leaving no space for Mother Nature, some not even a single tree or a blade of grass. They dwarf a small sterile garden that does nothing to filter and screen out the worst excesses of our summer heat and winter cold (Hahn, 2013). This type of non-sustainable aesthetic may unfortunately become more prevalent through socialisation and eventually a cultural norm. A problem identified and perceived in perspective is a problem half solved. After repainting the gutter and walls in off-white and subtle colours suitable to be backgrounds, I was able to focus on the garden again.

Although I appreciate the aesthetics of the Chinese garden, which are mostly behind enclosed walls, building a wall around my front garden does not reflect my values. The unnecessary waste of natural resources would increase my footprint on the planet; the visual effect of the wall would be a social statement indicating a desire to disconnect from my neighbours; and the financial cost could also be unwise and unnecessary. However, it is not aesthetically pleasing to look onto concrete curbs and tar road. Chinese garden masters advocate, "…making appropriate use of what is available" (Zheng, 1988, p. 31). What I had available was a few trees and bushes near the street end of the garden which I prune very carefully so that they "appear to be utterly natural" (Mizuno, 2006, p. 75). This technique is similar to what Arcadian landscapers use where "the hand of man is everywhere concealed" (Seddon, 1970, p. 13). These trees and shrubs provided screening from the street but not treated as walls; they were treated as plants. This sensibility is different to the one that treats plants as living architecture by cutting them into hedges where "we see the mark of the scissors on every plant and bush" (ibid, p. 25). Some of the pruning in the Perth neighbourhood is what I consider butchering; lopping branches so brutally as if the pruner wishes the tree dead (Figure 2). This kind of pruning is not sustainable materially or psychologically. It projects violence towards nature. Pruning is an art form which requires sensitivity and sensibility.

Figure 4: Harsh pruning in the Perth Neighbourhood . Photo: Huilin Sun.

View, in the context of gardening, is something interesting to look at, which is an important element in an aesthetically pleasing garden. I considered three Chinese techniques, *borrow view*, *block view* and *create view*. 'Borrow view' speaks about incorporating existing views into the garden. I included a few trees in the neighbourhood as background. To keep these distant trees in sight gives a sense of depth which allows for a perception of space and inclusion. This emulates a feeling of connection, wholesomeness and tranquillity when walking in the forest. This sense of depth and space is achieved by allowing the trees in the foreground to filter the view of the background. 'Block view' is the strategy I used the most. Functional structures such as power lines, chimneys and antennas are views to be blocked. In creating view, I built a pergola with recycled timber in order to provide a climbing structure for productive fruit vines. I initially painted the pergola with Pale Eucalypt, the same colour as the gutter. Although most visitors complimented the pergola, I questioned and contemplated upon the appropriateness of this colour, observing it in different light and from different angles. Reflecting upon the Chinese gardening principles of harmonising with nature, I plan to change the colour of the pergola so that the pillars will mimic and harmonise with the tree trunks in the garden.

Figure 5. Borrow view, block view and create view. Photo: Huilin Sun.

My garden invites and includes the visitor. Space and view are created within the garden so that the view changes as the visitor walks through. The Chinese garden designer manages to make possible a whole range of emotions that otherwise could be felt in nature, within the small space of a garden:

The garden designer strives to heighten his effects by contrast and juxtaposition – high leading to low, open to closed, narrow to wide, light to dark – in a constant, delicate pairing, on an infinity of levels, that echoes the elemental force of the yin and yang. In practice the designer manages so to confuse the visitor about how he came in, where he is and how he is to get out, and at the same time so to delight and lull his senses, that the space of his little garden seems to extend indefinitely. (Keswick, 1988, p. 24)

This sense of inclusion, delight and expansion is what I aim to achieve in my garden, for when one is allowed to be included in the garden and surrounded by the wonders of nature, one can feel at one with nature.

Harmony is the guiding principle of all aspects of my garden design including shape and colour. I removed spiky plants from my garden because they project visual discomfort and are not conducive to psychological and emotional wellbeing. The ancient Chinese science of Fengshui places the interaction of energies between people and places on a very profound level. The condition of our environment affects our internal state (Merle, 1998). Research shows: plants have awareness, language and emotions. For example, Clivia does not like to bloom in an inharmonious family; but it often blooms before a happy event (Liao & Chen, 2006). Plants with spiky or pointed leaves are not recommended unless placed in recessed areas where they cannot "bite" [disturb the well-being of] anyone passing by (Merle, 1998).

Although I did not build a wall to enclose the garden, I rendered the wall of the house an off-white colour which provides a backdrop for the garden. This colour is the same as the inside of the house, which harmonises the interior and the exterior–and gives a sense of unity. I study nature by listening, observing and responding with awareness and intuition.

'Allowing' is another guiding principle that I borrowed from Ester and Jerry Hicks (2006), who speak about the creation of wellbeing through tapping into good feelings. Allowing the trees to thrive and grow tall into the sky is to celebrate nature, to tune in, harmonise and reciprocate with nature. It is a beautiful feeling to see the trees in my garden growing to their full height rather than, as is the usual case in the suburbs, of keeping them below the gutter line. Although mainstream Australians seem to be entrenched in their 'traditional' values towards nature and gardening habits, some government agencies and popular TV programs are strongly advocating sustainable gardening practices (Lewis & Potter, 2011, pp. 231-243). This indicates a cultural shift and my study will contribute to the debate about new artistic and culturally diverse sustainable gardening.

Gardens speak. People do look at gardens and become inspired. To use hiking as a metaphor, once the trail blazer finds a good trail, she shares by leading others to walk it and enjoy the scenery. I view my research in garden making as discovering a new approach to gardening whereby a native garden combined with a vegetable and fruit garden can look aesthetically pleasing.

Aesthetics reflect values and play an important role in individual well-being which has profound social and material implications (Cold, 2001). By engaging in experiments in my own garden I will reflect on the links between well-being, sustainability and aesthetics. It is increasingly argued that in a sustainable world individuals should not only be concerned with the sustainability of natural resources but also consciously aware of their emotional bond with nature (Carlson & Lintott, 2009) and that this has an aesthetic dimension. Any discussion around sustainability should therefore be a holistic one.

Huilin Sun is an artist, entrepreneur and educator. She studied Graphic Design in Beijing and Visual Arts in Perth, Australia. She founded the pioneering hiking company 'Beijing Hikers' in 2001 and has been teaching at the University of Western Australia since 2010.

Endnotes

1. The methodology I have employed for this project is based on the action research cyclical process of planning, acting, observing and reflecting (Crouch & Pearce, 2012, pp. 143-147).

2. The root of the idea of the Post-Christian idea can be pinned down to Genesis, II, verse 27. "… and have dominion over every living that moveth upon the earth".

References

Ann, Y. S. & Du, D. (2002). 佛道文化与中国园林 Bhudhist and daoist cultures and Chinese traditional gardens. *Journal of Hebei Agricultural College, 22*(2). Retrieved from: http://www.cqvip.com/qk/91582x/200202/6235085.html

Carlson, A., & Lintott, S. (Eds.). (2008). *Nature, aesthetics, and environmentalism: from beauty to duty.* New York: Columbia University Press.

Cold, B. (2001). *Aesthetics, well-being and health: essays within architecture and environmental aesthetics.* London: Ashgate.

Crouch, C., & Pearce, J. (2012). *Doing research in design.* New York: Berg.

Department of Agriculture. (2001). *A Weed plan for Western Australia.* Department of Agriculture, WA, Australia.

Dzidic, P., & Green, M. (2011). Outdoing the Joneses: understanding community acceptance of an alternative water supply scheme and sustainable urban design. *Landscape and Urban Planning, 103*(3), 266–273.

Evers, A., & Hodgson, N. *(2011). Food choices and local food access among Perth's community gardeners.* Local Environment: The International Journal of Justice and Sustainability. 16*(6), 585-602.*

Gardening Trends. (2013, August 3). Digging in for the future of society. *The West Australian*, p. 7.

Hahn, S. (2013). *Hamilton Hill sustainable home:* Hand out. Perth: Open Gardens Australia.

Hicks, E., & Hicks, J. (2006). *Living the art of allowing* [CD]. California: Hay House.

Ji, Ch. (1988). *The craft of gardens.* (A. Hardie, Trans.). New Haven and London: Yale University Press.

Kalscheuer, B. (2009). Encounters in the third space: links between intercultural communication theories and postcolonial approaches. In K. Ikas & G. Wagner (Eds.), *Communicating in the third space* (pp. 26-48). New York and UK: Routledge.

Kellett, J. (2011). The Australian quarter acre block: the death of a dream? *Town Planning Review, 82*(3), 263-284. Liverpool University Press.

Keswick, M. (1988). *The craft of gardens.* New Haven and London: Yale University Press.

Layt, T. (2014). A short history of Buffalo Turf. *Ozbreed Environmental Turf and Plant Breeding.* Retrieved from http://softleafbuffalograss.com.au/buffalo-lawn-care-and-articles/buffalo-turf-history.php

Lewis, T., & Potter, E. (Ed.). (2011). *Ethical consumption, an introduction.* Oxon & New York: Routledge.

Lia, W. M., & Chen, F. P. (2006). 风水学与居住环境植物配. Geomantic omen and plant disposition in residential environment. *Journal of Anhui Agriculture and Science, 34*(22), 5830–5831. Retrieved from, http://www.nykxw.com/upload/loadimg/20061211163105329.pdf

Liu, X. H. (2002). 文心画境 - 中国古典园林景观构成的要素分析. *In the heart of a scholar and in the ambiance of a painting: an analysis of key elements in Chinese traditional gardens.* Beijing: China Architecture and Building Industry Press.

Lullfitz, G. (2002). *A new image for Western Australian plants.* Perth: Scott Print.

Mahnke, F. H. (1996). *Color, environment & human response.* New York: Wiley.

Merle, S. (1998). *Marvellous Feng Shui.* Retrieved from http://impzone.free.fr/mag/Feng%20Shui/Marvellous%20Fengshui-S.Merle.pdf

Mizuno, K. (2006). *Courtyard gardens of Kyoto's merchant houses.* Tokyo: Kodansha.

Morris, G. (2013). *Mandurah sustainable home and Josh's house:* Handout. Perth: Solar dwellings.

Seddon, G. (1970). *Swan River landscapes.* Nedlands, Australia: University of Western Australia Press.

Seddon, G. (2005). *The old country: Australian landscapes, plants and people.* Port Melbourne: Cambridge University Press.

Sustainable Gardening Australia. (2014). Retrieved from http://www.sgaonline.org.au/about/

The LifeStyle Magazine. (2014, April 5). *Geometric designs keep plants in line - minimalist garden design.* Retrieved from: https://picturesdotnews.wordpress.com/tag/minimalist-garden-design/

Urban Design, Cultural Heritage & Landscape Unit and Land for Wildlife. (2002). Guidelines for undesirable plants for natural bushland and waterways. (Fact Sheet 5). Retrieved from http://www.logan.qld.gov.au/__data/assets/pdf_file/0009/8568/policy1213-info5.pdf

World Commission on Environment and Development (1987). *Our common future*. Oxford: Oxford University Press.

Zheng, Y. (1988). Forward. *The craft of gardens*. (A. Hardie, Trans.). New Haven and London: Yale University Press.

CHAPTER NINE

NATURAL DYNAMICS

John Stanislav Sadar & Gyungju Chyon

Technology is not enough

In design, ecological sustainability is largely considered in terms of materials and processes. With increasing awareness of the dwindling health of our environment and the threat that poses to our very existence, we have focused on addressing this by developing technologies and systems such as green energy, green building, recycling, eco travel, eating local food, and car sharing. An ongoing critique of literature is required to keep one informed of the developments of new materials and processes designed to improve performance and efficiency, by making more out of less (Fuad-Luke, 2002). A plethora of agencies and ratings systems spanning the globe, monitor, grade, and publish technical reports on quantifiable attributes of our material world, from toxicity to recyclability, from volatility to embodied energy, and from by-products to the social conditions of manufacture. At the same time, we are making great strides in material efficiency by maximising the use of natural resources with new materials, such as engineered wood products or metallic foams; by developing forms derived from digital simulation that enable material to be placed only where needed to ensure structural or environmental performance; and by recycling artefacts. We have placed an emphasis on ethical appeals to reason. Our rational solutions have been to reuse more, travel less, have shorter showers, install solar panels, and to reduce paper usage by minimising printing. Yet, in following this trajectory we continue to focus on the material value of the natural world, and risk further alienating ourselves from it (Davison, 2001).

Technological development is a fact of human survival and development. It defines us as a species, and its results have been spectacular: the developments of engineering, and, more recently, nanotechnology and biotechnology have enabled us to live healthier, longer, more convenient, and arguably richer lives (Rifkin, 1998). Human development indicators, such as health, education and standard of living, are proxies of the degree of technological development and consumption. Development is intoxicating, as the most developed economies in the world consume ever faster, stronger, and newer artefacts to such an extent that, according to the World Wide Fund for Nature, we would require the resources of four planets were the entire planet's population to reach an equivalent level of development (WWF, 2012, p. 45). Yet, at the same time, we are aware that the very instrument of our survival is also an instrument of harm to the world in which we live. At a time of environmental crisis – the result of an incompatibility between our technologies and our environment – it is little wonder we look for a technological fix, as with replacing our energy resources with cleaner and potentially perpetual alternatives. However, as American philosopher Timothy Morton (2010) writes, in thinking of our technologies in isolation from our environment we have opened a rift between us and our environment.

Continuing this consumption- and technology-driven approach risks taking us to the point where we no longer recognise the very preciousness and fragility of the natural world, which we sought to protect in the first place (Morton, 2010). A key reference text would be useful here As Aidan Davison writes, this "ecomodernist" approach may also may not make us truly happier, instead merely substituting one track to greater efficiency with another (Davison, 2001). Architect Lance Hosey cites scientist and environmentalist David Suzuki's observation that "American parents spend six hours per week shopping and only 40 minutes playing with their kids," observing that while following a path which emphasises the consumption of material solutions has dominated our thinking, it has not ensured our happiness (2012, p. 97). Perhaps the ecomodernist approach of attending to our ecological dilemma with a technological fix risks missing the point, and is such an approach akin to prescribing drugs to stop the symptoms rather than addressing the cause of the problem?

In his 2012 book, *The Shape of Green: Aesthetics, Ecology and Design* Hosey argues that sustainability can not only have an aesthetic dimension, but that it must. For him, a problem with the ecological movement in design has been its tendency to downplay the role of aesthetics in favour of ethics (2012, pp. 27-29). Artefacts made from environmentally benign processes or with irrefutable material efficiency are obviously necessary, but if undesirable will not be adopted widely enough to effect real change, and if unloved, will not be cared for by their users. At the same time, Hosey writes, that human pleasure is not to be discounted out of hand, and need not be at odds with ecological design, but rather be a necessarily integral part of it (2012, pp. 39-47).

Our aesthetic needs do not come last, for, as Hosey argues, aesthetics are part of what it is to be human (Hosey, 2012, pp. 22-23). Contrary to opinions, such as those from American psychologist Abraham Maslow which state that aesthetic needs come after the satisfaction of other needs (Maslow, 1943, pp. 372-385), Hosey cites American writer Virginia Postrel when he argues aesthetic need "... is not a luxury, but a universal human desire". For example, jewellery, decorated basketry, pottery, and painting are found even amongst those who find daily nutrition a challenge. Hosey continues, "Art and design can feed the soul when even the body goes hungry" (2012, p. 23).

Similarly, designer David Pye argues that beauty is a primary need, essential not only to our survival, but to the "health of the soul," and has the power to move us deeply, inciting us to think, feel, and act (1978, p. 108). Perhaps because of this, a great deal of the work that goes into making any and every made object is for attributes (such as decoration, ornament or embellishment) that do not contribute to function, but enhance the conviviality of our relationship with our artefacts. Our lives would be greatly impoverished, if this was not the case (1978, p. 13). Beauty also has the power to provoke desire and motivate action. Artefacts and environments that move us are those for which we care, and are more likely to protect. As Hosey points out, attention to aesthetics is important for sustainable design as it heightens our engagement with our artefacts, resulting in greater longevity (Hosey, 2012, pp. 6-7). That is to say, beauty is important, and, if anything, will become more so. For, having achieved dependability and functionality of our artefacts and built environment, Anthony Dunne argues we now have "post-optimal objects," in which the "most difficult challenges... [lie in] the realm of metaphysics, poetry and aesthetics..." (2005). Beauty fills a need that our rational discussion about materials and resources does not. We must have both ethics and aesthetics, if we are to offer compelling design alternatives for tomorrow's world.

Towards an aesthetics of ecology

The question is not whether there is a connection between ecologically sustainable design and aesthetics, but what might constitute that aesthetics, and how that might impact upon our understanding of the world. One might start by working outwards from the designed interior spaces that are our living environments. As countless writers from Vitruvius through to architectural theorist Reyner Banham, design educator and theorist David Pye, and Spanish architect Luis Fernández-Galiano have noted, architecture's beginnings and prime raison d'être is the provision of environmental conditions distinct from those of the outdoors (Banham, 1984; Fernández-Galiano, 2000; Pye, 1978; Vitruvius & Morgan, 1960). The building works to keep the indoor environment static and stable, in the face of fluctuating outdoor environmental conditions. The world outside our building interiors is in constant flux, driven by planetary thermodynamic processes, such as the shifting winds that dramatically sculpt the land. Animal life, too, radically shapes and reshapes the earth, as oceanic algae influence global carbon dioxide levels, beavers create entire new habitats with their dams, and termites dramatically change the surface of the earth with their towering mounds. Taken as a whole, the individual contributions of the planet's organisms comprise the remarkably resilient, and complex, dynamic system that is the Earth's biosphere (Lovelock, 2000).

Timothy Morton writes that thinking ecologically rests on acknowledging our connectedness to the natural world (Morton, 2010, p. 1). It also rests on acknowledging that our technologies are part of that connection. He argues that while it may be disturbing for many of us, we need to let go of ideals both of technological cleanliness and hygiene, and of natural pristineness (2010, p. 9). The distinction between *nature* and *technology* has, in Morton's view, been unproductive for thinking and acting ecologically, as it has served only to further the divide between humans and our environment. Although defining nature as undisturbed by human activity may have drawn attention to the deleterious impact of our actions, it has also deepened a sense of our alienation from it, rather than our reconnection with it. In place of both, he poses a view in which humans, including our technologies, are completely and unbreakably entangled with our environment (Morton, 2010, p. 9).

Japanese designer Kenya Hara similarly argues that sustainability is not about returning an artificial condition to a natural state, but rather about how best to move forward (cited in Brownell, 2011). Like the organisms we share the planet with, humans also shape and modify the environment with our activities to ensure it is more amenable to our survival. Our technologies are our way of relating to our environment, and, like the actions of other organisms, they are inseparable from us (Hosey, 2012). For Hosey, as for former contributing editor for *Audubon* Robert Frenay, the issue is not that our technologies are incompatible with our environment, so much as we have not learnt enough from the natural world regarding their functionality; their development is incomplete and has not been informed by our deepening understanding of biology (Frenay, 2006). Hara is also hopeful we can bring our technologies into a more complete relationship with our environment, noting, "There is a difference between the artificial and the natural – but the more we develop technology, the boundary will blur" (cited in Brownell, 2011, p. 95).

For architectural critic Peter Buchanan the immediate consequence of our distancing of nature and technology, and of our particular line of technological development, is that our technological society undervalues our relationship with our environment, as demonstrated in the creation of alienating built environments, and a "general disenchanting of the world" (Buchanan, 2012). In his discussion of the mentally restorative qualities of the natural world, psychologist Stephen Kaplan concisely asserts, "It is only in the modern world that the split between the important and the interesting has become extreme" (1995), and Buchanan writes, "A necessary step to sustainability is to re-enchant the world and evoke reverence and connection with it" (2012). Perhaps it is not so much to re-enchant the world, as it is to re-discover what is enchanting for us and reconnect with that (Morton, 2010, p. 104). Perhaps an aesthetic of sustainability can aid this necessary enchantment.

The Dutch philosopher of technology, Peter-Paul Verbeek, writes that the aesthetics of products concerns not only what they look like, but their bodily presence and "the range of our practical dealings with them" (2005, p. 211). A seascape or landscape painting presents a fundamentally different aesthetic experience than swimming in the sea or walking through the woods. Both examples demonstrate that our aesthetic experiences with the natural world extend beyond the visual to non-visual, intangible phenomena, as Verbeek (2005) argues. As Hosey notes, aesthetic delight may even exert its most powerful influence in non-visual stimuli, such as smell or touch (2012, p. 63). Pleasure from a day spent at the beach or in the woods is not only derived from the view, but from the continuous, unpredictable dynamics of natural phenomena – air movement, odour, sound, daily and seasonal cycles – and their engagement with our range of sensory receptors. Pye describes beauty as something that you experience rather than something that you see, (1978, p. 96). "To say 'It is beautiful' is a statement not simply about the thing seen, neither is it simply about the seer of it. It is about the effect of the scene on the seers and many others too" he writes. (1978, p. 99). Furthermore, Pye notes that because beauty resides as much in the experience of the perceiver as in the designed object, it is not as much seen as felt. This resides as much in the experience of the perceiver as in the designed object, and encompasses multiple aspects of a particular environment. Rather than an appearance, beauty is an effect.

If design is to aid in rediscovering the enchanting qualities of the natural world, engaging these sensory receptors is essential. Perhaps another option is needed, one that foregrounds natural phenomena. When it comes to sustainability, aesthetic experience could evoke the preciousness of nature and compel us to protect it.

The aesthetics of processes and dynamics

If fulfilling our aesthetic needs is as important as Hosey and Pye claim, and if the aesthetic dimension of the natural world resides in our embodied, sensorial experience of its dynamics, designs that amplify an appreciation of nature and an understanding of ecological cycles, rather than a focus on materials and processes, might offer an important approach to sustainability. Returning to Buchanan's (2012) call to re-enchant our world, and Morton's (2010) call to rediscover and reconnect with those aspects of our world that are particularly enchanting as a necessary step towards sustainability, designers ought to consider what instinctively and primordially fascinates us.

For Kaplan, the natural world is paramount in its capacity for fascination (1995, p. 174). In discussing directed attention, whereby one has to perform taxing mental work to focus on a given task, as in an assembly line, Kaplan writes, "… much of what was important to the evolving human—wild animals, danger, caves, blood, to name a few examples—was (and still is) innately fascinating and thus does not require directed attention" (1995). Similarly in *Biophilia*, Edward Wilson argues that because it comprises the environment in which we evolved, we have an inherent affiliation with the natural world (1984). Observation would seem to bear this out, as we are continually interested and surprised by the behaviour of other species, such as our pets, by the changing light quality from dawn to midday to dusk, and by the atmospheric conditions of the forest or seaside. We routinely speak of getting out of the office and escaping from the city. This need to escape our own creations is indicative of the extent to which our designs fail to adequately serve our perceptual, psychological and aesthetic needs. Working with natural dynamics such as time, energy, and natural forces may give us an opportunity to connect our constructed world and the broader environment more forcefully. Morton (2010) writes, "… we could imagine technology as bringing phenomena to light" (p. 106). Perhaps artefacts and buildings might enable natural phenomena to make them more apparent and enriching in our lives. Furthermore, if our buildings were more responsive and alive rather than mechanical and static, we might feel in greater harmony with our world.

Ecological processes

Incorporating ecological cycles into the design of our environment could open up new possibilities for aesthetics of sustainability. For example, designs such as *Local River*, by the French designer Mathieu Lehanneur, and the *Microbial Home*, by Philips Design Probes, use an understanding of ecological processes to create living machines for the home, while the *Mussel Choir*, by Australian artist Natalie Jeremijenko, transforms ecological processes into a musical performance (Carbon Arts, 2013; Lehanneur, 2008; Philips Design, 2011).

Lehanneur's *Local River* is an aquaponic system that utilises a controlled co-habitat for plants and fish. The plants consume nutrients from waste excreted by the fish, thereby cleansing the water and ensuring the survival of the fish. *Local River* makes this codependency of fish and plants explicit by incubating them in a hybrid planter/aquarium of transparent glass, which is displayed in a living room where it becomes a piece of furniture. Lehanneur explains that the design combines an aquarium with a refrigerator, taking both to a different dimension with the aim "to reduce impact on the environment inherent to the transport of foodstuffs, while ensuring their traceability" (2008). The presence of living fish and growing plants housed in glass within a living room provides us with a very different perspective on our food, in comparison with stacked vegetables and frozen fish found in the kitchen refrigerator. Whereas food in the refrigerator is viewed only as materials for cooking and eating, *Local River's* presentation of living plants and fish remind us of the food chain in the natural world.

The *Microbial Home* by Jack Mama and Clive van Heerdan for Philips Design probes a new concept for a domestic living system by replacing conventional fuel sources with microbes (Philips Design, 2011). Comprising a bio-digestor, larder, apothecary, filtering toilet, plastic waste upcycler, bioluminescent light, and urban beehive, the *Microbial Home* makes William McDonough and Michael Braungart's "waste = food" mantra manifest in an ecological loop for the home (McDonough & Braungart, 2002). The bio-digester, produces methane during the bacterial digestion of our food waste, which provides gas for cooking, lighting and heating. The plastic waste upcycler uses fungi to break down toxin-free plastics and, at the same time, produce edible mushrooms. Thus, the microbes that we breathe and live with, but are typically associated with the science lab, assume a more engaging presence in our lives. If these invisible organisms are to become new energy sources, our artefacts harnessing them also need to sustain their lives. Thus, the ecological thinking necessary to design such artefacts needs to take into account both form and function, as artefacts become no longer inanimate products, but controlled habitats for the living workers cohabiting our dwellings.

Natalie Jeremijenko and Carbon Arts in Melbourne collaborated on the proposed public art project for Melbourne Docklands, *The Melbourne Mussel Choir*. Sensors wirelessly collect data from the mussels regarding the openness of their shells, as this is an indicator of water quality. The data is digitally transformed into sound, producing an audible performance for the residents of Melbourne, and thereby raising the awareness of pollution levels and health of the marine ecosystem. (Carbon Arts, 2013). The *Mussel Choir* is part of a larger body of work for Jeremijenko, which often employs organisms to diagnose, remediate and communicate issues of environmental damage (X Clinic: The Environmental Clinic and Lab, 2013). Her installations not only provide information on environmental damage, but also remind us of our entangled relationships with the creatures with which we cohabit the planet.

As with *Local River* and the *Microbial Home*, the *Mussel Choir* demonstrates that designing with ecosystems, necessarily calls for not only new ethics, but also results in a particular aesthetic quality in our built environment that is perhaps less dependent on form, and more predicated on experience and process.

Natural dynamics

Another possibility for developing an aesthetics of sustainability lies in engaging the vagaries of natural dynamics with the design of our constructed environments. Our artefacts are continually being acted upon and transformed by natural forces, from gravity to light to thermodynamics. Designs such as Triptyque's *Harmonia 57*, Ned Kahn's *Wind Arbor*, Philippe Rahm's *Domestic Astronomy*, and Little Wonder's *Liquid Sky* each make the dynamics of the natural world more apparent and enchanting (Chyon & Sadar, 2010; Kahn, 2011; Myers & Antonelli, 2012, pp. 22-25; Rahm, 2009).

Harmonia 57, an office building designed by Triptyque and built in São Paulo, Brazil, appears to be alive, as a constant growth of plants and blow of mist envelop the building like a living skin (Myers & Antonelli, 2012, pp. 22-25). Enveloped in a green wall, William Myers describes the building's exposed pipes, sprinklers, and plumbing tanks, which are used to create amenable weather conditions around the building by misting plants growing from the porous façade in a temporal cloud, as "… almost like veins and arteries" (Myers & Antonelli, 2012, p. 22). Rather than providing a protective, controlled barrier to the outdoors, the building façade becomes a miniaturised terrain that celebrates and harmonises with the ephemeral qualities of the natural environment (Fig. 1). Entering the building becomes an experience more akin to entering a forest that to entering a conventional building.

Figure 1: Harmonia 57 by Triptyque (2008). Photography by Nelson Kon.

Ned Kahn's *Wind Arbor* at Marina Bay Sands, in Singapore (like the *Wind Veil* in Charlotte, North Carolina, USA), is a façade constructed of thousands of aluminium panels, which transform the wind into a visual spectacle (Kahn, 2011). Depending upon the weather, the panels may be almost static, gently fluttering or rippling, or dancing chaotically. Furthermore, depending upon lighting conditions, the slight panels may appear dull, metallic grey, or sparkle in the sunlight, as they transform the wind into a dynamic, luminous seascape (Fig. 2). Kahn describes the function of *Wind Arbor* as akin to the leaves of a tree, blocking half of incident sunlight and attendant heat, while allowing for ventilation in the building beyond. Rather than achieving energy efficiency through complete environmental control, *Wind Arbor* proposes we develop technologies that work with environmental dynamics, and connect them with our lives.

Figure 2: Wind Arbor by Ned Kahn (2011). Photography by Ned Kahn.

Liquid Sky (2008), designed by Little Wonder (Gyungju Chyon & John Sadar), employs layers of textiles to capture the natural dynamics of wind and light, and brings evanescence beauty of natural phenomena indoors. Rather than simply blocking sunlight from penetrating the indoors, *Liquid Sky* projects sunlight as a pattern on the textiles that amplifies slight changes of light conditions and air movement, which accompany weather changes and seasonal shifts. The projected pattern resembles at times fog, rain, or the sparkling light reflected from the ocean. Its intention is to transport the viewer's imagination to the wilderness and bring the experience of being at the seashore into the home (Fig. 3). *Liquid Sky* amplifies the minute hour-to-hour, and day-to-day variations of our environment that we otherwise take for granted, as it paints the interior in an animate display of light (Fig. 4).

Figure 3: Liquid Sky by little wonder (2008). Image by little wonder.

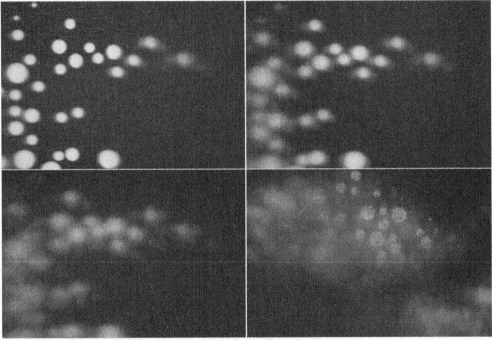

Figure 4: Liquid Sky by little wonder (2008). Photography by Gary Annett.

In *Domestic Astronomy*, Philippe Rahm (2009) uses the thermal gradients that naturally occur within our environments as a basis for spatial organisation. Using different thermal comfort requirements for different activities (such as cooking, bathing, sleeping, reading, or relaxing) and the tendency for warm air to rise and cool air to fall, Rahm locates his programme accordingly, within the three-dimensional confines of a loft interior (Fig. 5). The resulting space produces seemingly odd relationships – bathing and relaxing facilities are suspended from the ceiling, while cooking and sleeping are located at the ground level. In basing the spatial organisation on thermodynamics and human physiology, rather than architectural convention, Rahm foregrounds the role of our built environments in ensuring our thermal comfort and creating conditions in which our physiology can thrive. At the same time, he heightens our awareness of the non-visual attributes, or what Lisa Heschong called the "thermal delight" of our built environments.

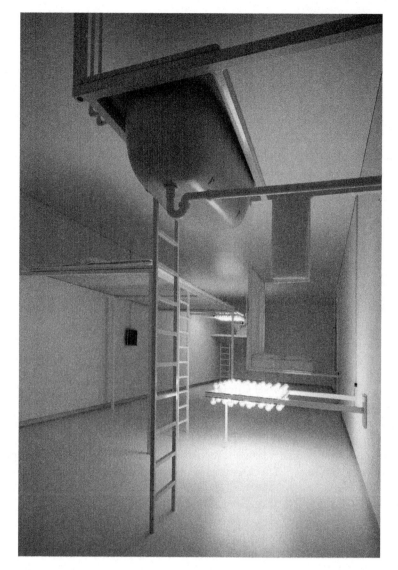

Figure 5: Domestic Astronomy by Philippe Rahm architectes (2009). Photography by Brøndum & Co.

Harmonia 57, the *Wind Arbor*, *Liquid Sky* and *Domestic Anatomy* each seek to re-forge connections with the natural world through amplifying its effects. By foregrounding an appreciation of the inherent aesthetic experience of the natural world, perhaps this approach would lead us a step closer to less consumption-oriented, healthier, and more sustainable lifestyles (Chyon & Sadar, 2013).

An aesthetic of natural dynamics

The approaches demonstrated in these projects (foregrounding ecological processes and natural dynamics) have the potential to move us beyond an aesthetics of form to one of experience and process. As Hosey writes, "More and more, new research reveals how everyday sights, sounds, smells, tastes, and textures influence the unconscious mind. Aesthetic delight is a powerful motivator, firing up the pleasure centers of the brain, the "hedonic hot spots," as neurobiologist call them" (2012, p.

63). Projects such as those discussed may move us closer to building a more ecological relationship with other living organisms and our built environment. If aesthetic delight is as powerful a motivator as Hosey argues, a greater experience of ecological processes and natural dynamics in our homes, offices, and cities may be the way to connect our lives with the enchantment of our environment, and to change our values to those of environmental stewardship (2012, p. 63). When it comes to design, aesthetic judgement lies not in how advanced or how cleverly recycled our materials are, but in how we connect our technological world with the natural world.

John Stanislav Sadar is a Senior Lecturer in architecture at Monash University and a partner of Little Wonder design studio. He is interested in the way our technological artefacts mediate the relationship between our bodies and the environment.

Gyungju Chyon is a Lecturer in industrial design at RMIT and a partner of Little Wonder design studio. Her research and practice is concerned with the relationship between objects and sensory perception.

References

Banham, R. (1984). *The architecture of the well-tempered environment* (2nd ed.). London: Architectural Press.

Brownell, B. E. (2011). *Matter in the floating world: conversations with leading Japanese architects and designers* (1st ed.). New York: Princeton Architectural Press.

Buchanan, P. (2012). The Big Rethink: Learning From Four Modern Masters. *Architectural Review, 231*(1384), 83-95.

Carbon Arts. (2013). Melbourne Mussel Choir. Retrieved 20 September 2013, from http://www.carbonarts.org/projects/melbourne-mussel-choir/

Chyon, G., & Sadar, J. S. (2010). Liquid Sky: Sensorial Experience as an Aesthetic of Objects. In J. Gimeno-Martinez & F. Floré (Eds.), *Design and Craft: A History of Convergences and Divergences* (pp. 158-161). Brussels: Koninklijke Vlaamse Academie van Belgie voor Wetenschappen en Kunsten.

Chyon, G., & Sadar, J. S. (2013). The Dematerialising and Rematerialising of Design. *Craft Research, 4*(1), 53-72.

Davison, A. (2001). *Technology and the contested meanings of sustainability.* Albany, NY: State University of New York Press.

Dewey, J. (1934). *Art as experience.* New York: Minton, Balch & Co.

Dunne, A. (2005). *Hertzian tales: electronic products, aesthetic experience, and critical design* ([2005 ed.). Cambridge, Mass.: MIT Press.

Fernández-Galiano, L. (2000). *Fire and memory: on architecture and energy.* Cambridge, Mass.: MIT Press.

Frenay, R. (2006). *Pulse: the coming age of systems and machines inspired by living things* (1st ed.). New York: Farrar, Straus and Giroux.

Fuad-Luke, A. (2002). *Eco design: the sourcebook.* San Francisco, CA: Chronicle Books.

Heschong, L. (1979). *Thermal delight in architecture.* Cambridge, Mass.: MIT Press.

Hosey, L. (2012). *The shape of green: aesthetics, ecology, and design.* Washington, DC: Island Press.

Kahn, N. (2011). Wind Arbor. Retrieved 20 September 2013, from http://nedkahn.com/portfolio/wind-arbor/

Kaplan, S. (1995). The restorative benefits of nature: Toward an integrative framework. *Journal of environmental psychology, 15*(3), 169-182.

Lehanneur, M. (2008). Local River. Retrieved 20 September 2013, from http://www.mathieulehanneur .fr/projet_gb.php?projet=127&PHPSESSID=db1b5836542ad9efec1507d427f81bf5

Little Wonder. (2008). Liquid Sky.   Retrieved 20 September 2013, from http://www.littlewonder-design.com/liquidsky.html

Lovelock, J. (2000). *Gaia: a new look at life on earth.* Oxford ; New York: Oxford University Press.

Maslow, A. H. (1943). "A theory of human motivation." *Psychological review, 50* (4), 370.

McDonough, W., & Braungart, M. (2002). *Cradle to cradle: remaking the way we make things* (1st ed.). New York: North Point Press.

Morton, T. (2010). *The ecological thought.* Cambridge, Mass.: Harvard University Press.

Myers, W., & Antonelli, P. (2012). *Bio design : nature, science, creativity.* New York: Museum of Modern Art ;.

Philips Design. (2011). Microbial Home.   Retrieved 20 September 2013, from http://www.design.philips.com/about/design/designportfolio/design_futures/microbial_home.page

Pye, D. W. (1978). *The nature and aesthetics of design.* New York: Van Nostrand Reinhold.

Rahm, P. (2009). Domestic Astronomy.   Retrieved 20 September 2013, from http://www.philipperahm.com/data/projects/domesticastronomy/index.html

Rifkin, J. (1998). *The biotech century: harnessing the gene and remaking the world.* New York: Jeremy P. Tarcher/Putnam.

Verbeek, P.P. (2005). *What things do: philosophical reflections on technology, agency, and design.* University Park, Pa.: Pennsylvania State University Press.

Vitruvius, P., & Morgan, M. H. (1960). *Vitruvius: the ten books on architecture.* New York: Dover Publications.

Wilson, E. O. (1984). *Biophilia.* Cambridge, Mass.: Harvard University Press.

WWF. (2012). *Living Planet Report 2012.* Gland, Switzerland: WWF International.

X Clinic: The Environmental Clinic and Lab. (2013). X Clinic: The Environmental Clinic and Lab. Retrieved 20 September 2013, from http://www.environmentalhealthclinic.net/

CHAPTER TEN

PICTURE FOR ILLUSTRATION PURPOSES ONLY

Chrissie Smith

Introduction

This chapter explores the existing relationships between aesthetics, consumerism and design, and how these practices can be reshaped and used as effective tools to bring about a shift towards a more sustainable future. It will explore the role of aesthetics in the service of consumer culture, highlight the urgent need for aesthetics and design to make a contribution to sustainability, and identify some ways in which this can be done. More specifically, in the context of food production, marketing and consumption, this chapter investigates how the relationship between the consumer and food is mediated by the processing, packaging and purchasing experiences, how this mediation deliberately confuses the 'real' and the 'artificial', and how this disconnection has an adverse impact on the sustainability of consumer choices.

An abundant world

The way we live and eat has changed more in the last 50 years than in the previous 10,000. In 1800, just three per cent of the world's population lived in towns with 5,000 inhabitants or more. In 1950 that percentage was still less than a third (Schoenauer, 2000). The past 50 years has seen these percentages increase dramatically with the global population becoming predominantly urban for the first time ever. The United Nations (2011) forecasts that eighty percent of people will live in cities by 2050. That is an extra three billion more people living in cities. These cities already consume seventy five per cent of earth's energy and resources. Currently the UK alone consumes 820 million chickens every year; that's enough chickens, at three chickens per metre, to wrap around the world seven times. The United States leads the developed world in meat consumption, with each American eating an average 125 kg of meat a year. Australia is the second largest at 116kg. Per capita, meat consumption in Europe averaged 74 kg, while the average UK citizen consumed 80 kg UN (2002) – equivalent to 1,400 pork sausages each year, or nearly four a day. By 2030, the UN (2005) predicts two thirds of worldwide meat and milk supplies will be consumed by developing nations, and by 2050, global meat consumption will have doubled. Because of our rapidly increasing global population, even if we wanted it, to supply ourselves with the amount of meat we eat today with free-range animals would be next to impossible in this urbanised future.

With these increasingly staggering numbers, the global food economy has evolved to produce and keep up with constant demands from city dwellers to supply cheap, predictable food. In the main, the food we eat today is not driven by local producers but by economies of scale, and those economies apply to every stage of the food supply chain. In order to make it onto the supermarket shelves, produce not only has to look good and big, it also has to be capable of withstanding the rigours of a global distribution system. This system aims to deliver fewer and fewer product types to more and more of us. These modernised food systems are capable of preserving food and transporting it anywhere in the world, and as a result they have freed the planning of cities from geographical concerns.

In the past, city sites were carefully chosen, ensuring that the rural hinterland was productive, fertile and able to feed the city. Although the romantic notion of countryside with lush fertile pastures and fluffy sheep is still encouraged and sustained, the modernised version of the rural hinterland is not designed for such public viewing consumption. These landscapes consist of fields of corn and soya stretching as far as the eye can see, plastic poly tunnels apparently so vast you can see them from space, and industrial sheds and feed lots full of factory farmed animals. By operating at this level of efficiency and economy of scale, factory food farming has resulted in a cheap and reliable food source, able to satisfy the seemingly endless urban appetite for consumption. For city dwellers these processes are largely hidden, allowing us to forget that we too are animals and the food we eat links us directly back to nature. We would throw a chicken kebab on the BBQ without a second thought, but if we were locked in a room with a live hen and a sharp knife, most of us would probably starve.

The global food economies hide such realities from us and have a lot invested in our complicity. In order to compete for market share, businesses engage in promotional activities filling their offerings with images, aesthetics, promises and symbols that are non-confronting and lull us into comfortable and unsustainable consumption beyond what we actually need. Böhme (2003) comments on a production system geared toward ever-increasing growth and consumption; "it creates one of the most serious impediments for sustainable development, especially when the business practices move away from addressing people's needs to exploiting their desires" (Böhme, 2003, p. 73).

There has been a lot written and researched on the unsustainable nature of the global consumer economy and the role that design and aesthetics have taken in both the service of it and the move toward a more sustainable future (Bohle, 2012; Braungart & McDonough, 2013; Fry 2009). Dobers and Strannedgard (2005) assert that design is becoming a central feature for companies to become competitive, and meanwhile a means for consumers to express their identities. As a result, there are far-reaching implications for the understanding of sustainable development in general and sustainable consumption in particular. This chapter seeks to further explore the cultural and social relationships and identities that are constructed by the food industry to shape unsustainable food choices and the confusion and subsequent disconnection that results. To do this it is necessary to consider:

- The 'real' identity of the food; what is it? Where is it from? How did it get here? What is it now?
- The constructed identity of the product through attached values, use of design and other aesthetic concerns.
- How these relationships between consumer and product are used to construct the collective and individual identifications of the consumer or consumer groups.

Consumption as identity and process

The supermarket is a highly structured arena where constructed appearance is everything and product placement is highly competitive. Circling around the outer fringes, the produce still bears some resemblance to the real thing; fruit, vegetables and freshly baked goods. But as you move further into the heart of the shopping aisles and past the refrigeration units you are faced with carefully packaged processed foods bearing little resemblance to its origins. The aesthetic of packaging and advertising purposefully removes us from the product and from the processes that it has gone through to get to the supermarket and on the shelves. In most cases, we see the food contained in packaging or an image of what the food might look like once prepared and served rather than experiencing the product itself. Barthes (2013) makes the point:

> ... the development of advertising has enabled the economists to become quite conscious of the ideal nature of consumer goods; by now everyone knows that the product as bought – that is, ex-

perienced – by the consumer is by no means the real product; between the former and the latter there is a considerable production of false perceptions and values. (p. 29)

In Barthes' statement he implies that we, as consumers, are complicit in the illusion. This complicity benefits us by replacing images of mass production and killing floors with happy farmers surveying fields of grain and sports personalities barbequing well done steak. Advertising may tell us that cows stand in green fields and contentedly munch grass. The supermarkets show us that steak comes in foam trays covered with plastic. What do we truly want to know of the intermediate stages of stock transport, slaughter, butchering and vacuum packing or gas preservation?

The following advertising campaigns put out by Meat and Livestock Australia and Beef and Lamb New Zealand serve as recent examples of this constructed identity. In both campaign examples, meat consumption is attached to nationalism and athletic activity. The New Zealand campaign 'Iron Maidens' was launched in 2012; the images depict female athletes who have a profile both nationally and internationally. The iron maidens become role models, almost goddess-like and an ultimate image of who we would like to be. This campaign sends a clear message that our exports are premium and therefore worthy of consumption. The Australian meat campaign also exploits our sense of nationalism, cashing in on its own stereotypes by depicting colorful characters at a poolside party, 'throwing another steak on the barbie'. In both cases, the emphasis moves from the product to the function, with meat taking on the function of vitality and mateship. In relation to that function, they reflect back a version of who we think we are.

On a deeper level, this identity that is constructed for us is re-constructed by us as we connect to the images and create another identity around how we see ourselves in relation to them. In new or 'postmodern' paradigms of consumption, the idea of the self-constructing consumer is emphasised. They are active in reinterpreting and accommodating signs of their own culture (Uusitalo, 1996). Further to this idea, Mike Featherstone (1991) argues that products and services potentially signal a particular lifestyle and the style has become a 'life project' where customer's individuality is displayed in an assembly of artifacts, appearances, experiences and practices. These practices may include eating out at a particular restaurant, choosing a particular form of transportation, being a vegetarian or meat eater and becomes a way of building identity and constructing a 'lifestyle'. Douglas and Isherwood (1979) put forth the idea of consumption as essentially symbolic activities, which create order in the mental world of individuals.

Creating 'lifestyle' has been a significant occupation of design and communications industries. In the service of competing companies and corporations, it has seduced people to lead a wasteful lifestyle and has created regularity about always wanting more. As stated earlier by Bohme (2003), the move from 'need' to 'desire' creates serious impediments for sustainable development. As long as we live in a system geared toward ever-increasing growth and consumption, it is difficult to imagine this changing. Need and want can become blurry when faced with the endless temptations of the commercial powers of design and aesthetics based consumption. It makes it a difficult task to understand that the practices of lifestyle and aesthetic consumption are a threat to public health and to sustainable practices on the whole. These practices of consumption have been, despite growing evidence of its unsustainable nature, largely under problematised as a social process. If it were taken just as seriously as the campaigning against smoking and regulations of the tobacco industry, it could give agency to the individual to make decisions around more sustainable consumption choices, something which is now discussed in the context of choosing what is marketed as 'organic' food.

Authentic values co-opted

Alternative food choices can signal a strong set of values and beliefs, in opposition to industrialised agriculture systems; examples of such alternatives include the ideas of slow food, low miles, urban gardens, organic, home grown, local and the value of production systems that require minimal use of packaging and processing. These systems and values enable connections to the people and the environment where the food is produced. For many people it is a 'life project' constructed around these values and beliefs. As Pederson (2000) put it, "We do not only eat to survive, we also eat to socialise and feel well. An example is the increased interest in organic food, which has led to remarkable changes in retail profitability and changing consumption patterns".

In the last three decades (Clunies-Ross, 1990), large supermarket chains have begun stocking organic brands, further expanding their availability. This growth has seen the organics industry evolve from a local food movement to an international industry. The organic industry is the world's fastest growing food sector, with worldwide sales estimated to be worth US$20 billion and growth of between 20 and 50 percent per annum (Lyons, 2001). In Australia, the value of organic production has expanded ten-fold between 1990 and 2000, and is currently valued at around A$250 million, of which about $80 million worth is exported (RIRDC, 1996; Palaszczuk, 2000). Despite these figures, organics account for less than one percent of the total value of Australia's agriculture production.

This rapid expansion of the organic food market has made huge changes to the structure and composition of the industry. The entry of entities associated with industrial food systems like food processes, supermarkets and government departments has made a significant impact.

The resulting transformation of organics from 'sandals to suits' has incited much division and debate in the industry (Lyons, 2001) and competing visions for the future. With the increased growth and mainstreaming of organic agriculture, the scaling up of these values can become problematic. The industrial food production model disconnects consumers from the physical and social context of where the food is produced, potentially undermining the viability of sustainable organic local food production and networks.

Because of the expansion of the organics industry into the mainstream marketplace, it has taken a significant departure from its historical opposition to the industrialised system of agriculture. Can the organics industry expand into a much bigger marketplace without departing from its original values or will it take on the sanitised flavour of big business? When a consumer consciously selects an organic food product, they are making a statement about their relationship with the history of that product. However, on the supermarket floor it's unlikely we would really know if we are looking at the real thing with the history we think of as 'organic' or yet another representation of a idealised agrarian fantasy. Are food retailers bringing the organic aesthetic to a wider audience, or has the brand 'organic' been co-opted with this increased growth into the mainstream food economy?

Conclusion

The way we eat and relate to food has changed tremendously as the world's population becomes increasingly urbanised. There are fewer product types, we eat out of season produce, and modern food-preserving technologies means food can travel long distances and be stored longer, with cities no longer needing to be situated around productive food growing land. As the gap between rural producers and urban consumers widens, we lose touch where our food comes from and prefer maintaining a romantic version of lush productive hinterlands rather than face up to the realities of how the global food economies operate in producing and delivering food to us in urban environments. This distancing of consumers from the physical and social contexts of what they are consuming is a repeating pattern common in the modern industrialised world.

In contrast, an increasing number of alternative food movements address the alienation of the consumer from the product; the ideas of slow food, low miles, urban gardens, organic, home grown and local are becoming more familiar. Care is taken to grow and prepare the food, and a slower and a more sensual approach to food and consumption is celebrated. This individual action can draw attention to the need for change, but only systemic, organisational modifications can effect society wide change. So far, mainstream supermarkets only mimic these ideals in imagery and slogans but with little authenticity.

As this chapter suggests, given what we know, communication design and the use of aesthetics in the service of perpetuating the industrialised food economy has been hugely successful. We have learnt to define ourselves by the type of lifestyle a food product signifies, from convenience foods to wholesome organics. We pay less than the cost it takes to produce and distribute food through these systems and have learnt to expect it. We replace images of mass production and killing floors with an agrarian pastoral fantasy we know cannot possibly be true. Within this context, this chapter closes by highlighting some issues that communication design must address in order to embody more authentic aesthetic qualities that connect us more closely to the environment and support a wider culture of sustainability. Issues requiring urgent attention include a focus on how communication design can positively impact on each of the following:

- How individual agency, and functioning of the system overall, is being distorted by the under problematising of our disconnection from what we know and how this impacts on our lives. There are examples in other fields that point the way to giving agency to the individual and supporting incremental change at the system level – such as smoking cessation and obesity awareness.

- The use of aesthetics to reconnect us with our food, by building awareness about where our food comes from and why it makes sense to eat food that is in season locally. To use aesthetics as it relates to all senses, by relating food to taste, by re-exploring its texture and colour, and by creating visual relationships with food and weather.

- Embedding ethics and philosophy into design courses so that emerging designers have a sense of awareness about the career choices they make and how that impacts on sustainability and the way we live.

Our relationship to food is fundamental to our lives. As this chapter highlights, the reasons we have become disconnected from our food, and consume food in unsustainable ways, are complex and are shaped by powerful forces that use design and visual communication very effectively. Since it is clear that visual communication is a powerful mechanism, this chapter advocates for the deployment of design, aesthetics and visual communication in general in the services of more sustainable consumption. This is complex work, but to design means to deal with paradoxes and contradictions. In order to design for a more sustainable future designers and design educators need to facilitate individual agency and system level change so as to change patterns of consumption; connecting with our senses and establishing more authentic relationships with food; and embed ethics and philosophy into design education. In this way, the relationship of the production, distribution and consumption of food with aesthetics, design and consumerism can be highlighted and these practices reshaped to bring about a shift toward a more sustainable future.

Originally from New Zealand, Chrissie Smith currently lives, works and studies in the central highlands of Victoria. She lectures in Communication Design and in Digital Art, Fine Arts, at Federation University and is undertaking a PHD by research in visual communication and cultural sustainability.

References

Barthes, R. (2013). *Toward a psychosociology of contemporary food consumption.* In C. Counihan & P. van Esterik (Eds.), *Food and culture: a reader* (3ʳᵈ ed., pp. 23-30). New York, USA: Routledge.

Böhme, G. (2003). Contribution to the critique of the aesthetic economy. *Thesis Eleven* (73), 71–82.

Braungart, M. & Mc Donough, W. (2013). *The upcycle: beyond sustainability-designing for abundance.* New York: Charles Melcher.

Clunies-Ross, T. (1990). Organic food: swimming against the tide. In T. Marsden & J. Little (Eds.), *Political, social and economic perspectives on the international food system.* Aldershot: Avebury.

Counihan, C. & Van Esterik, P. (Eds.). (2013). *Food and Culture: a reader.* New York, USA: Routledge.

Dobers, P. & Strannedgard, L. (2005). Design, lifestyles and sustainability. aesthetic consumption in a world of abundance. *Business strategy and the environment. 14*(5), 324-336.

Featherstone. M. (1991). *Consumer culture and post modernism.* London: Sage.

Fry, T. (2009). *Design futuring: sustainability, ethics and new practice.* New York: Berg.

Gergen K. J. (1991). *The saturated self.* New York: Basic.Globalization and Livestock (2005, April). *Spotlight.* Retrieved from http://www.fao.org/ag/magazine/0504sp1.htm

Hudson, R. (1996). *The domestic market for Australian organic produce: an update / a report for RIRDC.* Barton, ACT: Rural Industries Research and Development Corporation.

Lyons, K. (2001). *The culture and politics of organic food: an Australian perspective.* Retrieved from http://www.australianreview.net/digest/2001/10/lyons.html

Meyer, A. (2001). What's in it for the customers? successfully marketing green clothes. *Business Strategy and the Environment,* 10, 317-330.

Peterson, L. H. (2000). The dynamics of green consumption. A matter of visibility? *Journal of Environmental Policy and Planning, 2*(3), 193-210.

Schoenauer, N. (2000), *6000 years of housing.* New York: W.W. Norton.

Schouten, J. W. & McAlexander, J. H. (1995). Subcultures of consumption: an ethnography of the new bikers. *Journal of Consumer Research, 22*(1), 43-61.

Uusitalo, O. (1996). Consumption and the environment. *Electronic Journal of Business and Organization Studies, 1*(1). Retrieved from http://ejbo.jyu.fi/articles/0101_5.html

World Resources Institute. (2002). *Agriculture and food-meat consumption: per capita.* Retrieved from http://www.wri.org/our-work/topics/food

World Urbanization Prospects: The 2011 Revision. *Department of Economic and Social Affairs, United Nations.* Retrieved from http://esa.un.org/unup/pdf/WUP2011_Highlights.pdf

Chapter Eleven

Graphic Design and the Aesthetics of Sustainability

Johanna Niessner

Introduction

In the discourse of sustainable design, graphic design is frequently neglected. Other design disciplines have developed viable strategies and theories in response to sustainability, such as Design-for-Disassembly and Adaptive Re-Use (Madge, 1997). These strategies, however, do not translate to the field of graphic design. The existing strategies for sustainable graphic design are reactive in nature. They are a response to the difficulties of the current situation but make no strides to envisage or create an alternative situation. To date, "proposals for change have been all too modest" (Margolin, 1998, p. 86) and do not address the complexity of sustainability and the vast changes that are needed. This chapter attempts to straddle both the academic/theoretical and commercial/practical contexts of graphic design. It is not the intention of this chapter to polarise the well-intentioned efforts of graphic designers between 'sustainable' and 'not sustainable enough.' Rather, the aim is to critique existing and widely accepted theories and practices of sustainable graphic design in order to demonstrate the true complexity of sustainability and the need for a radical reconceptualization of the discipline. In doing so, this chapter makes a distinction between the issues of style and aesthetics. Style is taken to mean the purely visual quality of graphic design whereas aesthetics refers to a holistic approach to understanding and relating to the concept of sustainable graphic design.

Graphic Design

Graphic design is an exceptionally broad field. Graphic designer Tibor Kalman (1994) defines graphic design as "a medium [...] a means of communication" that consists of "the use of words and images on more or less everything, more or less everywhere" (Kalman, 1994, p. 25). A more detailed definition is given by Graham (2013) who defines graphic design as "a form of visual communication that uses typography, illustration, photography, and technical processes such as printing and interactive design for the purposes of persuasion, information, or instruction" (Graham, 2013, p. 170). Graphic designers are skilled image-makers who communicate through their aesthetic choices; they transform appearances, and in doing so, construct and attach meaning. As Dobers and Strannegard (2005, p. 327) state, "an aesthetic image serves as a stimulus, a sign or a representation that drives cognition, interpretation and preference." The aesthetic function of graphic design is to generate attention and interest. The aesthetic image is designed to convey a message and that message is intended to elicit some form of change.

Graphic design is inextricably linked to consumption and waste. Graphic design output can take any number of forms, including posters, logos, business cards, brochures, signs, fliers and product packaging. While this list is in no way exhaustive, it clearly demonstrates that the vast majority of graphic design can be categorised as ubiquitous, visual ephemera; it has a short lifespan and is highly disposable (Keedy, 1998). Jacobs explains the transitory nature of graphic design by stating that the majority of the output is literally "garbage" (Jacobs, 1994, p. 185). Graphic design is constant, inescapable, instantly forgettable, and produces an enormous amount of waste. Furthermore, Jacobs cynically notes that graphic designers are obligated to consider the ecological impact of their practice "not just because [they] are so intimately involved with the disposable, but because it is now the style to be environmentally concerned" (Jacobs, 1994, p. 190).

Graphic design is a fundamental part of consumer society. Of course, the same could be said of all design: "Design, its very meaning, its raison d'être, its philosophical core is, today, synonymous with the business of producing, selling and consuming" (Fuad-Luke, 2007, p. 20). However, graphic design is perhaps implicated in this to a greater degree than other design disciplines. While its function may be broadly given as communication, graphic design predominantly operates in the "service of advertising and a capitalist system that encourages consumption" (Davis, 2012, p. 204).

Graphic Design and Sustainability

The definition of sustainability outlined in the Brundtland Report, the findings of the UN established commission on sustainable development released in 1987, suggest that sustainability must be viewed from a broad systems based approach. By considering social, cultural and economic and environmental factors, the goal of sustainability is to "meet the needs of the present without compromising the ability of future generations to meet their own needs" (United Nations General Assembly, 1987). This remains the most widely accepted and cited definition of sustainability.

The Society of Graphic Designers of Canada has formulated a definition of sustainable communication design that is closely aligned to the Brundtland Report: "Sustainable communication design is the application of sustainability principles to communication design practice. Practitioners consider the full lifecycle of products and services, and commit to strategies, processes and materials that value environmental, cultural, social and economic responsibility" (GDC Sustainable Design Principles, n.d.). This definition correctly frames sustainability as a multifaceted and complex dilemma which requires a systemic approach. Indeed, complexity is central to sustainability and refers to the interactions between interdependent systems (Davis, 2012).

Sustainable design is far broader and more complex in scope than what might otherwise be referred to as "green" or "eco" design. Green or eco design is typically "project-based, single issue and relatively short-term" (Madge, 1997, p. 52). In contrast, sustainable design is long-term, systems-based and adaptive. Rather than searching for singular solutions at the project level, sustainable design requires fundamental changes in the culture of design. This is described by Kagan (2011, p. 66) as "the search for alternative sets of values and knowledge of the world". Sustainable design is can also be described as inclusive, participatory and equitable. As John Thackara (2007, p. xviii) notes "sustainable design means co-design of daily life with the people who are living it". Sustainable design also recognises the need to alter the existing patterns of consumption. Dobers and Strannegard (2005, p. 325) argue that "a production system geared towards ever-increasing growth and consumption creates one of the most serious impediments for sustainable development, especially when the business practices move away from addressing people's needs to exploiting their desires".

The Current State of Sustainability in Graphic Design

Materials
Current literature on sustainable graphic design tends to focus almost exclusively on using sustainable materials and processes. Choosing non-toxic inks, unbleached or recycled paper, and low energy printing are presented as practical steps designers can take to reduce the environmental impact of their output. These practices, referred to by Hosey (2012, p. 18) as "invisible green" techniques, are the most common efforts graphic designers make towards sustainability. These changes can be easily regulated and measured and they do not necessarily impact on the artistic or visual outcome of the design (Hosey, 2012).

While clearly beneficial, the shift towards using more ecologically sound materials and processes is a relatively small accomplishment for graphic designers, and by all accounts, a relatively easy one to achieve (Margolin, 1998; Sargent, 2013). These measures are more accurately categorised as *green* graphic design rather than sustainable graphic design as they operate on a reactive, short-term, project-based level (Fry, 2009; Madge, 1997; Sargent, 2013). That is, using more environmentally sustainable materials represent only one component in a broader system of sustainability.

Messages

Beyond materials and processes, current theories and practice of sustainable graphic design also focus on the discipline's communicative function, particularly in the form of sustainability campaigns. These campaigns generally follow a single model: A clear message of sustainability communicated in attractive and informative graphic design stimulates debate, increases public awareness, and encourages action. The logic behind this is very straightforward and is essentially identical to traditional graphic design. The aim is to attract attention, impart a message and, as a result of that message, to effect change.

Given how closely these forms of graphic design align to traditional graphic design process it is essential to question how successfully they respond to the complexity of sustainability. Klanten, Ehmann and Bohle (2012) state that "successful sustainable communication sensitizes people, puts it's finger on the problem and creates a sense of awareness". John Thackara (2007, p. xvii) disputes this claim, stating that "posters and ad campaigns that tell people to behave sustainably are a pointless diversion". Thackara contends that sustainable graphic design campaigns and messages contribute to the existing image-glut and its desensitizing effects as described by Susan Sontag: "Image-glut keeps attention light, mobile, relatively indifferent to content" (Sontag, cited in Thackara, 2013). That is, while these images may be informative and well intentioned the sheer amount of visual communication we are exposed to on a daily basis renders the viewer passive to the message being presented. Designs promoting messages of sustainability are competing with up to 5000 advertising messages that an individual is exposed to in the course of a single day (Story, 2007). Furthermore, sustainable graphic design messages are disseminated in the same manner and form as advertising-based graphic design. Posters calling for us to "Reduce, Reuse and Recycle" are placed on bus stops where we are used to seeing posters telling us to buy Coke. It follows that these messages would thus be received and filtered in the same way.

Thackara (2013) also points out that the majority of these sustainability messages are too modest and frequently undermine the scope of the problem. The underlying suggestion is that "we can have or cake and eat it – where "cake" means a perpetual growth economy" (Thackara, 2013). These messages are pedagogic in nature and generally focus on altering individual behaviour. Encouraging consumers to use re-usable shopping bags, for example, overlooks the bigger picture. The current system of consumption is being reinforced by these images. Furthermore, consumers are given the impression that if, for example, they use re-cycled shopping bags, they have done their part (or all they can or need to do) to ensure the future of the planet. These are feel-good campaigns which serve to deflect attention from the bigger picture and undermine the complexity of sustainability.

Style

To a certain extent, graphic designers have succeeded in creating the style or "look" of sustainability. A green and brown colour palette, while a cliché, does evoke a cognitive connection to nature, and by extension, suggest ecological awareness. The intention of this overt style of sustainability is that consumers will be able to identify and choose the more sustainable options (Dougherty, 2008). This style has become culturally integrated as a signifier of sustainability. Doing what they do best, graphic designers have succeeded in *branding* sustainability.

On the surface, the proliferation of products marketed through a sustainable graphic design style is exceedingly positive, suggesting the market has recognised and complied with a growing consumer demand for more sustainable products. In some regards this is true. It can be argued, however, that the growing visual presence of sustainability in the form of product packaging and other graphic design merely serves to create an illusion of progress among producers, consumers and designers (Chapman & Gant, 2007). There is a presumed correlation between reality and image: "The modern injunction to believe only what one sees [...] confusingly coexists with awesome technical powers to produce convincing spectacles" (Slater, cited in Dobers & Strannegard, 2005, p. 328). The illusion of progress is exacerbated by *greenwashing*, the practice of deliberately misrepresenting products as environmentally sustainable when they are not (Dougherty, 2008). Whether mendacious, such as the unethical practice of *greenwashing*, or through the desire to be recognised and congratulated for making efforts towards sustainability, the use of an overt style of sustainability acts as self-applied stamp of approval, and is a viable and often very successful marketing tool.

Beyond creating an unrealistic impression of progress and action, the notion of a visual style of sustainability is still problematic. This conspicuous visual style simply reinforces the existing consumer culture by turning sustainability into a "commodity to be bought and sold" (Davis, 2012, p. 204). Sustainability is "addressed via modified and targeted consumption" rather than through changes to the current patterns of consumption (Reinmuth, 2010). In this sense, the existing consumer culture which is driven by desire rather than need is reinforced by positioning sustainability as a desire rather than an imperative. As Jacobs (1994, p. 186) notes "style is the most disposable thing there is". Therefore, by tying sustainability to a visual style "we are in danger of turning sustainability into nothing more than a passing trend rather than a deep cultural shift that makes sustainability sustainable" (Chapman & Gant, 2007, p. 13). The sustainable product becomes the new object of desire, and as such, is susceptible to stylistic obsolescence like all the objects of desire that came before it (Burdick, 1994).

Towards an Aesthetic of Sustainable Graphic Design

As a branch of philosophy, aesthetics refers to the "the science of the sensual perception of the world" (Reinhardt, 2013). It is a form of inquiry, a way of understanding and interacting with the world, and an arena for conducting social and cultural experiments (Kelly, 1998).

The role aesthetics play in sustainable design has been broached by several theorists. Manzini (1994, p. 43) discusses the importance of aesthetics for sustainability as a facilitator of change, as a means of clearly and formally expressing the complexity of the challenge, and as a "social attractor" that can sway the decisions of individuals. Meyer (2008) similarly mentions the power of aesthetics in transforming consciousness and altering perceptions and values. Kurt (2004, p. 239) finds that aesthetics are vital in moving sustainability from a narrow discourse of environmentalism to a broader understanding of sustainability as a "cultural challenge". In a more practical sense, theorists have noted that aesthetics also contribute to sustainability by increasing the longevity of a design artefact by creating an enduring emotional response (Hosey, 2012). The more aesthetically pleasing an object, the less disposable it is.

To date, graphic design has not succeeded in creating an aesthetic of sustainability. What they have created is a "style" of sustainability. The question is, what does an aesthetic of sustainable graphic design look like beyond "fad, trend or fashionable styling" (Papanek, 1995, p. 236)? This new aesthetic of sustainability must be based on more than an "arbitrary invented style [...], appearance, flamboyant 'gesture' or semiotic 'statements'" (Papanek, 1995, p. 235). That is, sustainability should not be addressed through the incremental parts of the graphic design process but by reorienting our conception of the discipline. What is required is a focus on the needs of the end-users and "a deep spiritual concern for planet, environment, and people" (Papanek, 1995, p. 235).

Rather than being preoccupied with materials, messages and style, an aesthetic of sustainable graphic design will focus on the designing of systems and processes by which people relate to information, context and experience. This is described by Papanek (1995, p. 7) as a "change [in] the driving question behind design from "how does it look" to "how does it relate".

Relational design recognises the complexity of the contemporary context and emphasises "performative, pragmatic, programmatic, process-oriented, open-ended, experiential and participatory elements" as well as social and human interactions (Blauvelt, 2008). Relational design provides a multifaceted approach for envisaging an aesthetic of sustainable design, one that prioritises the needs of the users and accepts that sustainable graphic design is an iterative and open-ended process.

The participatory nature of relation design is particularly relevant to forming an aesthetic of sustainable graphic design. Traditionally, graphic design positions the consumer in a passive role. Sustainability requires action and as such, the new sustainable graphic design aesthetic should demand (or coax) participation and action from its audience. Graphic designers must create opportunities to involve end-users in the act of creation. In commercial graphic design this is already being employed to create a sense of brand loyalty, to simulate an intimate connection between the consumer and the product. If these techniques could be employed for environmental and socially constructive graphic design, the impact could be immense. Encouraging participation positions the audience to engage with the message being presented and to be more mindful and critical of images in general. The audience becomes complicit, personally invested; they begin to develop a sense of ownership of the problems of the unsustainable world and the potential solutions. "Action requires grasping, doubting, negotiating, deciding, altering and creating" (Meurer, 1997, p. 120). As such, the aesthetic of sustainable graphic design should be participatory and provocative rather than passive and pedagogic.

Co-design demands input from all stakeholders during the design process. By encouraging participation and collaboration between designers, organisations and end-users, this approach recognises that "sustainability has to be a cooperative ambition, a societal ambition" (Fuad-Luke, 2007, p. 37). Sustainable co-design takes in to account the social, financial and environmental requirements of all interested parties with the aim of creating new outcomes that meet specific needs.

What will set a sustainable graphic design practice apart from an unsustainable one is the adherence to a core philosophy of eliminating waste wherever possible. In the current context this may be achieved by graphic designers trying to persuade their clients away from print media towards digital technology. Graphic designers could work more closely with systems designers to find new ways of transmitting their visual communication that doesn't involve an enormous amount of waste. This will require both graphic designers and the public freeing themselves from the tactile allure of printed graphic design and embracing new and potentially more convenient and effective solutions in the form of programmatic, digital and open-source technologies. Graphic designers must start thinking about the things we take for granted, such as the poster or business card, and ask how these can be turned into different products that still achieves the same end goal but in a sustainable way.

Conclusion

It is beyond the scope and ability of this chapter to provide an absolute solution or methodology for sustainable graphic design. Indeed, it is essential that the search for a singular vision of sustainable graphic design be abandoned: "[D]oubting what exists, what one thinks and what one does is the most important aspect of creative action. Doubt is a prerequisite for creativity" (Meurer, 1997, p. 126). Sustainability offers an unprecedented opportunity for graphic designers to expand the boundaries of their practice beyond the traditional focus of materials, messages and style. As Chapman and Gant (2007, p. 142) suggest, designers "have the ability to engage with more overarching, systemic approaches that develop new consumer paradigms (and even socio-cultural movements and behaviours) to provide a further layer of intervention for creative practitioners to engage with". The participatory, programmatic, user-centred and open-ended nature of relational design provides an interesting foundation on which to conceive a new aesthetic of sustainable graphic design.

Johanna Niessner is a graphic designer, design researcher and academic. She has previously taught at the Université Sorbonne Nouvelle in Paris and is currently working as an academic and research administrator at the School of Design & Art, Curtin University.

References

Blauvelt, A. (2008). Towards relational design. *Design Observer*. Retrieved from http://designobserver.com/feature/towards-relational-design/7557/

Burdick, A. (1994). Neomania: feeding the monster. In M. Bierut, W. Drenttel, S. Heller & D. K. Holland (Eds.), *Looking closer: critical writings on graphic design* (pp. 135-143). New York, USA: Allworth Press.

Chapman, J. & Gant, N. (Eds.). (2007). *Designers, visionaries and other stories: a collection of sustainable design essays*. London, UK: Earthscan.

Davis, M. (2012). *Graphic design theory*. London, UK: Thames & Hudson.

Dobers, P. & Strannegard, L. (2005). Design, lifestyle and sustainability: aesthetic consumption in a world of abundance. *Business Strategy and the Environment, 14*(5), 324-336.

Dougherty, B. (2008). *Green graphic design*. New York, USA: Allworth Press.

Fry, T. (2009). *Design futuring: sustainability, ethics and new practice*. Sydney, Australia: UNSW Press.

Fuad-Luke, A. (2007). Re-defining the purpose of (sustainable) design: enter the design enablers, catalysts in co-design. In J. Chapman & N. Gant. (Eds.), *Designers, visionaries and other stories: a collection of sustainable design essays* (pp. 18-52). London, UK: Earthscan.

GDC Sustainable Design Values and Principles. (n.d.). Society of graphic designers of Canada. Retrieved from http://www.gdc.net/about/index/articles/711.php

Graham, L. M. (2012). Towards a more sustainable graphic design philosophy. *The International Journal of the Arts in Society, 6*(5), 169-176.

Hosey, L. (2012). *The shape of green: aesthetics, ecology and design*. Washington DC, USA: Island Press.

Jacobs, K. (1994). Disposability, graphic design, style, and waste. In M. Bierut, W. Drenttel, S. Heller & D. K. Holland (Eds.), *Looking closer: critical writings on graphic design* (pp. 149-152). New York, USA: Allworth Press.

Kalman, T., Miller, J. A. & Jacobs, K. (1994). Good history/bad history. In M. Bierut, W. Drenttel, S. Heller & D. K. Holland (Eds.), *Looking closer: critical writings on graphic design* (pp. 25-33). New York, USA: Allworth Press.

Keedy, J. (1998). Graphic design in the postmodern era. *Émigré*, 47. Retrieved from http://www.emigre.com/Editorial.php?sect=1&id=20

Kelly, M. (Ed.). (1998). *Encyclopedia of aesthetics*. Oxford, UK: Oxford University Press.

Klanten, R., Ehmann, S. & Bohle, S. (Eds.). (2012). *Cause and effect: visualising sustainability*. London, UK: Gestalten.

Kurt, H. (2004). Aesthetics of sustainability. In H. Stretow (Ed.), *Aesthetics of ecology: art in environmental design, theory and practice*. Boston, USA: Birkhauser.

Madge, P. (1997). Ecological design: a new critique. *Design Issues, 13*(2), 44-54.

Manzini, E. (1994). Design, environment and social quality: from "existenzminimum" to "quality maximum." *Design Issues, 10*(1), 37-43.

Margolin, V. (1998). Design for a sustainable world. *Design Issues, 14*(2), 83-92.

Meurer, B. (1997). The transformation of design. In J. Frascara (Ed.), *User-centred graphic design: mass communication and social change* (pp. 119-126). London, UK: Taylor & Francis.

Meyer, E. K. (2008). Sustaining beauty. the performance of appearance: a manifesto in three parts. *Journal of Landscape Architecture, 3*(2), 6-23.

Papanek, V. (1995). *The green imperative: ecology and ethics in design and architecture.* London, UK: Thames & Hudson.

Reinhardt, K. (2013, November 25). *Aesthetic sustainability: Kurt C. Reinhardt at TEDxKreuzeskirchvirtel* [Video File]. Retrieved from http://www.youtube.com/watch?v=enRE B DzX7bw

Reinmuth, G. (2010). Sustainability as an aesthetic problem. *Conditions Magazine.*
Retrieved from http://www.conditionsmagazine.com/archives/1567

Sargent, D. (2013). Green design as unsustainable design. *Studio Research, 1*(7), 78-86.

Story, L. (2007, January 15). Anywhere the eye can see, it's likely to see an ad. *The New York Times.* Retrieved from http://www.nytimes.com/2007/01/15/business/media/15everywhere.html?pagewanted=all&_r=0

Thackara, J. (2007). Foreword. In J. Chapman & N. Gant. (Eds.), *Designers, visionaries and other stories: a collection of sustainable design essays* (pp. xvi-xviii). London, UK: Earthscan.

Thackara, J. (2013, November 23). Desert of the real. [Web log post]. Retrieved from http://www.doorsofperception.com/notopic/desert-of-the-real/#more-5142

CHAPTER TWELVE

THE IMPORTANCE OF AESTHETICS IN SUSTAINABLE INTERIOR DESIGN FOR RETAIL SPACES

Eko Pam

Introduction

In my work as an Interior Designer I have been involved in regular discussions and debates about the importance of sustainability in design. A growing worldwide concern for the environment is evidenced by designers, architects, engineers and theorising about and creating designs that, as outlined in the Brundtland report, "meet the needs of the present without compromising the ability of future generations to meet their own needs" (United Nations General Assembly, 1987). However, despite the identification of sustainability in the 1980s as an issue requiring immediate action, sustainability is often neglected when decisions are made about final design outcomes in an industry driven by budgets, deadlines and client briefs. In addition, sustainable environmental design has developed a rustic, raw visual trend, which limits the exploration of aesthetics in the broader application of design. The tendency for designers to conform to fashionable aesthetics limits the durability and economic and social impact of sustainable design. My upcoming PhD project will investigate ways to approach renovations of retail fit-outs from a triple bottom line approach to sustainability that affords the economic concerns of retailers the same importance as the positive environmental and social aspects of the design. In this chapter I will explore and contest the aesthetics of sustainable design in retail environments in terms of its importance in the success of sustainable interior design practice.

Aesthetics: definition and politics

Aesthetics implies a wide variety of meanings and is difficult to define (Castronovo, 2007, p. 10). This is perhaps because an aesthetic is "not necessarily a rational element" (Guillen, 1997, p. 709). It is connected to several philosophical theories regarding beauty, personal experience and style (Douglass, 2008, p. 5). Discussions of aesthetics have long been connected to artwork rather than design and have involved much philosophical debate on the question of how to define concepts connected to aesthetics such as ideas of beauty and taste. Traditionally, discussions of aesthetics have involved questions of unity, form and balance or the composition of something visual (Castronovo, 2007, p. 2). The purpose of this paper is not to open a discussion of what aesthetics means, but rather to acknowledge that aesthetics are important and shape the meanings that consumers invest in design projects.

The aesthetics of an object or building are a vital part of creating an emotional connection (Walker, 2006, p. 142). As Le Corbusier said in *Towards a new architecture* (1989), aesthetics in the context of architecture is similar to the way we view art. It is a "phenomenon of the emotions, lying outside questions of construction and beyond them". In light of how powerful a reaction they can produce, beautifully designed products and buildings are more likely to be maintained and cared for than those where aesthetics are given little thought. Ralph DiNola, Principal of Green Building Services in America, points out that "aesthetics is very much a part of longevity, and longevity is key to sustainability" (Garris, 2007, p. 44). Ironically, when the focus is only on sustainable outcomes, thoughts of the beauty of an object, space or building are often secondary.

An object or building that is used for many years is ultimately much more sustainable than one that has been designed with positive environmental outcomes in mind but is only used for a short period. McLennan gives the example of warehouses and factories that were built at a time, during the late 19th and early 20th century, when beauty and attention to detail was given to even the most functional of buildings, and which are now being used as offices and apartments. When the amount of time that the materials have been used for is considered, these buildings have a much lower embodied energy than even the most environmentally friendly recent building projects (McLennan, 2004, p. 236). Buildings for trade today are often not given the same aesthetic attention, and as a result are not always geared towards re-use in the future. Instead, we are living in an increasingly disposable, consumerist society which generates high levels of waste and aesthetic obsolescence and is driven by the need to provide affordable, functional products or buildings in short time frames. My doctoral research will explore the role that aesthetics plays in the way that a design is perceived by its target audience and how the aesthetics associated with sustainability can have a negative impact on the acceptance of a design. These considerations are important in the context of retail design, my area of focus, where the aesthetics of a shop fit-out make an important contribution to the economic success of a retailer.

It seems little consideration was given to aesthetics in early sustainable design projects from the seventies and eighties. McLennan points out that these early models focused "little on anything other than performance" (2004, p. 227). As an example, sustainable design pioneer Victor Papanek designed a radio made from a transistor that used an energy source of paraffin wax and a wick housed in a recycled juice can. The design gained a lot of media attention and worked well as a radio using recycled materials and an alternative energy source, but "invited criticism from the design world at the time because of its ugly appearance" (Knight, 2009). More recent sustainable design projects have paid more attention to aesthetics but these general impressions do not seem to have changed much. Hosey says, "the ugly truth about sustainable design is that much of it is ugly" (2012a, p. 2). Hybrid cars models have been criticised for how ugly they are (Heffner, Kurani, & Turrentine, 2007) and architectural surveys of the world's most beautiful buildings lack examples of green architecture (Hosey, 2012b). The role of aesthetics in architecture according to Larson (1993) is to inspire the public "and not offend it". As these recent examples demonstrate, there is clearly still some negativity about the aesthetics of sustainable design.

Leaving this negativity to one side, examples of sustainable design do seem to share a strong aesthetic link. As Lance Hosey (2012a) points out, eco-friendly design has become an aesthetic cliché featuring "hemp shirts, rattan furniture, unbleached paper, wood-pulp walls, wheat-board cabinets and the like" which point to the idea "earth friendly should look earthy". Certainly in some cases designers seem to have gone out of their way to make their building or product visibly environmentally sustainable (McLennan, 2004, p. 230). These visual cues are an important part of design communication. Aesthetics are not only a way of creating pleasure through beauty but also a way of passing on information or influencing an audience in some way (Buchanan, 1985, p. 4). This form of visual communication and connection that aesthetics promotes is why the aesthetics associated with sustainability is so important.

Aesthetic and rhetoric

Sustainable aesthetics take on an almost pedagogic or constructive role in that they instruct or persuade consumers to think about the importance of sustainability. This is why the way a design looks is so important. Design as a form of visual communication through appearance or aesthetics has been widely discussed. Visual rhetoric can be closely linked to semiotics. This tradition was initiated by

Roland Barthes (1977) and Guy Bonsiepe (1965) who focused on the relationship between image and text and the way images can communicate messages. Buchanan argues that due to the rise of technology in the twentieth century, objects through their design have the power to shape society and change the course of individuals and communities. These are the aims of many sustainable designers, so clearly the aesthetics of design play a key role in that desire for change. Some of the aesthetic elements that are closely related to sustainable design are by-products of the design rather than purposely arranged visual cues. These could include solar panels on buildings and raw unfinished materials used in furniture and interiors. These design elements then form part of the visual rhetoric of design and communicate a message of sustainability. Visual rhetoric, defined by Foss as "a product individuals create as they use visual symbols for the purpose of communication" (2005, p. 143), is therefore an important aspect of the success of sustainable design.

However, the aesthetics of sustainable design are not always communicated as effectively or purposefully as this. In some instances, a designer goes out of his/her way to add unnecessary features to a product, interior or building to make it look sustainable either as greenwashing or because the existing sustainable design decisions are not visible. As Ehses points out, "shaping the appearance of any visual object involves rhetoric" (1988, p. 6). In this way, all designers have the challenge of creating a design that is appropriate for particular clients and audiences (Ehses, 1988). By deliberately placing sustainability into a recognisable aesthetic, a designer risks communicating a message that is disliked or part of a visual trend that will soon become unfashionable. Dobers and Strannegård (2005) believe that consumers are becoming progressively more fashion sensitive and therefore aware of whether a certain aesthetic appears redundant. If sustainability is represented in a design in the form of a short-term visual trend that eventually falls out of fashion, the values and principles behind the sustainable approach will also be lost.

Aesthetics of sustainable (retail) design

Companies and retailers realise the importance of this visual rhetoric and are now using aesthetics as a way to sell products as part of the trend cycle. Ironically, the disposability of products and the desire to create instant consumer appeal is the main reason why a strong visual aesthetic has come to be associated with sustainability. More recently, the semblance of an eco-conscience has become a powerful marketing strategy, as a significant proportion of the population favour greener products and services (Grant, 2008). High profile corporate scandals over the last decade and the climate crisis gaining increased media attention have sensitised the public to ideas of ethics and effective governance in business (D'Souza, Taghian & Lamb, 2006; Reimer, 2012; Stieg, 2006) and as a result most large companies today are aware of the global concern for the environment and adhere to the idea of corporate responsibility as being important for the success of their business (D'Souza et al., 2006, p. 162). For this reason, companies seek to project a clear positive environmental message to consumers. This has led to the greenwashing problem, with companies making claims about the greenness of a company or product that are not backed by rigorous testing or research (Douglass, 2008; Stieg, 2006, p. 34). Greenwashing points to the value in promoting an environmentally friendly image to the public.

The result of companies wanting to appear environmentally friendly is that the features that make the product, building or company sustainable are displayed to the public so that they can recognise the visual symbols of sustainability. This is because design aesthetics are visible and recognisable whereas, interestingly, a lot of sustainable design choices are invisible and implicit (Kisek, 2002). McLennan gives this example from architecture: "A building with the right orientation will have a much lower environmental impact than the exact same building facing due east-west" (2004, p. 230). Instead of using these small but powerful design choices, designers feel compelled to create designs that have more overt displays of sustainability, such as green roof or solar panels in architecture and raw materials or visibly-recycled aspects of a design in interiors. This seems oddly reminiscent of 'Featurism' that Robin Boyd refers to in his 1960 book *The Australian ugliness*; unnecessary ornamentation which is "applied at the expense of unified functional design" (p. 9). McLennan echoes Boyd's sentiments when he states, "we have become a features society" (2004, p. 230). This idea of adding features, or purposely designing something to seem more sustainable, seems at odds with definitions of sustainable design which seek to reduce the amount of materials used as the first step towards creating a less environmentally destructive design (Smith, O'Farrell, & Brindley, 2012).

This aesthetic trend associated with the environmental movement attracts a range of connotations, not all of them positive. Many consumers identify what Hosey (2012b) calls the "hippie-aesthetic" as ugly and pretentious. This is partly due to the fact that early adopters of the sustainability movement in design were more concerned with high-tech engineering methods and chemistry rather than aesthetics (McLennan, 2004, p. 227). This excluded initial designs with a broader appeal and set the precedent for sustainable design as being different-looking to traditional design aesthetics. Today, many sustainable designs still look different. Examples of sustainable residential architecture often feature building materials and facades that are very different to what most suburban houses look like. These traditional house designs dictate a particular external façade that usually features a pitched tiled roof and brick or rendered brick walls. Hawley (2003, p. 2) claims that this 'sameness' in design, "brings a certain comfort, security, and a sense of true community" (p. 2). Robin Boyd (Fiske, Hodge, & Turner, 1987, p. 27) believes that "servility and conformism are two strong messages about the national character". So for sustainability to be a truly mainstream movement in Australia, perhaps the very features that differentiate sustainable design from traditional design are actually preventing sustainability from being accepted in the best possible way – as normal.

Despite the unnecessary extra ornamentation that comes with this new sustainable aesthetic, these approaches are a positive sign that companies and designers are being compelled to make more environmentally friendly decisions due to public demand. At present sustainability is such an emotive buzzword that in the field of economics it is being referred to as 'green gold' (Berger, 2011). This points to sustainability and the obligatory green aesthetic being a fashion or trend of the twenty-first century. Mike Featherstone (1991) makes the point that society is becoming more and more concerned with aesthetics because companies' marketing efforts have led to consumers being constantly on the search for new fashions, styles and experiences. The implication for this is that consumption today is very trend oriented (Dobers & Stannegard, 2005). Designers have long known the power of aesthetics and as a result the success of the industry is driven by intentional aesthetic obsolescence and a way to fuel consumption (Walker, 2006, p. 142). As we live in a society where perceived obsolescence drives the design industry, trends and fashions need to be carefully considered when approaching sustainable design.

Conclusion

This is the risk that this recognisable design aesthetic poses to the future of sustainability. If the emphasis of the aesthetics is to remind people of how eco-friendly something is "then the designs that result will risk looking quickly passé" (Hosey, 2012). McLennan (2004, p. 5) believes that sustainable design should be viewed as an approach to design rather than an aesthetic style so that it never goes out of style or is seen as a fad. The success of the triple bottom line approach depends on careful consideration of the aesthetics of the project and the contribution of aesthetics to economic growth and social inclusiveness. If the design appears out of date or is unable to create a mood or experience that attracts their customer base, the economic and social factors will be negatively impacted.

For this reason, it is quite likely that the sustainable aspects of my retail design might not necessarily be visible and will certainly not dictate the aesthetic of the shop, but will still be the principal component. It is therefore very important that the aesthetics are driven by a brief set by the client in response to current trends and fashions rather than by an agenda from the designer to make the environmental sustainability of fit-out a visual feature. The main benefit of a more invisible and implicit approach to sustainable design for retail, compared to an ornamental and therefore wasteful approach, will help sustainability in design to be more sustainable.

Eko Pam has worked as an interior designer on significant projects including the Grove Library in Cottesloe, the Albany Entertainment Centre and the Supreme Court in Perth. She is currently working as a lecturer in Environmental and Spatial Design at Edith Cowan University and is undertaking her PhD on the topic, 'Aesthetics and sustainability in retail design: considering environmental, ethical and economic objectives', which explores retail interior design from a triple bottom line perspective and the role that aesthetics plays in the success of designs for sustainable outcomes.

References

Barthes, R. (1977). The rhetoric of the image. In S. Heath (Ed.), *Image, music, text.* (pp. 32-51). New York: Hill and Wang.

Berger, R. (2011). *Green growth, green profit. how green transformation boosts business.* Hampshire, United Kingdom: Palgrave Macmillan.

Bonsiepe, G. (1965). Visual/verbal rhetoric. *Journal of the Ulm School of Design, 14*(16), 23-10.

Boyd, R. (1960). *The Australian ugliness.* Melbourne: The Hawthorn Press.

Buchanan, R. (1985). Declaration by design: rhetoric, argument, and demonstration in design practice. *Design Issues, 2*(1), 4-22.

Castronovo, R. (2007). Aesthetics. In B. Burgett & G. Hendler (Eds.), *Keywords for American Cultural Studies.* New York: New York University Press.

Corbusier, Le. (1989). *Towards a new architecture.* London: Butterworth Architecture.

D'Souza, C, Taghian, M, & Lamb, P. (2006). An empirical study on the influence of environmental labels on consumers. *Corporate Communications: An International Journal, 11*(2), 162-173.

Dobers, P. & Stannegard, L. (2005). Design, lifestyles and sustainability. Aesthetic consumption in a world of abundance. *Business Strategy and the Environment, 14,* 324-336.

Douglass, D. B. (2008). *Defining a sustainable aesthetic: a new paradigm for architecture* (Master's dissertation). Retrieved from https://arch.usc.edu/sites/default/files/mbs/papers/david_douglass.pdf

Ehses, H. (1988). Rhetoric and design. *Design Papers 5: Rhetorical Handbook.*

Featherstone, M. (1991). *Consumer culture and postmodernism.* London: Sage.

Fiske, J., Hodge, B. & Turner, G. (1987). *The myths of oz: reading Australian popular culture.* Sydney: Allen & Unwin.

Foss, S. K. (2005). Theory of visual rhetoric. In K. Smith, S. Moriarty, G. Barbatsis & K. Kenney (Eds.), *Handbook of visual communication: theory, methods, and media* (pp. 141-52). Mahwah, New Jersey: Lawrence Erlbaum.

Garris, L. (2007). A smart approach to sustainability. *Buildings, 3*(7), 44-50.

Grant, J. (2008). Green marketing. *Strategic Direction, 24*(6), 25-27.

Guillen, M. (1997). Scientific management's lost aesthetic: architecture, organization, and the taylorized beauty of the mechanical. *Administrative Science Quarterly, 42*(4), 682.

Hawley, J. (2003, August 26). Crowded land of giants, *Sydney Morning Herald, Good Weekend.* Retrieved from http://www.smh.com.au/articles/2003/08/26/1061663776473.html

Heffner, R., Kurani, K. & Turrentine, T. (2007). Symbolism in California's early market for hybrid electric vehicles. *Transportation Research Part D: Transport and Environment, 12*(6), 396-413.

Hosey, L. (2012a). *The shape of green; aesthetics, ecology and design.* Washington DC: Island Press.

Hosey, L. (2012b, 6th June 2012). The shape of green: aesthetic imperatives. Retrieved from http://places.designobserver.com/feature/the-shape-of-green-sustainability-and-aesthetics/34518/

Kisek, T. (2002). Perspectives on sustainablility. Retrieved from http://www.canadianarchitect.com/news/perspectives-on-sustainability/1000149467/

Knight, A. (2009). Hidden histories: the story of sustainable design. Retrieved from http://www.csa.com/discoveryguides/design/review2.php

Larson, M. (1993). *Behind the postmodern facade: architectural change in late twentieth century America.* Berkeley: University of California Press.

McLennan, Jason. (2004). *The philosophy of sustainable design: the future of architecture.* Canada: Ecotone LLC.

Reimer, M. (2012). Unsettling eco-scapes: aesthetic performances for sustainable future. *Journal of Landscape Architecture, 5*(1), 24-37. doi: 10.1080/18626033.2010.9723428

Smith, K., O'Farrell, K. & Brindley, F. (2012). *Waste and recycling in Australia 2011.* Sydney, Australia: Department Of Sustainability, Environment, Water, Population And Communities.

Stieg, C. (2006). The sustainability gap. *Journal of Interior Design, 32*(1), 7-20.

Walker, S. (2006). *Sustainable by design.* London: Earthscan.

CHAPTER THIRTEEN

THE 'HOUSE OF THE FUTURE' AND THE TOYOTA PRIUS (MkII): PERSPECTIVES ON SUSTAINABILITY

Henry Skates & Peter Wood

Introduction

Aesthetics, image and feedback not only shape perceptions of sustainability but also influence behaviour. This has variously been referred to as the 'Prius Effect' (Wood & Skates, 2006) and 'Conspicuous Conservation' (Sexton & Sexton, 2011). Since its introduction, the Prius has received two major revisions and a facelift, and, perhaps more importantly, it has received popular support as a responsible vehicle choice for drivers who wish to minimise the impact of their driving on the environment. Leonardo Di-Caprio drives one, as do many of his celebrity friends. The Prius is no longer regarded as a small car, and a new model called the Prius 'c' has filled the gap left by the now somewhat obese standard Prius. It doesn't really look obese, as it has been streamlined further to reduce air resistance, but despite the technologically aesthetic corset it has put on weight. This effect is referred to in the automotive industry as 'The Bloat Law' (Dykes, 2012). The second version is always larger than the first. Perhaps this applies to fields other than the automotive industry, but let us continue for a moment with cars.

At the other end of the automotive spectrum is the Hummer – a behemoth sport utility vehicle (SUV) favoured by that other behemoth, Arnold Schwarzenegger. So, who costs the environment more – Leonardo or Arnold? According to a 2005 CNW Marketing Research, Leo does (CNW Marketing Research, 2005). Taking into account the full range of energy usage required to conceive, produce, drive and dispose of a car, CNW marketing concluded that the hybrid Prius consumes 1.6 times more energy over its lifetime than the 2 tonne H3 Hummer. Toyota have since responded with their own figures to show that the CNW figures are misleading, and that the assumptions made are not accurate, but nevertheless, the report raises some interesting questions. So we may well ask the question; which mode of transport is the most sustainable? But before we do that, perhaps we should examine what lies behind the question. Do we ask the question because we want ourselves, or other people, to know that we are saving the planet when we are driving? Perceptions of sustainability are important. For the moment, let us assume that it is self-satisfaction.

Feedback is a well-recognised ingredient in regulating perceptions and hence behaviour. After all, what is the point of saving the world if no one knows you are saving the world? When driving the Prius the dashboard display tells you when you are using the electric motor rather than the petrol engine, letting you know when you are saving the planet so you can try even harder to save it more. This has also been referred to as the Prius effect, but for this paper we will define the Prius effect as the feedback that allows you to feel better when driving your car, even though driving any car can be viewed as environmentally threatening. In the popular American animated television series *Southpark*, this self-satisfying feeling has been referred to as the 'smug effect'. (In the 2006 'smug alert' episode of *Southpark*, Gerald buys a Prius, buys into the whole progressive movement and, deciding to move his whole family to San Fransisco, a cloud of smug follows his move where it meets up with other smug clouds including George Clooney's own personal smug cloud to create the perfect storm of self satisfaction [smug is defined in the episode as "the self satisfied garbage being spewed into the air to replace the other emissions not being spewed"].)

Perhaps there are other metrics for measuring sustainability rather than the car one drives. It is too easy to use the phrase 'sustainability' as a topical anaesthetic to dumb ourselves to the reality that almost every part of Westernised living is highly unsustainable, and that the very raison d'etre of our civilisation has been expansion through consumption. We might hope that it is otherwise, but as Ronald Wright observed in his study on the collapse of civilisations, "Hope, like greed, fuels the engine of capitalism" (Wright, 2004, p. 123).

Sustainability, like any political movement, benefits from aesthetic or visible codes that represent its ideological motivation. These aesthetic codes elicit emotional responses, some blatant and powerful, some subtle and somewhat weaker, but they exist nonetheless, Hitler used the swastika, Stalin the hammer and sickle, Chairman Mao managed to popularise appallingly bad olive drab clothing, and the environmentally self-conscious of the third millennium drive the Toyota Prius.

The Prius Effect

Perhaps another green celebrity, Julia Louis-Dreyfus, who played Elaine Benes in the successful television sitcom 'Seinfield', provides the best example of the Prius Effect. In one episode, a superficial TV executive, Russell Dalrimple, becomes so infatuated with Elaine that he joins Greenpeace in an attempt to win her affections after mistakenly overhearing that she is into environmentalists. Alas, Russell is lost at sea after being hit by a wanton whaling harpoon. By contrast, Elaine is elated to find she is free from his unwanted attentions (Griscom, 2004).

But there is more to this story. In the world that celebrities call reality, Julia Louis-Dreyfus and husband Brad Hall are outspoken environmentalists who remodeled their beach house as a case study in environmental responsibility. What began as an improvement to the living quarters ended up a tour de force of leading active and passive energy systems that are expected to pay for themselves in only 23 years. Like the Prius, this is a house that uses more and costs more in the interests of promoting the sustainable practice of others. In other words, it follows the automotive bloat law. As Brad acknowledges, "having a second home is itself an appalling excess, so we figured if we're going to do it, we better be as environmentally responsible as we can" (cited in Griscom, 2003, p. 1). They did however, have the forethought to donate the recyclable timber from the old house to a builders' exchange. To finish the picture they have not one, but two Prii(1) parked outside, so that Julia and Brad can maintain their independence (Griscom, 2004).

Louis-Dreyfus is a part of a group of prominent Hollywood women whose environmental concerns have brought them together as the Natural Resources Defence Council (NRDC). It may seem shallow, but the group has made much of the Prius over the Hummer as a platform for environmental responsibility. NRDC spokesperson, Laurie David (wife of Seinfeld co-creator, Larry David), recalls stopping her Prius in a School parking lot to accuse a Hummer-mum of putting children's lives at risk with her giant car (Bagley, 2004, p. 139). In a moment that makes Seinfeld look normal, Prius owner David managed to arrange a face-to-face meeting with Hummer driving Schwarzenegger, then Governor of California, to plead her case for allowing hybrid cars on commuter lanes. Afterwards she stated with conviction that, "Getting that man in a hybrid car would be one of our great victories [and] I'm not giving up on that hope" (David cited in Bagley, 2004, p. 140). Hope, it seems, springs eternal, but Arnold for his part, bless his heart, sold all but one of his eight-Hummer fleet and converted the remaining one to run on bio-diesel.

The emptiness of celebrities arguing over hybrids or SUVs is a point well illustrated by Howard Drake, the owner of a Hummer dealership in San Fernando Valley. He recalls a well-known actress who was concerned about the environment and thought she should buy a Prius. Drake asked her how big her house was, listened to her answer, and then replied, "I don't know what's less correct. Having three people live in a 20,000 square-foot house, with a pool and heaters and air-conditioning, or me driving my Hummer 500 miles a month" (Waxman, 2004, n.p.). And that, in a nutshell, is how we define the Prius Effect - the desire to appear and feel hopeful about the world even if ones actual impact on the earth is detrimental. The Prius Effect replaces guilt with hope.

Appropriately enough for their professions, Julia Louis-Dreyfus and Brad Hall are acting out a situation that in another context French philosopher Gaston Bachelard called the 'hut dream' – the desire to escape overcrowded houses and city problems to a 'real' refuge (Bachelard, 1964, p. 31). For Bachelard, that refuge was a psychological one available to all, but in an affluent society it is inevitable that the privileged replace philosophical escapes with physical sanctuaries to dilute their environmental guilt. It is the temptation to buy environmental salvation that has made the Toyota Prius the pin-up of energy efficient transportation, and it operates in at least two emotional ways: firstly, it alleviates the guilt of extravagant living, and secondly, it does not demand change. In the end, replacing a Hummer with a Prius alters the mode of transportation without challenging the rationalisation of transportation as a whole.

Automobile Society

Central to this debate is a fundamental impasse: Westernised society is synonymous with the car. Indeed, the automobile is a standard of westernised development, as the economic boom and explosion in car ownership in China is illustrating so comprehensively (Watts, 2003). Inevitably, the development of an automobile culture brings with it that other sign of westernised living - urban sprawl. As the proponents of New Urbanism have so vocally pointed out, the automobile is a mode of modern survival that makes the sprawl of the suburbs possible (Duany et al, 2000, p. 14).

In a treatise for New Urbanism, Duany, Plater-Zyberk and Speck observe that while a disproportionate number of suburban Americans visit Disneyland every year, very few of these visitors actually spend more than 3% of their Disney experience on the rides (Duany et al, 2000, p. 63). Confirming Jean Baudrillard's remark that Disneyland exists to persuade us the rest of America is real (Baudrillard, 1999, p. 34). Duany, et al., argue that the remaining 97% of their time in Disneyland is spent enjoying the qualities so lacking in the suburban neighbourhoods they live: "pleasant, pedestrian-friendly, public space and the sociability it engenders" (2000, p. 63). They conclude that in the modern suburb there is no reason to walk other than for exercise, and I might add that more often than not suburbanites find themselves driving to health clubs anyway. As one of the authors recently discovered, the availability of car parking is a major selling point in gym memberships.

Issues such as these were behind the decision of Michael Eisner, Disney CEO, to build the New Urbanist town of Celebration in Florida, so famously used as the set for the satirical movie The Truman Show. As Robert Beuka has shown, this film brought together the latest movements in American suburbanisation: the neo-traditionalism of New Urbanism, and the rising popularity of gated communities. He suggests that together they lead to social isolation, which in turn breeds a greater sense of fear as even more unidentifiable threats lie in the 'outside' world (Beuka, 2004, pp. 230-231). Austin has argued that in comparing Disneyland and Celebration there exists a paradox brought about by conflicting values of memory. Disneyland, he writes, works because it closes each day with fireworks, is serviced and cleaned overnight, and then starts afresh with a new group of visitors as if for the first time. By contrast, Celebration attempts to maintain an experience of timelessness with a permanent population as though memory can be made stable (Austin, 2005, p. 33).

Austin continues that Disneyland and Celebration are appositional in this regard, but it is also possible to consider these states as examples of the Prius Effect. As conditions of occupancy, Disneyland and Celebration create internal worlds in which new rules reset the parameters for guilt free living. As another French philosopher, Maurice Merleau-Ponty, put it, the outside has certain ways of invading us, we have certain ways of meeting this invasion, and memory serves the purpose of separating the framework of our perception of the outside from the actuality of that intrusion (1962, p. 317).

If Celebration is an example of how we might repel the assaults of suburban alienation, then Disneyland offers a temporary respite from the battle. Both are architectural examples of the Prius Effect. Following Merleau-Ponty's argument, both are instances where the creation of a new perception of reality is more important than reality itself. In Celebration and Disneyland there is a willing, indeed, wilful, forgetting of the larger world, just as the Prius owner prioritises the display of an environmental awareness over a reality of energy conservation.

Jurca has suggested that the temperament of suburbanites has long been characterized by qualities of alienation, anguish, and self-pity (2001, p. 161). A significant reason for suburban disillusionment might be the great distances suburbanites travel to link the disparate parts of their living (Duany et al, 2000). After all, what better place is there to build a persecution complex than the endless hours spent driving between the distant elements of a fractured world?

This was not something that worried Walt Disney however. One of the original rides from 1955 that is still operating today is Autopia; a miniature motorway on which Disney wanted children to learn to be better drivers. Today people drive to Disneyland, catch a shuttle from the car park to the theme park. Such paradoxes prompted Margaret J. King to describe Disneyland as traditional values disguised in futuristic form (King, 1981).

The House of the Future

Designed by MIT researchers, the House of the Future was conceived of as a genuine attempt to predict what form domesticity for future generations might be by making generous use of innovative plastics provided by the exhibit sponsor, Monsanto. The pristine white shell with its curved surfaces may not have been homely in a conventional sense but it certainly spoke of the future. There was plastic furniture, a working microwave oven, and a wall-mounted television for which actual working technology had not yet caught up. The future, Monsanto loudly declared, was synthetic.

During the 10 years that it was on display, millions toured the home touted as the archetypal house of 1987 (Scanlon, 2005). Through 1957 the exhibit was widely successful, with 60,000 people a week visiting, but while public opinion was favourable it was not enough to create a viable market. As Monsanto manager Robert Whittier recalls, "This is a pretty radical proposal for a very conservative housing market" (Whittier cited in Scanlon, 2005, n.p.).

A particularly novel feature was an air conditioning unit that offered the option of selecting a fragrance to accompany air distribution. With a choice of flowers, pine trees or sea air, the House of the Future was well equipped to banish any lingering odour from the plastic construction. Yet, beyond some new materials, and the promise of new technologies, and despite its' billing, the inside of the House of the Future was not as radical a domestic arrangement as many might have thought from the outside. Beneath the thin fibreglass shells lay regularly shaped rooms that replicated domestic conventions of the time. It may have looked unconventional, but in practice it was quite traditional.

Due largely to its association with Disneyland, the Monsanto House of the Future was never really taken seriously as a proposal. As Borden has observed, it was all too easy to dismiss it as fantasy (Borden, 2001). Tellingly, by 1967 it was deemed too 'old fashioned' to remain at the entrance to Tomorrowland despite no changes to the housing industry at large, and the decision was made to demolish it (McPherson, 2005). However, the House of the Future did have one last surprise. The wrecking ball brought in to tear it down bounced off the plastic shell and two weeks of laborious and expensive demolition was necessary to remove it. It is now known in Disney lingo as an 'extinct attraction'.

Unlike Celebration, Disney's House of the Future is not an example of the Prius Effect. While it captured popular imagination as a theme park exhibit, people did not see themselves living their lives in it. Following Merleau-Ponty's thinking, it lacked a memory for how we have lived, and importantly, it also lacked a garage. The House of the Future was not connected – neither physically nor symbolically – to Disney's triumph of future transportation: Autopia. It was as though the world of the future had split into those who drove continuously, and those who stayed at home.

To complicate matters further, five years after the installation of the House of the Future biologist and writer Rachel Carson first published *Silent Spring* (1962), a seminal study on the systemic effects of damage caused by chemical pesticides. This book is widely acknowledged as the beginning of the environmental movement, and in it she names Monsanto (among others) as a key benefactor in the million dollar pesticide industry. It would be some years before the image of Monsanto would be muddied by its association to Agent Orange and other chemicals used during the Vietnam War, but the House of the Future does become emblematic of a conflict between the values of healthy living and modern living. Indeed, one of the greater paradoxes that can be found with hindsight in Carson's writing concerns the suburbs. More than a decade before Vietnam would be sprayed with harmful defoliants, American suburbanites had been liberally dosing their own front lawns with related chemical compounds to remove crabgrass (Carson, 2002, pp. 146-147). Disney's House of the Future did not have a front lawn, and this made it even harder to present a desirable image of suburban hope. As architectural theorist Beatriz Colomina has observed, "The lawn is a medical hazard and yet the lawn stands for health: mental and physical" (Colomina, 2007, p. 107).

Dilbert's Ultimate House

Someone not known for his optimism is Dilbert, a fictional character of the syndicated cartoon series of the same name. An engineer eternally trapped within a hopelessly ineffectual bureaucracy, Dilbert stumbles from one psychotic workmate to the next in an endless cycle of inefficiency that many find humorously familiar.

But in 2004, as though to compensate him for the desperate existence he leads, Dilbert's creator, Scott Adams, announced his intention to build Dilbert a virtual home, calling on fans to contribute ideas for its development. As Adams wrote in a latter press release: "Dilbert is single and needs the all the help he can get ... We wanted him to have a house so impressive that some woman would overlook his personality just to live in it" (Adams, 2005).

This sardonic tone was integrated into the DUH project as a number of additions to the standard house. 'Innovations' included; a storage closet for a fake Christmas tree so that it could be wheeled out every December, a urinal in Dilbert's en-suite, a basketball court in the basement, and a bathroom for children that can be hosed down. Externally, the most obvious feature of the 'unusual' is the observatory shaped like Dilbert's head. By September 2005 Dilbert's Ultimate House- known as 'DUH' was online as a fully realised digital model.

While Scott has established himself as a satirist of office life, it would be a mistake to dismiss this project as simply an elaborate joke. The original specification, issued by Scott on the Dilbert web site, made a point of emphasising zero energy usage, green building materials and healthy air quality. Its ideological framework is therefore consistent with sustainable building practices. The point of this in a virtual domain is perplexing – what gain is there from an energy saving design that does actually use any more energy than it takes to run a computer? Yet the specification is quite specific on this point. The house is orientated for maximum solar energy gain, the roof has PV panels, the walls use structural insulated panels, windows are double glazed, and so on (Adams, 2005). The full room specification goes so far as to provide hyperlinks to actual suppliers, and it is at this point that the ideological undercurrent of the DUH is visible. The DUH project is a showcase of all those features that Adams feels others should be integrating into their homes in the interests of responsible living.

Unlike Disney's House of the Future, Dilbert's Ultimate House does not rely on future technologies or lifestyles. DUH utilises current technologies that are readily available, and this is why a virtual house is so effective – it need not prove itself. Anyone interested in some part of the proposed material fabrication of the house can follow a hyperlink to a real supplier for his or her own needs. In this way the virtual house is more a virtual shop providing information, links, and, most importantly, inspiration on available healthy home products. But we should not confuse responsible specification with responsible living. After all, DUH also contains a home theatre, three-car garaging, and a golf practice area.

Like the Prius, DUH promotes a model of responsible living that does not ask that any thing be given up, not even ones bourgeois aspirations. This is where the House of the Future got it so wrong. As a part of Disneyland, the seriousness in the MIT designed house was undermined by the fantasy environment it was a part of. Visitors had fully expected to find a home whose design and fittings were completely foreign, but the familiar aspects meant that they would return to their suburban houses comfortable in the knowledge that the future was not all that weird. The DUH project does exactly the opposite. Its sustainability message rides in on the back of a much-loved graphic character whose popularity is found in the way others identify with him. The project invited the ideas of Dilbert's fans and so presented itself as a democratic rather than autocratic approach to future living. It then integrated available rather than promised technologies, thereby making it possible for others to make smaller changes to their own homes. And finally it did all this without suggesting for a moment that it might be environmentally undesirable to have ones own swimming pool, or home gym, or a 'quiet room' where you can escape the bustle of your own home.

Conclusion

Like the Prius, Dilbert's Ultimate House makes overtures to sustainable living that do not challenge how we have been living, but while it makes the idea of sustainable practices more palatable, it also perpetuates westernised lifestyles that have been at the forefront of environmental degradation. It may be that Disney's House of the Future becomes more prophetic than anyone expected; the failure of a vision for the future to read true has about it the same hollowness as making dream homes sustainable.

In conclusion, it is suggested that architecture like the automobile is also bound by the automotive industry's 'Bloat Law' and that we continue to add more and more in order to achieve less and less. We replace ever-increasing guilt with ever-increasing hope. This we submit is the underlying driver for the Prius Effect.

This chapter was first published as *The 'House of the Future' and the Toyota Prius – Looking to the Future of Sustainable* Housing in 2006 in the proceedings of the 40th Annual Conference of the Architectural Science Association ANZAScA.

Dr Henry Skates is a Senior Lecturer in Architecture the Griffith School of Environment, Griffith University, Gold Coast, Australia.

Dr Peter Wood is a Senior Lecturer in the School of Architecture, Victoria University of Wellington, New Zealand.

Endnotes
1. Prii is Toyota's preferred plural of Prius.

References

Adams, S. (2005). Dilbert's ultimate house. Retrieved from www.dilbert.com/comics/dilbert/duh/press_release.html

Adams, S. (2005). Original specs. Retrieved from www.dilbert.com/comics/dilbert/duh/specslindex.html

Austin, M. (2005). Celebration with some mention of Napier. In *Celebration: XXII Annual Conference of the Society of Architectural Historians, Australia and New Zealand* (pp. 31-34). Napier, New Zealand.

Bachelard, G. (1964). *The poetics of space.* Boston, Massachusetts: Beacon Press.

Bagley, C. (2004). The naturals. *W Magazine*, pp. 138-40.

Baudrillard, J. (1999). Truth or radicality? the future of architecture. *Blueprint 157*(1), 30-35.

Beuka, R. (2004). *SuburbiaNation.* New York: Palgrave Macmillan.

Borden, G. P. (2001). The house of tomorrow for today. *The Independent Weekly.*

Cambron, M. (2006). Gig spotlight: a chat with Will Wright. Retrieved from ww.gignews.com/goddess_wright

Carson, R. (2002). *Silent spring.* New York: Houghton Mifflin Harcourt.

Chan, David. (2003). The philosophy of the sims. Retrieved from http://web.stanford.edu/group/htgg/cgi-bin/drupal/sites/default/files2/dchan_2003_1.pdf

Colomina, B. (2007). *Domesticity at war.* Cambridge Massachusetts: The MIT Press.

CNW Marketing Research. (2006). Dust to dust: the energy costs of new vehicles from concept to disposal. Retrieved from www.cnwmr.com/nss-folder/automotiveenergy

Duany, A., Plater-Zyberk, E., & Speck, J. (2000). *Suburban nation: the rise of sprawl and the decline of the American dream.* New York: North Point Press.

Dykes A. L. (2012). Review: 2012 Toyota Prius c. *The Truth About Cars.* Retrieved from http://www.thetruthaboutcars.com/2012/04/review-2012-toyota-prius-c/

Foreman-McLean, J. (2006). An interview with Will Wright. *Gamasutra.* Retrieved from http://www.gamasutra.com/view/feature/134754/the_replay_interviews_will_wright.php?print=1

Gonzalo, F. W. (2001). The sims: grandmothers are cooler than trolls. *Game studies: The International Journal of Computer Game Research. 1*(1).

Griscom, A. (2003, April 10). At home with: Julia Louis-Dreyfus and Brad Hall; a house that any tree would hug. *The New York Times*, sec. F.1.

Griscom, A. (2004). Comfortably conscientious. *Mother Earth News, 205*(7), p. 34.

Jurca, C. (2001). *White diaspora: the suburb and the twentieth-century novel.* Princeton and Oxford: Princeton University Press.

King, M. J. (1981). Disneyland and Walt Disney world: traditional values in futuristic form. *Journal of Popular Culture, 15*(1), 116-40.

McPherson, C. G. (n.d). The house of the future. Retrieved from www.plasticliving.com/hotf/f.html

Merleau-Ponty, M. (1962). *Phenomenology of perception.* (Smith, C., Trans.). London: Routledge and Kegan Paul.

Sexton S., & Sexton A. (2011). Conspicuous conservation: the prius effect and willingness to pay for environmental bona fides. Retrieved from http://www.works.bepress.com/sexton/11

Scanlon, L. (2005). The house of the future that wasn't. *MIT Technology Review.* Retrieved from http://www.technologyreview.com/article/403523/the-house-of-the-future-that-wasnt/

Watts, J. (2003, August 18). China takes to capitalist road with a vengeance. *Guardian Unlimited.*

Waxman, S. (2004, March 7). WA Prius-Hummer war divides oscarville. *Los Angeles Times*, pp. 1-3.

Wood P. & Skates H. (2006). The 'house of the future' and the Toyota Prius – looking to the future of sustainable housing. In *Proceedings of the 40th Annual Conference of the Architectural Science Association: Challenges for architectural science in changing climates*. Adelaide, Australia: The University of Adelaide.

Wright, R. (2004). *A short history of progress*. Melbourne: Text Publishing.

CHAPTER FOURTEEN

SUSTAINABLE FASHION: FROM ORGANIC FORM TO DIGITALLY MANMADE PATTERN

Fanke Peng & Peter Hill

Introduction

Sustainable practices for fashion designers include a wide range of issues. Design strategies encompass using new technologies to save energy and materials in production, reducing return rate in e-commerce and m-commerce, and encouraging participation and inclusion of consumer and designer awareness and knowledge about the environment and social impacts of fashion/textile products. In addition, there are other phases of the life cycle of products, according to the fashion supply chain, that need examination. The fashion supply chain is diverse and complex, encompassing a number of tiers, including design, raw material harvesting, spinning, yarn production, dyeing, weaving, cutting, stitching, final garment construction and sales. It can incorporate handcraft and cottage workers, as well as high-volume technology, intensive facilities (Boone, 2012).

This project utilised the unique role of the Fashion Digital Studio (FDS) at the London College of Fashion, (LCF), UK. FDS is at the forefront of these developing trends and has been examining how such social and technological innovations will define the coming 'collective' fashion landscape and backdrop.

At FDS, emerging designers and researchers use digital print and 3D printing to their full potential, throughout a wide range of applications. They are also beginning to combine 3D scanning, plus additive manufacturing (AM) and digital print with generative design, to create a new digital pattern. The authors have witnessed these efforts, and helped many designers and design students, whose primary medium is not specifically software/digital media. Design processes, harnessed through the medium of 3D scanning, 3D CAD, digital printing and 3D printing, allow designers to generate increasingly complex visual forms otherwise unimaginable, let alone capable of delineation.

Designing a 2D textile pattern often involves a very different sensibility from that inherent in pure 3D printing/AM, in terms of the design thinking and the design process. In this chapter, the authors examine design's rootedness in nature, as well as defining the organic form and digital design process for pattern design. The chapter is organised into six sections: design's rootedness in nature, defining organic form and its application in AM, towards a new approach to digital fashion design, methods and methodologies, ending with discussion and a conclusion. The first two sections set the context, by defining terms and introducing basic concepts. The methods and methodologies used are intrinsic to action research and generative design. Each stage in the digital design process is firstly classified, and then continues with software, equipment and applications in the current market, to clarify and evaluate the potential of digital design at each stage. The chapter concludes with illustrated examples of 3D prototypes.

Design's rootedness in nature

Can it be said that all design originally comes from nature and can be understood by observing nature? If so, what is meant by the term, nature? It seems likely that sociologists, historians, theologians, environmental theorists, cultural theorists and art theorists, along with philosophers have, over the years, studied various aspects of humanity's relationship with nature (Marshall, 2002). It should be understood, however, that it is not necessary to be a philosopher or theorist, to understand the theory and secret of nature. The secret is hidden within nature and can only be found by seeing with the heart and practising with hands (Cumming, 2007).

Designers/makers work closely with nature, having their own ways of seeing, which help them to explore the theory of nature and express it in their design practice. Although essential points may be invisible to the eye, it is difficult, if not impossible, to get close to the designers/ makers' intention without careful observation. 'When the power to see does not accompany the power to know – when the power to see is blunted – art historians, critics, and collectors all fall into the same kind of confusion' (Yanagi, 1972, p. 111).

McHarg (1995) demonstrates in *Design with nature*, how humans can copy examples of nature to design and build better structures. Irwin (2007) considers both the biological and environmental principles that govern the natural world and develops meta-level principles that can be used as the basis for sustainable/ecological design. She argues (2007) that human-made forms must follow the same processes and life cycles as natural forms, in order to be in harmony with nature.

Design's rootedness in nature places a greater emphasis on designers' relationship and participation with nature to create a direct experience. This holistic relationship between design and nature can be understood in terms of 'functional - form' and 'expressive -form'. Functional-form connects nature with design's form, materials and techniques. Risatti argues that all, "design/craft's basic forms, basic materials, and basic techniques existed everywhere in nature" (2007, p. 62). If we examine the facts – we find that form in nature is conveyed not so much by the 'geometric-technical' properties of the percept as such, but by the forces they can be assumed to arouse in the nervous system of the observer (Risatti, 2007). Therefore, a designer looks at the forms and patterns in nature, not only intending to concentrate on the 'geometric-technical' qualities of what he/she sees but also to contemplate the expressive qualities. The concentration merely on 'geometric form', without the understanding of 'expressive qualities', is but an imitation of the form in terms of the exact length and direction of contour lines, the relative position of points and the shape of masses. Only when the expressive qualities are married to the geometrical qualities, can a designer communicate his/her experience with nature in his/her visual work (Risatti, 2007; Lane, 2003).

Defining organic form and its application to additive manufacturing

> "It inspired us to design algorithms that could map physical movement and material behavior to geometrical form and morphological variation in a seamless and continuous wearable surface" – Neri Oxman

In this chapter the authors define organic form as being the forms and spatial structures of any living thing in nature. Numerous designers study and adopt organic form extensively in their practice. As mentioned earlier, good design practice combines functional and expressive form.

AM boosts designers'/pioneers' practice and offers exciting digital advantages, by blending organic forms with algorithms and new materials, to define new patterns, forms and possibilities. The pioneers printed various 3D prototypes, including shoes and seamlessly manufactured dresses, to tissue and organs. Anthony Atala (2011) demonstrated an early-stage experiment that may someday resolve the organ-donor problem: a 3D printer that uses living cells to output a transplantable kidney. Van Herpen and Julia Koerner (2013) presented 3D-printed dresses as part of their runway show at the Paris Fashion Week. The structure of garments uses multiple layers of thin, woven lines to, "animate the body in an organic way" (Oxman, Herpen & Koerner, 2013).

Bohnacker, Gross and Laub (2010) define generative design as being a revolutionary new method of creating artwork, models and animation, from sets of rules or algorithms. As design educators, the authors see great potential for generative design (GD) in a design process. There are many good GD practices already in existence in various design disciplines, such as architecture, product design, sculpture, type design, as well as graphic and interaction design. GD also has the potential to be a suitable design method for digital fashion, as it fills the gap between the code and image in a holistic way (Bohnacker, Gross & Laub, 2010). Firstly, combining generative design and 3D technology, the organic form generated by 3D scanning can be repeated and rescaled while printing coded graphics. Generative Design provides a holistic approach to learning the organic forms of nature and creates that which is more likely to integrate with many creative processes.

Defining the digital fashion process: stages and technologies in the digital design process

	Stages in the design process	Equipment, Software and application
Input	Capture it / 3D Scan	Focus on low-cost equipment and applications, such as Autodesk 123D catch and Next Engine desktop 3D scanner
	Modelling / 3D Design	3Ds Max Grasshopper Processing
Output	Make it / Rapid prototyping & Direct Manufacturing 1. 3D to 2D 2. 3D to 3D	2D Digital fabric printing 3D printing
	Present it	Virtual try on (VTO) apps

Table 1: Stages and technologies in the digital design process.

This research divides the digital design process into four main stages. They are capture (input), model (input), prototype (output) and presentation & evaluation (output). Both stages in the input phase have been examined and evaluated in terms of various 3D scanning equipment, processing and modelling approaches (repetition, transformation, parameterisation and simulation). The two stages in the output phase will be examined in a future study.

In order to review the entire design process, different stages in the digital design process have been identified and classified, which sets the ground for examining the new types of design freedom in fashion design. Low-cost 3D scanners were adopted, along with 3Ds Max, 2D digital printing and 3D printing, so as to create new dimensions and solutions, which are only possible using computerised modelling and programming tools. It is this exciting digital advantage, which has paved the way for digital innovation in fashion. The four types of coding (repetition, transformation, parameterisation and distribution) are presented with the aim of explaining how a single geometric 'cell' could be processed and transformed, as 3D modelling becomes more accessible for manipulation. "The continuous 3D environment from input to output should reduce the time from design to realization, and the reduction of waste material, logistical issues and the consequent reduction of environmental impact could be significant" (Delamore, 2004).

The research team is enthused about the potential for capturing from low-cost mobile phone applications. Being able to manipulate and transform an organic form digitally, means that incorporating 3D modelling and printing into textile and fashion design is now much more sympathetic to the nature of growing processes. The author's aim is that this chapter will inspire design professionals and students to think further about the organic form and GD in their design practice.

Capture it: 3D scanning

A series of 3D organic forms (leaves and flowers) were scanned to test the qualities and capacity of the low-cost 3D scanners currently available on the market. 3D scanning technology has been rapidly developed over the last two decades. At the FDS, we have a wide range of 3D scanning equipment, including TC2 3D body scanning, a foot scanner, iFashion hand scanners, Kinect and a Next Engine desktop 3D scanner. The scanners are suitably adapted for different applications. Through the years of experience in developing size and fitting applications for fashion e-commerce, the authors have built tangible and intangible knowledge of 3D body scanning. For this study, the focus is not on specialist high-cost equipment but on low-cost equipment and applications. The concern is not with a body-scaled object but a small and delicate object. As a result, an Autodesk 123D catch and a Next Engine desktop 3D scanner have been selected for this pilot study, due to their affordability and portability.

To use 123D Catch, it is possible to use an iPhone, iPad, Web or desktop app, to upload the photographs onto the Autodesk cloud, where they are converted into realistic 3D models. In this case, the researchers and designers used an iPhone to take 20-40 photographs sequentially of a stationary subject (leaves and flowers), before the photographs were uploaded to the Autodesk cloud. In order to compare the visual quality, a desktop 3D scanner has been used to scan the same leaves and flowers.

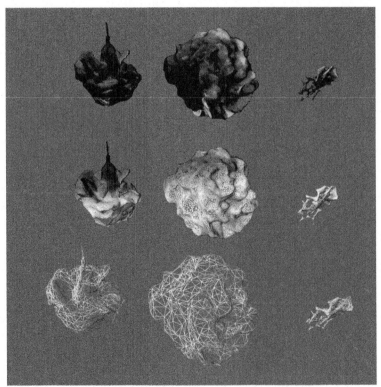

Figure 1: 3D scanning images and polygon mesh.

Visualisation and modelling – repeat, transform, parameterise and distribute

After digitising all the samples of organic forms by using 3D scanning applications and equipment, the next stage in the digital design process is modelling and visualising. The 3D forms (Polygon mesh and density of points) generated by 123D catch and Next Engine first need to be tidied up, to remove the noise (such as any background which has been captured) and repair the holesin the mesh (see Figure 1). In order to achieve a refined and polished form, 3Ds Max was used.

Pattern-making involves drawing the same shape over and over again or producing a group of related, self-similar shapes. Programming languages in 3Ds Max can repeat any action infinitely. When one repetition sequence is embedded within another, the effect multiplies. This simple technique can be used to explore many patterns. While this type of repetition makes a predictable pattern, adding a small amount of randomness to the shape/form lengths, sizes, degrees of rotation, can produce apparently organic forms (see Figure 2).

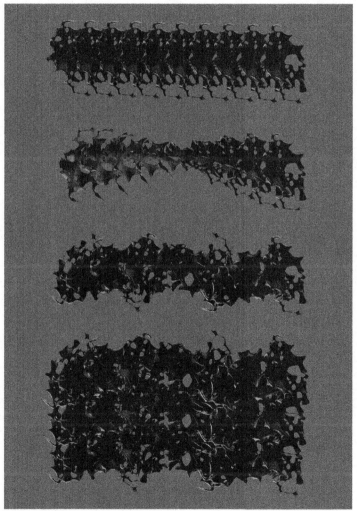

Figure 2: Image generated by repetition sequence.

The digitalised forms generated by 3D scanning can be a rich source of data. Transcoding and parameters can be used to interpret this data from a different perspective (Reas & McWilliams, 2010).

The designers can contemplate how a group of these objects might combine to create a larger form, rather than just the individual objects – in this case a leaf. The rotation of each leaf is linked to the rotations of those adjacent. This type of parameterisation lends itself to the creation of complex patterns. The pattern begins with a row of leaves, each slightly rotated at a random angle. At first, the rotations proceed clockwise but to avoid overlap, the direction reverses, if the new rotation value is too large or small. This creates a dimensional surface that the programme slowly turns, to present it from infinite angles.

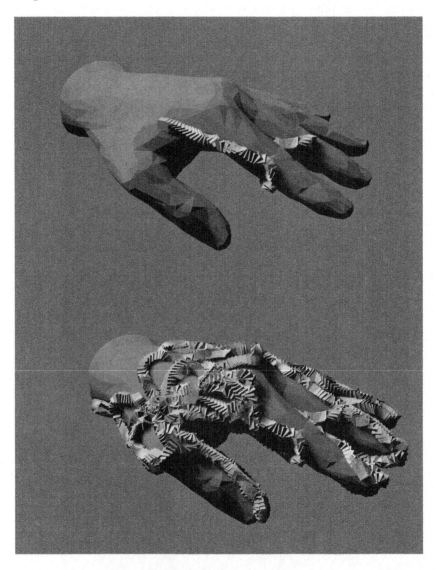

Figure 3: Two examples of a distribution object (hand) by using particle systems, which distribute an instanced geometric shape across each triangular face, edge or vertices, which defines the shape of the distribution object in 3D computer graphics.

Grow your own organic pattern on the body

The traditional method of making a form or sewing 2D patterns to fit the body is bypassed. This innovative approach requires a 3D design environment to be developed, in which designers can scatter and distribute a single organic form across the surface of an avatar or a body-scan. The pattern would, thus, grow along a distribution object, move through space or stick together, on colliding (see Figure 3). The form is built up over time, as more and more particles collide and gather together. The aggregated form often has a complex structure.

The basic pattern is created by making multiple copies of a simple form. Each scanned 3D form retains specific data regarding its exact position in space, speed and the rate at which its speed is increasing or decreasing. At each stage in the distribution process, every form calculates its next position, by means of its present location, speed and rate of variation in the speed. Finally, each organic form is drawn to the polygon surface of the distribution object, which can be divided into different numbers of vertices, edges and polygon faces. 3D scanning and 3D design enable a direct construction in a 3D environment, by maintaining and transforming data and design, between a 3D organic form and a 3D body-scan.

This research is exploring a process for generating organic forms from a few simple rules. Repetition, transcoding, parameterisation and distribution, can combine to produce a variety of dynamic visual effects and depending on the source and perspectives, can often reveal interesting patterns for both the digital fabric printing and 3D printing.

A series of organic patterns have been created in the prototyping stages. The prototypes will be further tested in a future study, to explore the digital presentation and its application to garment design. The digital design process generated in this research project will be further tested and developed-at LCF, in order to explore its potential for design education in digital fashion.

Conclusion

In this chapter, the approach to sustainable design is pursued through a strategy of digital innovation and technology. The focus is on improving the fashion product's footprint through design, developing the interface between digital innovation and design, and optimising digital aesthetics, design enhancement and convergence. This research examines design's rootedness in nature, defines organic forms and their application in the additive manufacturing (AM) and verifies a new digital approach to pattern design. This proposed innovative approach aims to achieve new types of design enhancement, which AM and generative design (GD) enables fashion professionals and designers to embed in their design process. Thus, we consider how an existing low-cost 3D scanner can be used to capture organic form and how to further process the forms for AM, by using 3D CAD. This proposed innovative, yet principled approach, is to offer a framework to define, verify and explain the designer's approach towards digital innovation and digital aesthetics for sustainable fashion.

Dr Fanke Peng is an experienced interactive media designer and researcher. She originally trained as a Fashion Designer and Interactive Media designer. She holds a PhD in Interaction Design and Visual Communication. She has been heavily involved in extensive research projects in the UK and is currently based at the University of Canberra.

Peter Hill is a 3D artist and designer with a professional background in motion graphics, interface design and fashion illustration. His research interests are in real-time 3D for print design and online experience. He lectures on web design, fashion graphics and 3D for the Fashion Media Production MA and the Digital Fashion MA at the Fashion Digital Studio, London College of Fashion.

References

Atala, A. Printing a human kidney. Retrieved from http://www.ted.com/talks/anthony_atala_printing_a_human_kidney.html, 2013

Bohnacker, H., Gross, B. & Laub, J. (2010). *Generative design: visualize, program, and create with processing*. New York: Princeton Architectural Press.

Boone, T. (2012, July 17). Fashion industry: a story of consumption and waste. Retrieved from http://www.rediff.com/money/slide-show/slide-show-1-special-fashion-industry-a-story-of-consumption-and-waste/20120717.htm

Bloch, M. (1998). *How we think they think: anthropological approaches to cognition, memory and literacy*. Oxford: West View.

Cumming, E. (2007). Hand, heart and soul: the arts and crafts movement in Scotland, UK: Birlinn Ltd.

Delamore, P. (2004). *3D printed textiles and personalised clothing*. London: The University of the Arts.

Donald, L. (2010). *Mind the gap – an advanced practice model for the understanding and development of fine craft*. (Doctoral dissertation). Retrieved from http://discovery.dundee.ac.uk/portal/files/1306937/Donald_phd_2012.pdf

Dormer, P. (1997). *The culture of craft: status and future*. Manchester, UK; New York: Manchester University Press.

Dresser, C. (1978). *Development of ornamental art in the international exhibition*. New York, Garland Publishing.

Edgerton, S. Y. (1976). *The renaissance rediscovery of linear perspective*. New York; London: Harper and Row.

Irwin T. (2007). *A curriculum for sustainable design: principles from holistic science*. University of Dundee.

Lane, P. (2003). *Ceramic form: design & decoration*. New York: Rizzoli.

Marshall, A. (2002). *The unity of nature: wholeness and disintegration in ecology and science*. London: Imperial College Press.

McHarg, I. L. (1995). *Design with nature*. London: John Wiley & Sons.

Oxman, N., Herpen, I. V. & Koerner, J. (2013, January 22). *Wearable stratasys and materialise 3D printed pieces hit Paris fashion week at Iris van Herpen show*. Retrieved from http://www.materialise.com/press/wearable-stratasys-and-materialise-3d-printed-pieces-hit-paris-fashion-week-at-iris-van-herpen

Reas, C. & McWilliams, C. (2010). *Form+code in design, art, and architecture (Design Briefs)*. New York: Princeton Architectural Press.

Reason, P. & Bradbury, H. (Eds.). (2008). *The SAGE handbook of action research: participative inquiry and practice*. London: Sage Publications Ltd.

Risatti, H. (2007). *A theory of craft: function and aesthetic expression*. Chapel Hill: University of North Carolina Press.

Yanagi, S. E. & Leach, B. (1989). *The unknown craftsman: a Japanese insight into beauty*. Tokyo, London: Kodansha International.

CHAPTER FIFTEEN

THE ORDINARY AS A PRECEDENT FOR SUSTAINABILITY IN ARCHITECTURE

Martina Novakova & Tony Lam

The architecture we encounter today tends towards the overt, the exaggerated and the pronounced. The mere mention of ordinary stimulates defiant recoil (Berke, 1997) – we should be as extraordinary as the times and our place in history dictates. Accompanying this energetic propulsion into the unknown is the potential risk of an indiscriminate disregard for the natural environment. Set aside for a moment this desire for expression, and consider that perhaps what society needs is not wanton excess, but rather something more restrained, more innate, something which resonates more deeply and honestly with the human condition – something more ordinary.

The architecture of the ordinary is informed by the everyday, and the vernacular, which is typically associated with ecological sensitivity and sustainability. Often developed out of local customs, which carry an inherent reverence for nature and its tentative capacity to meet human needs, vernacular buildings typify oneness with the natural environment. They epitomise such architectural ideals as those commonly referred to by preeminent architectural theoreticians ranging from Marcus Vitruvius to Christopher Alexander and Bernard Rudofsky (AlSayyad & Arboleda, 2011) such as hyper contextualism, wholeness, pragmatism and ecological efficiency.

More recently however, the validity of this belief is under threat with these typified traditional communities now experiencing unprecedented pressures imposed by global, social, economic, geographical, political and environmental shifts which are occurring faster today than ever before (AlSayyad & Arboleda, 2011). As a result these communities have resorted to more modern means of building, which meet the increased demands imposed by these pressures, however, sadly at the expense of their traditional concerns for the environment.

In response to this drawn out departure, an aesthetic that is inspired by the ordinary, everyday and banal (Danto, 1981) is beginning to develop amongst artists and architects which captures the sustainable principles encapsulated by vernacular architecture, but which simultaneously responds to present socio-political pressures and concerns.

In the 1980s, Swiss architect and theorist Martin Steinmann used the words "simple" and "ordinary" to describe new architecture (1980). Steinmann's use of the word "ordinary" referred to architecture which was based on symbols that referenced the ordinary. An important feature of this architecture was present in its use of trivial materials which held the possibility of inducing mood and thus becoming the holder of meanings. This resulted in the genesis of a new and unusual approach in architecture which was most clearly evidenced in the work of architects such as Robert and Roger Diener, Adolf Krischanitz, Peter Zumthor, Annette Gigon and Mike Guyer, Peter Märkli and many others. Steinmann considers the sudden emphasis placed on the existing surroundings, the absolute connection between forms and objects that were determined by the environment, as crucial components informing the birth of the new architecture (Steinmann, 2003).

Particular to this new architecture is an incisive effort to discover new qualities hidden within the known, everyday, vernacular products and materials, and then through their reinterpretation, to extract and display these qualities. This tendency manifested itself in the mundane commissions these architects received from local clients, which included storage houses, social housing developments and family houses in anonymous suburban settings. The buildings that resulted from these commissions were often consciously filled with references to their everydayness (Wang, 1992, p. 7).

This is demonstrated in an office building from Diener and Diener, where they produced work which resembled investor driven architecture. Adolf Krischanitz was known for his commissioned remodelling of the gaunt row housing on the outskirts of a city, while Herzog and de Meuron received mundane commissions which included houses located "in the middle of an area defined by a concentration of average family houses, in the architectural nothingness," as well as the cladding of an old warehouse in an industrial area (Strathaus, 1998, p. 8). The inevitable and ordinary reality of the surroundings, was not only accepted, but also served as an originator for their respective artistic profiles (Steinmann, 1990, p. 83). By ignoring major theoretical and ideological streams, these architectural offices referenced their architecture directly from the banal and ordinary things requisite of everyday life.

They commonly developed their architectural ideas from unattractive, secondary, drama-less, ordinary everyday images, or from mundane elements found in the contextual environment. Ordinary things such as the physical context along with the limitations imposed by building materials, the site and the building programme, once again became an important impetus in the architects' work. An important moment occurs in the transformation of everyday life into something of an artistic quality (Danto, 1981).

This artistic quality systematically resulted from a modern understanding of production, tectonic density and strength of composition. It also demonstrates a strong recognition for local conditions as well as a confident and critical approach to the modern avant-garde (Hays, 1991). It responds to the desire for purity and truth and often reinstates a repressed social and cultural reality. These collectively reaffirm an aesthetic position which values a similar set of environmentally sustainable principles as those inherent within vernacular architecture, whilst also being sensitive to its present historical context.

The aesthetic of this architecture can be characterised by a single key desire for concreteness and reality. The immediate consequence of this desire is an explicit absence of style. The architecture it creates possesses an inherent aversion to the extraneous and the superimposed, precisely the wastage generated by trends and commercial movements grown through an irreverence towards reality and material preciousness. This is a characteristic also commonly associated with the vernacular as outlined in Ivan Illich's definition of the term "everything in the Roman domus made for domestic consumption and not for market is vernacular" (as cited in Frey & Bouchain, 2010, p. 45). In other words: the "Vernacular is whatever stands peripheral to or outside the global flows of capital and everything that, willingly or not, escapes the control of these flows" (Frey & Bouchain, 2010, p. 45). Exactly the same can be said of ordinariness. Common features of this "ordinary" architecture may be either subtle or explicit, and will generally fall within the following three most commonly recurring characteristics: site appropriate and climate responsive expression, architecture with a material focus and architecture with a socio-economic focus.

Socio-economic focus

Architecture with a socio economic focus begins with architects in whose work is demonstrated a clear and successful tendency towards ordinariness. Most of these architects had a close affiliation with the Swiss Federal Institute of Technology (ETH) Zürich and entered the professional architectural field in the late 1970s and early 1980s. Their ideas were strongly influenced by the neo-rationalist theories of Aldo Rossi as well as the neo-realist theories and vernacular of Robert Venturi and Denise Scott Brown. The context within which these architects met however, was not Rossi's city (Rossi, 1982). In addition to Swiss modernism, where they saw their roots, there was a periphery, which served as an additional reference point, which lay somewhere between the anonymous landscape of everyday life and the vernacular. This second reference point became more prevalent in their work since their designs did not usually deal with city centres (Tschanz, 1995, p. 88).

Unlike some of their colleagues who turned away from the architectural nothingness of the periphery turning instead to internal private worlds, some architects in Europe, as did Robert Venturi (Venturi 1966; Venturi, Brown & Izenour, 1977) in the United States, tried to take the periphery seriously and sought to utilise its "discrete charm". What they were looking for were not design rules, but rather images, impressions of the random and seemingly accidental. They found inspiration in films and literary works, where the protagonists roamed the wilderness of the endless suburbs common in big cities, or established homes in large industrial areas (Tschanz, 1995, p. 88).

Within the periphery they tried to solve socio-economic issues and react to the current sociocultural shifts and impulses. They preferred ordinary commissions such as social housing at the edges of cities, auxiliary infrastructure, park houses, warehouses and ordinary family houses over prestigious projects in city centres. In dealing with housing, these architects sought to solve the question of how to regulate the relationship between the individual and others in these conditions, which traditionally did not afford the individual with any reasonable private space external to the living unit (Steinmann, 1988). By assigning this importance to the peripheral zones of the city, these architects acknowledged the concept of a broader sustainable agenda, which encompasses communities and their long-term viability to meet the needs of a growing population.

Materials

The architecture of the periphery is characterised by inexpensive, everyday materials such as corrugated steel, plywood and various synthetic materials. Collectively, these materials are used to convey an atmosphere and aura of randomness and temporariness. The architects typically favour vernacular, forgotten, worthless materials such as roughly cast in situ concrete, PVC panels as well as semiproducts from hardware stores, roofing felt, nylon mesh or ordinary fencing. The familiar yet unconventional nature of these materials makes it easier to discover the sensorial quality of the selected construction methods in a new and impartial manner. It is not primarily an image of a shed or a hut and temporary buildings, which they intend to draw attention to, but rather the surprising and often hidden sensuous qualities of the materials used for these structures (Steinmann, 1994).

The possibility for new interpretations of everyday materials and construction methods occurs with the advent of societal and economical change. The proportional cost of materials in relation to the overall structure has declined, and a growing range of transport options and new technologies, have led to a significant depreciation of the perceived value of many "precious" materials. Price does not seem to factor in the decision making for or against the use of a luxury timber, special bricks or exotic tiles. Natural stone in all colours and patterns are now available in remote corners of the world, taken for granted, and are expected even on the facades of office buildings in the suburbs, just as the marble bathroom has become a standard feature in the houses of the middle class (Tschanz, 1995, p. 88). As a result, the use of simple and seemingly poor material or conventional construction is a method of differentiation from this phenomenon. Plywood and bitumen moved into houses, design studios and fashion boutiques, and perhaps soon, to the lobbies of international banks (Tschanz, 1995). The value therefore is no longer expressed through materials and products in and of themselves, but purely through the conscious hand of the architect. This has nothing to do with the quality of architectural details, but rather the ability to recognise and consider the optical, tactile, acoustic, olfactory potential and full range of inherent design possibilities of the material. This allows new materials, products and construction methods, as well as those with which we are already familiar from everyday life, to appear in unusual and often surprising contexts, which brings new and fascinating ways of seeing (Tschanz, 1995).

These architects, by instilling the habit and ability to extract the intrinsic physical and symbolic qualities of a material, create the opportunity for delight with otherwise mundane means. In so doing the act of architecture becomes inherently supportive of the environment. Waste materials suddenly become attractive and local materials precious. This drastically minimises the embodied energy of the building by largely eliminating the cost of logistics, as well as helping to sustain the local industry, which has obvious benefits for the sustainability of the community.

Expression

In accepting readily available materials within the local building industry and adopting a playful approach to their deployment, these architects create a disaffected architectural language, which interestingly has subsequently resulted in numerous commissions. Their critical approach avoids the need to create unique architecture –which results in unnecessary and expensive solutions – while still enabling them to be presented as important, avant-garde architects in the global architectural scene. By adopting a supply of materials commonly available from "off the shelf" and an explicit intention to reduce the buildings expressive possibilities, these architects focus on revealing the architecture intrinsically.

The distinct lack of gestures and meanings provides many of these buildings with an almost ascetic quality. Unlike their ideologically influenced predecessors, these architects are beginning to respond to the realities of randomness and site specificity, where the programmes associated with conventional models are interpreted in a new and organic way. Their work takes into account the following areas: "special nature of the detail, the aura of the material, the static and constructive parts" (Kapfinger, 1993, p. 16). The aim of these interventions is moderation in the detail, in order to allow the favouring of new spatial qualities. Adolf Krischanitz – along with many other architects – invite us "to finally accept that the modern world already has its own style or non-style and it doesn't need any architects to be able to appreciate it" (1993, p. 15).

In opting for a common or a simple form which alludes to a vernacular character, the architect precludes the modern, which is effectively temporary and in a constant state of flux. The ordinary is the opposite of modern and fashionable. It is in itself timeless.

Conclusion

A sustainable ordinariness seeks intrigue in the mundane, surprise in the usual, sophistication in the simple and peacefulness in the ad hoc. It elevates the role of the existing over the role of the new and encourages invention within the dictates of our world with limited resources. It acknowledges the basic human need for shelter, as well as the spiritual desire for artistic fulfillment.

"Ordinary architecture" finds inspiration in the vernacular, in second-class architecture, not the great, often publicised models or canonical examples observed in architectural history, but within everyday reality and the commonplace. Although this architecture engages with banal, ordinary and seemingly secondary things, it must be understood that we are unequivocally dealing with architecture.

Thus the ordinary in and of itself does not constitute a sustainable aesthetic. The images, the genes, the principles present within the ordinary, as well as the vernacular, inform the aesthetic, but ultimately it relies on appropriately focused action to realise it.

Martina Novakova works in the field of architecture in Sydney, Australia. She obtained her degree in architectural design in Germany as well as a degree in sustainable design in Slovakia. She is currently undertaking research focused on the ordinary and its significance in architecture as part of her doctoral studies.

Tony Lam also works in the architecture industry in Sydney, Australia. He obtained his Masters degree in architecture after studying in both Australia and Germany. He has a passion for architectural design, architectural theory as well as sustainability in design.

References

AlSayyad, N. & Arboleda, G. (2011). The sustainable indigenous vernacular: interrogating a myth. In S. Lee (Ed.), *Aesthetics of sustainable architecture* (pp. 134-151). Uitgeverij: 010 Publishers.

Berke, D. (1997). Thoughts on the everyday. In S. Harris & D. Berke (Eds.). *Architecture of the everyday* (pp. 222-226). New York: Princeton Architectural Press.

Danto, A. C. (1981). *The transfiguration of commonplace: a philosophy of art.* Cambridge: Harvard University Press.

Davidovici, I. (2013). *Forms of practice.* German-Swiss architecture 1980-2000. Zurich: gtaVerlag.

Frey, P. & Bouchain, P. (2010). *Learning from vernacular. towards a new vernacular architecture.* Arles: Actes Sud.

Hays, M. (1991). Ready to travel: a note on the architecture of Roger Diener. In U. Strathaus, M. Steinmann & K. H. Hüter (Eds.), *Diener & Diener* (pp. 9-11). New York: Rizzoli.

Herzog, J. & de Meuron, P. (1992). The hidden geometry of nature. In W. Wang, (Ed.), *Herzog & de Meuron* (pp. 142-146). London: Ellipsis London Press.

Humbel, C. (1995). *Junge Schweizer architekten und architektinnen.* Zürich: Artemis.

Kapfinger, O. (1993). *Dazwischen.* In A. Krischanitz & Krischanitz, A. (Eds.), (pp. 12-20) Zürich, München, London: Artemis.

Krischanitz, A. (1993). Adolf Krischanitz. Zürich, München, London: Artemis.

Kuma, K. (2011). Natural architecture. In S. Lee (Ed.). *Aesthetics of sustainable architecture* (pp. 179-185). Uitgeverij: 010 Publishers.

Rossi, A. (1982). *The architecture of the city.* Cambridge, Mass: MIT Press.

Rudofsky, B. (1964). *Architecture without architects: a short introduction to non-pedigreed architecture.* Albuquerque: University of New Mexico Press.

Steinmann, M. & Boga, T. (Eds.). (2010). *Tendenzen: neuere architektur im Tessi. tendencies - recent architecture in Ticino. Tendenze - architettura recente nel Ticino.* Basel: Birkhauser Verlag.

Steinmann, M. (1980). *Von 'einfacher' und 'gewöhnlicher' architektur. Archithese 1, 8-13.*

Steinmann, M. (1990). Neuere architektur in der deutschen Schweiz. In M. Steinmann, M. (2003). *Forme forte. Écrits/Schriften 1972-2002* (pp. 93-109). Basel: Birkhauser Verlag.

Steinmann, M. (1994). Die Gegenwartigkeit der dinge: bemerkungen zur neueren architektur in der Deutschen Schweiz. In M. Steinmann, M. Gilbert & K. Alter (Eds.), *Construction, intention, detail: five projects from Swiss architects* (pp. 8-14). Zurich: Artemis.

Steinmann, M. (1998). You see what you see. zu einem neuen werk von Peter Märkli. In M. Steinmann (2003). *Forme forte. Écrits/Schriften 1972-2002* (pp. 267-278). Basel: Birkhauser Verlag.

Steinmann, M. (2003). Forme forte. Écrits/Schriften 1972-2002. Basel: Birkhäuser Verlag.

Strathaus, U. J-S. (1988). Herzog & de Meuron. In U. J-S, Strathaus, J. Herzog & Archotekturmuseum in FBasel (Eds.). *Herzog 7 de Meuron. architektur denkform. eine ausstellung im architekturmuseum vom 1. Oktober bis 20. November 1988.* Basel: Wiese Verlag.

Tschanz, M. (1995). *Gentle perversions. daidalos. nr. 56. magic of materials.* Berlin: Bertelsmann. 85-90.

Venturi, R. (1966). *Complexity and contradiction in architecture.* London: The Architectural Press.

Venturi, R., Brown, D. S. & Izenour, S. (1977). *Learning from Las Vegas: the forgotten symbolism of architectural form.* Cambridge: MIT Press.

Wang, W. (1992). *Herzog & de Meuron.* Zürich: Artemis.

CHAPTER SIXTEEN

APPLYING TRANSECT METHOD AS A CATALYST TO MAKE A SUSTAINABLE URBAN LANDSCAPE

Maryam Izadi

Introduction

At least 90% of the earth's landscape has been influenced and dramatically changed by humankind, and natural landscapes have been dramatically transformed by the process of urbanisation. Further environmental stress is caused through the interaction of people with the built environment and townscape. Ongoing contemporary changes of environmental, socio-cultural and spatial conditions need new insights into the forms of the physical, functional and ecological urban development we deploy. The last two centuries' rapid global urbanisation especially causes concerns about the sustainability of cities. Sustainability is a broad term that includes social, economic and environmental concerns but it can be thought of as a kind of development that seeks to meet human needs presently and for generations to come (Ritchie & Thomas, 2013). Urban growth has transformed the landscape in recent decades and caused significant impact on ecosystems. Landscape design has artistic and scientific aspects in creating an environment. It addresses both ecological issues and cultural values. Both living and non-living materials are used for in design and planning, therefore the outcome is always dynamic and changing. It is not possible, nor desirable to prevent change. Change can have different effects on places and how change is managed will determine what these effects might be. Urban alteration has profound impacts in physical, environmental and (by implication) aesthetic aspects (Memluk, 2012).

This chapter discusses the urban landscape as a mixture of nature zones and townscape. Whatever we can see in cities, from a mass of buildings and urban forms to public and green spaces are all parts of the urban landscape. The physical character of a city, or perhaps it is better to say its urban form - which includes architectural style, streetscape, urban block structure, public spaces, street pattern, sense of enclosure, and movement patterns - contributes greatly to townscape features. Natural and cultural dynamics both form the urban landscape. Therefore the urban landscape is not entirely independent of buildings and structures and yet it could be stated that it is more than green spaces. It is comprised of a variety of land use such as streets and squares, playgrounds, railway and canal corridors, cemeteries, bicycle and pedestrian paths, and waterfronts (Memluk, 2012). Equally, the natural or semi-natural characteristics of a city, such as trees, gardens, hedge lines, small woods, fields, commons, parks, hills, wetlands and forests have a visual and emotional impact on how we see our urban visual environment (Walsh, 2012). Biological systems and organic architecture can change urban structures and make them more agreeable to live in.

A sustainable townscape

Gordon Cullen states that to townscape is an artistic act undertaken in order to organise the buildings, streets and spaces that makes up urban environments, and give them visual coherence (Cullen, 1995). Indeed, it is an artistic shaping of the physical aspects of a city or urban area. In this case the townscape is the urban equivalent of a landscape. The townscape involves all the components seen in urban areas, but to be able to explain the details in this chapter, the townscape will be used to describe those urban features that are not related to ecological zones and green spaces.

Non-ecological features in a cityscape are classified further into 'physical' and 'identity' categories. The term 'urban form' can be used to describe a city's physical characteristics. The physical dimensions of urban form may include size, shape, land uses, scale, density, urban block layout, the configuration and distribution of open space and also green areas – a composite of a multitude of characteristics, including a city's transportation system and urban design features. However, urban form is not constituted solely by physical features, but also encompasses non-physical aspects such as socio-economic issues and density that also have physical impacts upon the urban fabric (Dempsey et al, 2012). A good townscape helps to balance urban and human scale in the urban core where the vertical effect of buildings and structures dominates (Memluk, 2012). To make a sustainable city, urban block orientation and density can be manipulated to decrease the adverse environmental effects. Aesthetic indicators in architecture such as proportion and building height can also be deployed across cultures (Ashira, 1985).

The identity of urban areas is influenced by urban history, and cultural and natural heritage should be protected to preserve the landscape (Antrop, 2006; Neil, 2004). The man-made environment, the cultural landscape, has been created by a particular group of people, so it follows that shared beliefs made manifest through daily activities will be evident in a spatial form and physical setting (Nunta & Sahachaisaeree, 2010). Social experience of climatic conditions, religious beliefs, traditions and local fictions all are parts of the cultural landscape. They are made manifest in landmarks, great buildings and their façades, architectural style and urban inherited character, focal points and visual corridors as well as detailed things such as construction materials revealed in the colour of roof roofs and walls. Sustainable places preserve their heritage, traditional values, and shared symbols. These have aesthetic qualities.

Ecological sustainability in urban areas

Is it possible to think of, and deploy 'natural capital' in the same way it is possible to define and use social capital (Selman, 2008). Natural capital is a component part of environmental sustainability and landscape ecology, and natural elements are a significant part of urban ecology (Bo et al, 2011, p. 415). In turn, urban form has an effect on ecological factors. Specific elements of urban form that impact upon patterns of biodiversity include the type of development, the amount of impervious man made surfaces, the distance to the city centre from the suburbs, natural vegetative cover and the density of residential areas (Irvine et al, 2010, p. 216). The ecological sustainability of landscapes can only be achieved on the base of large-scale cohesive patterns of ecosystems (Opdam et al, 2006, p. 325).

In the case of the urban environment as ecosystem, it is possible to either define the city as a single ecosystem or to see the city as composed of several individual ecosystems, such as parks and lakes. We can use the term urban ecosystems for all natural green and blue areas in the city, including street trees and ponds; although street trees are too small to be considered ecosystems, and should be regarded as elements of a larger system. Examples of ecosystems in urban areas are, suburban lawns and urban and suburban parks, urban woodland, cultivated land, wetlands, lakes, seafront and streams. However, almost all city areas are manipulated by man and their natural coherence is compromised (Bolund & Hunhammar, 1999, p. 294).

Since changing the diversity and abundance of natural species may have functional consequences, the importance of maintaining the integrity of the natural components of the city should be considered (Andersson, 2006). Preserving natural green spaces on a large scale is the first step to achieve a sustainable ecosystem. Flora should be protected not only as essential ecological elements but can also enhance local character and aesthetics in each specific ecosystem (Fenton, 1992). Flora species in an area can be an example for planners and designers to choose species for planting in that city

(McCormick, 1999). Native plants in a landscape bring local identity to urban spaces, and they can have practical applications as wind and sound barriers. On the other hand, urban residents frequently have private land around their home for a personal aesthetic contact with nature. They make independent decisions about how to manage their own garden, even if they let the garden grow wild or pave it entirely (Jenks & Jones, 2010, p. 225). There are many coastal cities and many other cities through which a rivers runs. Access to the waterfronts should be designed in a way that does not close visual corridors, as these also have aesthetic impact.

The transect as a design method

The transect (a line that cuts through the landscape along which the observer records phenomena) was formulated in the 18th century (Duany, 2002). A transect of the natural environment was first conceived by Alexander Von Humboldt at the close of the 18th century to analyse natural ecologies as a sequence of environments. It is now used to show the varying characteristics through different zones such as wetlands, shores, uplands, and plains (Land Use Law, n.d).

In environmental issues a transect means a cross-section that helps identify the change in use sequences in the environment. By using transect planning methods, many components in urban spaces can be identified and then discussed. Near the close of the 20th century new Urbanists such as Andres Duany and Elizabeth Plater-Zyberk began to extend the natural transect to include the built environment. They segmented the transect continuum into six eco-zones based on normative U.S. urban patterns which provide immersive contexts running from the rural to the urban. These zones vary in their environmental, physical and social character. The six eco- zones are; natural zone, rural zone, sub-urban zone, general urban zone, urban center zone, urban core zone (Center for Applied Transect Studies. n.d). The major criterion for identifying each zone or loops is the intensity of urbanisation taking place. For instance the urban core has the high population density meanwhile the rural zone has very low density. The zones are not formed according to Euclidean shapes, and the scale of the location and the shape of the zones are further determined by qualitative indicators. It follows that while planners usually use a straight line in making creating transects, lines need be neither straight, nor single, but can follow aspects of the physical and demographic topography that is being examined.

Applying transects

Transects can be used for both analysis and planning in urban studies. Obviously, a line cannot be a sample of whole city, therefore it is important to strategically choose the best line or lines. To usefully select lines in an area, planners and designers need to identify which one has more data to contribute achieving the goals of their project, in the case of this chapter, it would be data for creating a sustainable and aesthetically pleasing environment. In most planning projects aiming to develop a landscape that is both sustainable and imparts a sense of aesthetic wellbeing, the visual dimension of the design can be significant. Therefore in choosing a transect planners should concentrate on visual aspects.

Studying urban form, urban morphology and street networks demonstrates that two types of transect lines are best suited to analysing and planning the aesthetic character of the urban environs. Firstly, lines that section along streets and pathways are the best lines to determine the physical aspects of cities. Since streets are the heart of social life, the data deriving from these lines play a central, flexible role in the analysis and design of liveable cities. Appropriate places for landmarks and focal points, the control of building height and construction material, architectural style, and quality of urban furniture can be achieved by a choosing a carefully determined line along the streets. Lines in different orientations also help planners to find the relationship of an area with different parts of a city. It helps them to come over the limitations of this two dimensional analysis method.

Secondly, lines which cross from urban cores to rural zones are useful in controlling the urban skyline, urban silhouette and preserving nature assets, especially in the urban outskirts. Before drawing these lines planners should first identify the six transect zones in the project area. Several transect lines of different orientation give planners an image of a city. They contain much physical and identity information contained in different eco-zones inside the city. They can inform quickly what the urban values in an especial zone may be, and what integrating decisions might be made about the district. As well as the analysis of plans, building, and architectural standards, decisions can be made at this stage about the way in which the natural world can be a component part of any design.

Conclusion

This chapter has placed an emphasis on the way that planners can control urban form, the built environment and natural zones, and thereby maintain the socio-cultural landscape and shape an aesthetically sustainable one, all achievable by the use of transect as a method. The transect is an infinitely flexible tool, a means of enquiry that can be applied in numerous ways. It is not a straight-forward task to define an aesthetically sustainable town and landscape, because of the differing physical and cultural contexts in which it is framed, but it seems the transect is a sophisticated process able to address multiple issues in a practical, applicable way.

Maryam Izadi was born in Iran, and is currently based in Australia. She graduated in Architecture from Azad University and took her masters of Urban Design in the Iran University of Science & Technology. Working professionally in architecture and urban design, she also taught in Azad University in Iran.

References

Andersson, E. (2006). Urban landscapes and sustainable cities. *Ecology and Society 34*(11) 34. Retrieved from http://www.ecologyandsociety.org/vol11/iss1/art34/

Antrop, M. (2006). Sustainable landscapes: contradiction, fiction or utopia? *Landscape and Urban Planning,* 75,http://www.sciencedirect.com/science/journal/01692046/75/3 187-197.

Ashihara, Y. (1985) *The aesthetic townscape.* Cambridge, Mass: MIT Press.

Bo, H., Shu, L. & Shu-hua, L. (2011). Ecological landscape planning and design of an urban landscape fringe area: a case study of Yang'an District of Jiande City. *Procedia Engineering,* 21, 414-420. Doi: 10.1016/j.proeng.2011.11.2033

Bolund, P., & Hunhammar, S. (1999). Ecosystem services in urban areas. *Ecological Economics,* 29, 293-301. Retrieved from http://www.earthsake.ca/articles/urban_ecology_1_bolund1999.pdf

Burdette, J. T. (2004). Form-based codes: a cure for the cancer called euclidean zoning? (Master's dissertation). Retrieved from http://scholar.lib.vt.edu/theses/available/etd-05122004-113700/unrestricted/BurdetteFINALmajorpaper.pdf

Center for Applied Transect Studies. (n.d.). *The transect.* Retrieved from http://transect.org/transect.html

Cullen, G. (1995). *The concise townscape.* Oxford: Architectural Press

Duany, A. & Talen, E. (2002). Transect planning. *Journal of the American Planning Association,* 68, 245-266.

Fenton, D. (1992). Dimensions of meaning in the perception of natural settings and their relationship to aesthetic response. In L. Nasar (Ed.), *Environmental aesthetics: theory, research, and application.* Cambridge: Cambridge University Press.

Irvine, N., Fuller, R. A., Devine-Wright, P., Tratalos, J., Payne, S. R., Warren, H., Lomas, K. J., Gaston, K. J. (2010). Ecological and psychological value of urban green space. In M. Jenks & C. Jones (Eds.), *Dimensions of the sustainable city.* London, New York: Springer.

Jenks, M. & Jones, C. (Eds.). (2010). *Dimensions of the sustainable city*. London, New York: Springer.

Land Use Law. (2009). *SmartCode version 9.2*. Missouri, USA: University of Washington in St. Louis. Retrieved from http://landuselaw.wustl.edu/3000-BookletSC.pdf

Memluk, M. Z. (2012). Urban landscape design. In Ozyavuz, M. (Ed.). *Urban landscape design, landscape planning*. Retrieved from http://www.intechopen.com/books/landscape-planning/urban-landscape-design

McCormick, F. (1999). Principles of ecosystem management and sustainable development. In Peine, J. (Ed.). *Ecosystems management for sustainability*. London: CRC Press.

Nunta, J. & Sahachaisaeree, N. (2010). Determinant of cultural heritage on the spatial setting of cultural landscape: a case study on the northern region of Thailand. *Procedia Social and Behavioral Sciences, 5*, 1241-1245.

Opdam, P., Steingr, S. & van Rooij, S. (2006). Ecological networks: A spatial concept for multi-actor planning of sustainable landscapes. *Landscape and Urban Planning*, 322-332.

Ritchie, A. & Thomas, R. (Eds.). (2013). *Sustainable urban design:* an environmental approach. Abingdon: Spon Press.

Searns, R. M. (1995). The evolution of greenways as an adaptive urban landscape form. *Landscape and Urban Planning, 33*, 65-80.

Selman, P. (2008). What do we mean by sustainable landscape? *Sustainability: Science, Practice, & Policy, 4*(2), 23-28.

Swaroop Singh, S. (2010). Form-based codes: an alternative method for development regulation. *Institute of Town Planners, India Journal, 7*(2) 27-33.

Watson, D., J. Plattus, A. G. & Shibley, R. (2003). *Time-saver standards for urban design*. University of Minnesota: McGraw-Hill.

Walsh, D. (2012). *Historic townscape characterisation: the Lincoln Townscape assessment: a case study*. Lincoln: The City of Lincoln Council.

CHAPTER SEVENTEEN

CULTURE AND NATURE:
THE LANGUAGE OF SYMBOLS AND NATURE IN THE OEUVRE OF THE
CONTEMPORARY POLISH ARCHITECT, MAREK BUDZYŃSKI

Julia Sowińska-Heim

Introduction

For forty years of communist rule in Poland (and a dependence on the USSR), issues pertaining to environmental protection and taking care of human-friendly urban areas were pushed into the background and ignored. Contemporary policy was instead aimed mainly at industrial development, with a visual culture communicating ideas of the superiority and "rightness" of a communist system. At the same time, Poland's industrial programme was an important propaganda tool of the Cold War. The intensification of industry, especially of heavy industry, as well as the scale and low quality of mass housing resulted in substantial degradation of urban areas and considerable environmental pollution (Crampton & Crampton, 1996; Czepczyński, 2008).

After the thorough political transformation in Poland in 1989, political, economic and social systems were completely altered. As early as 1989, actions were taken in order to establish efficient and modern sustainable development policy (Prace Komitetu Obywatelskiego przy Przewodniczącym NSZZ Solidarność nr 2 Protokół Podzespołu Okrągłego Stołu ds. Ekologii, 1989). The most important legal act, summarising various minor activities (Uchwała Sejmu Rzeczypospolitej Polskiej, 1991; Uchwała Sejmu Rzeczypospolitej Polskiej, 1995; Uchwała Senatu Rzeczypospolitej Polskiej, 1994), was a regulation introduced in *The Constitution of the 3rd Republic of Poland*, which obliged the state to protect the environment in accordance with the guidelines for sustainable development.

Currently, Polish architects increasingly want to gain a positive assessment of a building in terms of its influence on the environment; they also use unconventional sources of energy in their projects (such as the Copernicus Science Centre in Warsaw, the FIS-SST Company office block in Gliwice, and the Gesterbine design for Wielkopolska region). In Poland, sustainable architecture is generally associated with two trends: high tech and low tech, and thus with two different aesthetics: on the one hand – dazzling with modernity and advanced technology, on the other – the simplicity of a thatched roof over a clay house.

The projects of Marek Budzyński architectural team constitute an individual and characteristic element of the urban landscape. In the architect's opinion, certain aspects of sustainable design are of equal importantance; these being the coexistence of architecture and nature, and supporting natural processes as well as contributing to the preservation of cultural values (Bartoszewicz & Goźliński, 2001; Bartoszewicz, 1999; Janowska & Mucharski, 2007); since Budzyński considers nature and culture (perceived as all human activities) to be two crucial elements conditioning human life (Budzyński, 2013d). Yet, he thinks that a balance between nature and culture has been currently lost; instead of coexisting, these two elements remain in conflict (Budzyński, 2013d; Budzyński, 1994, p. 73). Culture is starting to dominate nature and destroy it, and according to Budzyński, architecture is one of those things that can restore the lost symbiosis (Boniecki, 2001; Budzyński, 2013a).

Productions and designs – selected examples

An architectural building should be, according to the architect, designed in a way which does not destroy what already exists, but contributes to sustaining the natural continuity (biosphere), without which life on the Earth would be impossible, and at the same time it should help to maintain cultural continuity (Bartoszewicz & Goźliński, 2001).

Budzyński respects both cultural and ecological contexts. In his designs and productions, he uses a distinct aesthetic language referring to a centuries-old cultural tradition. One such example is the University of Warsaw Library. A competition design was held in 1993, and the production of the building was completed in 1999. The garden completed in 2002, the design of landscape architect Irena Bajerska.

Figure 1: University of Warsaw Library main entrance. Photo, J. Sowińska-Heim.

According to Budzyński's original idea, the internal form of the building is an exemplification of coexistence of architecture, nature and culture. The building has got three, so-called ecological (Budzyński, 2013c), elevations, whose walls, made of raw concrete, are covered with a net of patinated copper. This serves multiple roles: as a decorative element, a frame for climbers overgrowing the walls, and an element for distributing water over the roof. Plants also appear in other places, since a public garden is an integral part of the library complex, which "climbs" the building's roof.

This building provides Warsaw, a big and busy city, with an enriched and spacious (the surface of the garden itself is 15 000 m²/3,3 acres – lower level and 2000 m²/0,2 acre – upper level), biologically active coating, simultaneously creating a convivial space for leisure and rest in the city centre (O Bibliotece. Gmach i ogród, 2013).

Figure 2: One of the "ecological" elevations and part of the garden. Photo, J. Sowińska - Heim.

Figure 3: A view from the side of the main entrance. Photo, J. Sowińska - Heim.

This combination characterises many projects by Budzyński, who believes that it is an architects' task to create a healthy microclimate in the city and at the same time design new spaces contributing to the establishment of interpersonal relations and bonds (Janowska & Mucharski, 2007; Śmierzchalska, 2011). Such an approach is stimulated by a perceived crisis in relation to the modern public space of Polish cities, as well as global problems of environmental pollution (Bartoszewicz & Goźliński, 2001; Budzyński, 2013b). It also corresponds to priorities accepted by the creator, since according to Budzyński, architecture is converting the space for people's need in the way that does not destroy natural conditions created by nature and favours development of social life (Janowska & Mucharski, 2007).

Figure 4: A part of the roof garden with the picturesque view overlooking the city and the Vistula River. Photo, J. Sowińska - Heim.

One of the library buildings is inscribed with iconographical contexts, outside, the fourth, so-called cultural, elevation (the façade) conveys additional meanings. Its main feature is eight tablets made of patinated copper with inscriptions written in different languages, such as Old Polish, Old Russian, Hebrew, Arabic, Sanskrit and Greek. There is also a musical extract and a mathematical formula. Passers-by see (it is hard to assume that they will be able to decipher all the texts) passages from the Old Testament, the Koran and Plato's works. Emphasising the Polish context, is a musical extract from the eminent Polish composer, Karol Szymanowski. The tablets reference cultural heritage from different times and traditions, revealing the complexity of cultural images and civilisation. All of this is crowned with a frieze with the inscription *BIBLIOTEKA UNIWERSYTECK* [UNIVERSITY LIBRARY].

Figure 5: The main entrance and view of the "cultural" elevation. Photo, J. Sowińska - Heim.

Interestingly, there is a commercial space inside, directly behind the façade of "culture". Its placement is not accidental, but results from Budzyński's characteristic tendency to create additional symbols and references. He "expresses hope" that it is possible to redefine strictly commercial activities and recall the role of tradition in establishing identity (Sowińska-Heim, 2011). Inside, according to the architect's conception, the library and commercial parts symbolically combine and unite, being connected with a so-called "street" (Budzyński, 1994, 2013c), a kind of internal passage topped with a glass roof, whose concrete, grey walls are overgrown with plants.

The University of Warsaw Library is considered to be one of the most interesting architectural productions completed in Poland after 1989. It was showcased during a foreign exhibition *"Polska. Ikony architektury"* [Poland. The icons of architecture] organised by the monthly magazine "Architektura-murator" together with the Ministry of Foreign Affairs – presenting twenty buildings recognised as crucial achievements of Polish modern architecture. It also won fourth place in a poll organised in Poland in 2012, to choose the masterwork of Polish architecture of the last two decades (Sarzyński, 2012). In 2002, the production was honoured by the Minister of Infrastructure with the first prize in the field of "Architecture and Building" for a unique combination of ecological architecture and the latest technique and technology.

The building has been appreciated not only for the ecological values, but also for its pro-social functions, creating a convivial space in the city. A park and a botanic garden established on the library roof is where professors and students, as well as Warsaw citizens walk and rest. (In 2005, their votes contributed to honouring it with first prize in a poll for a positive place in the city organised by Clear

Channel as part of the project Positive City Bęc Zmiana Foundation and *Gazeta Stołeczna* newspaper in 2005).

The temple of divine providence

The Temple of Divine Providence, a Christian and Polish nationalist project, has a long history of starts and setbacks since 1791. At its most recent iteration in an architectural competition of 1999, a design prepared by Budzyński's architectural team won one of three *ex aequo* first places and chosen to be developed. However, the design gave rise to great controversy, which resulted in abandoning construction. Currently, the temple is being erected in accordance with a conservative design of another architectural team.

According to In Budzyński's conception, the structure was to resemble a mountain-mound (20-metre-high) overgrown with greenery with architectural accents referring both to Christian origins and to ecumenical spirit, and to the tradition of other faiths and cultures (Bartoszewicz & Goźliński, 2001)In his design the language of forms and symbols used by Budzyński are intended to have a direct impact on the passer-by, to be legible for everyone, not only for the inner circle (Budzyński, 1994, p. 53). Plants were selected to reconstruct a natural landscape. The architect thought it would be perfect if they could grow without any human interference (Bartoszewicz & Goźliński, 2001, p. 14). Other parts were to be filled with trees and bushes typical of the Polish countryside; the church was intended to be overgrown mainly by plants that are both easy to cultivate and decorative, such as Cotoneaster plants or wild rose bushes. The design also included a typically Polish landscape of meadows with colourful flowers: poppies, daisies or cornflowers, which, growing on the roofs of several buildings, were going to change them into soft slopes.

Using numerous direct references to Christianity was a conscious act. It creates an atmosphere which is felt with different senses – more felt than understood. First of all, using aesthetic language should result in creating bonds with tradition (Bartoszewicz & Goźliński, 2001, p. 8; Budzyński, 1994, pp. 53-59).

Awarding Budzyński's team first place, the competition jury decided that ideological background was paramount, and should constitute a deeply symbolic sign – both universal and connected with Polish tradition and national identity, whilst conforming with the main idea and the objective of the competition (Jury, n.d., p. 14).

According to the complex design, the architecture was to coexist with natural plants (greenery was to cover 9,000 m²/2,22 acres) (Boniecki, 2001, p. 9). In this way, the architect intended to shape a piece of landscape, connecting nature created by God with city scenery created by man. Furthermore, it was seeking unity in oppositions, equilibrium between nature and city, or modernity and tradition. The architect openly declares that the basic idea was to shape the landscape, not to erect a building (Bartoszewicz & Goźliński, 2001, p. 9). For Budzyński, architecture and nature constitute unity here – the "sacred landscape", exemplifying the idea of creation and human activity understood as co-creation based on the harmony and respect towards the environment (Bartoszewicz & Goźliński, 2001, p. 11; Boniecki, 2001, p. 8). In other words, this design is a sign of human ability to cooperate with God in an unending act of creation (Bartoszewicz & Goźliński, 2001, p. 10). The temple was to constitute an integral part of the architectural and landscape layout. The complex would have perfectly matched the space where the project was going to be carried out – a housing estate planned ultimately for 35–50 thousand inhabitants. Creating additional quality in the area deprived of greenery and public places.

For the architect, an important starting point of the project was an idea of sustainable development, understood as seeking unity in differences, such as nature and city, modernity and tradition, or utility and art (Bartoszewicz & Goźliński, 2001, p. 9). However, the concept of combining the sacred with nature appeared to be too brave, as after heated discussion, the project was abandoned (Boniecki, 2001, p. 8; Budzyński, 2001; Mikulski, 2001; Kanon, 2001; Kucza-Kuczyński, 2001, p. 11).

An urban complex of the judiciary with the seat of the Supreme Court in Warsaw

An important element of the design of both the University of Warsaw Library and the Temple of Divine Providence is text. The words integrated into the architecture, are integral to the overall design and are an important carrier of meanings. Text also plays a significant role in another prestigious project: erecting the Supreme Court in Warsaw. In 1991, Budzyński's team won first prize in the architectural competition, and the project was completed in 1999.

Figure 7: The seat of the Supreme Court in Warsaw. Photo, J. Sowińska - Heim.

The architectural body of the Supreme Court consists of a glass main part, hidden behind massive pillars of patinated copper, called by its authors "the pillars of law" (Bartoszewicz, 1999). They are the main compositional accent of the body of the building and determine the perception of the whole. Words and sentences are inscribed on the pillars. Roman sentences (seen both from the street and from inside) are not the only decorative elements, as in the examples discussed, but, more importantly, they convey a deep message, emphasising cultural continuity, unchanging form of truths, and rules of law and human life.

Importantly, the architect did not suppose that the texts would necessarily be read but their presence alone is aimed at creating a bond with traditions and the past, being the source of our culture and thus inducing to reflection (Bartoszewicz & Goźliński, 2001, p. 12).

This is also the role of the monumental, neo-classical pillars – "the pillars of law" (Bartoszewicz, 1999). According to the architect, they are also an exemplification of prestige and rank of the Supreme Court, and, together with a regular rhythm, they illustrate objectivity and readability of decisions (Budzyński, 2000, p. 28). They are also an element of the dialogue with cultural and historical context of the place, since the Court was built opposite a historic baroque palace. The square where the building was erected was in need of maintenance for a long time. The pillars, referring in their proportions and rhythm to pilasters from the palace façade, are just a tool for organisation and merging the area of the square. The architect was inspired by Greek agora (Bartoszewicz, 1999, p. 38).

Figure 8: A dialogue of tradition and culture. Part of a baroque palace and a contemporary building of the Supreme Court. Photo, J. Sowińska - Heim.

The design of the Supreme Court also includes an ecological aspect in the form of a garden on the roof (for safety reasons it is not widely accessible) and "a living ornament" made of (Spiraea) plants growing on entablature on the axis of each pillar. They introduce a level of individualism and unpredictability to the rigorous composition of the façade layout. A formal and ideological urban concept of the judiciary with the seat of the Supreme Court in Warsaw prepared by Budzyński's architectural team, aroused great controversy and extreme opinions especially among Polish architects. On the one hand, the project has been awarded various prestigious prizes, as such from the

Society of Polish Architects for the best architectural object built for public money in 2000), on the other hand, it has been harshly criticised or even accused of having a form characteristic of socialist, or even fascist architecture (Rozwadowska, 1999).

Figure 9: A passage over the street referring to a former historical solution. Photo, J. Sowińska - Heim.

Conclusion

Marek Budzyński has created an original and recognisable style of architectural expression. The essence of his work, according to him, is combining the new with the old and permeating them with nature, merging the natural with the artificial, in creating forms adopted both by nature and by cultural heritage (Budzyński, 1994, p. 73). These ideas can be seen in numerous designs prepared by Budzyński's architectural team, of public objects, churches, and multifunctional housing complexes or office blocks. The prestigious designs of the University of Warsaw Library, the Temple of Divine Providence and of the Supreme Court in Warsaw are good examples for understanding Budzyński's architectural concepts and design methods.

Budzyński continually carries out a dialogue with artistic tradition and cultural heritage. He is the supporter of a "speaking architecture" idea (Bartoszewicz, 1994, p. 10; Budzyński, 1994, p. 53). In his opinion, architecture is not the space for total functional purity, since each form says something (Bartoszewicz, 1994, p. 10; Budzyński, 1994, p. 53). He has frequently stressed (Budzyński, 1994, p. 73; Bartoszewicz, 1994, p. 6) that a language of symbols should be possibly readable and sometimes even literal as not to become only a subject of elite disputes. This does not mean, however, a simple transfer of styles from the past to modern times. According to Budzyński, an architect should know how to introduce cultural heritage into the subconsciousness and receive enriched associations from there (Budzyński, 1994, p. 53).

At the same time, the main objective of his designs is creating a human-friendly environment by enhancing the quality of the environment outside a building, or creating internal semi-public spaces with arranged greenery. "Green" roofs and walls are a reservoir of rainwater, and they also improve the city microclimate. Therefore as stated, the designs are both pro-social and pro-ecological.

Symbol-permeated architecture connected with greenery expresses fascination with sustainable development with emphasis placed on the aesthetic aspect of the designs. Budzyński's concept is based on a triad of priorities being, in his opinion, the origin of all architectural activities; these are: cooperating with culture, establishing places with favourable conditions for interpersonal communication and creating a new biotope (i.a. Budzyński, 2013a). The architect has also frequently emphasised that these combinations are possible thanks to using the latest technological solutions in his projects (e.g., Bartoszewicz & Goźliński, 2001, p. 8; Bartoszewicz, 1999, p. 39).

Budzyński's architectural concept and the imperative of putting the idea of sustainable development into practice does not result from fashion, but from a deep conviction that creating architectural objects does not have to be destructive. Harmonious coexistence of natural and man-made creations is possible; and instead of destroying things, an architect can and should do his/her job in order to restore the symbiosis of nature and architecture.

Dr Julia Sowińska – Heim is an art historian and lectures at the Department of Art History, University of Lozd. The area of her research especially concerns the problems and ideas of 20th Century architecture particularly focusing on issues of ideologies of architectural and urban space production in a socialist and post-socialist city.

References

Bartoszewicz, D. (1994, June 17). Architekt państwowych marzeń. [Interview with Marek Budzyński]. *Gazeta Wyborcza. Magazyn*, pp. 6-10.

Bartoszewicz, D. (1999, October 7). Sprawiedliwość z autorskim orłem. [Interview with Marek Budzyński]. *Gazeta Wyborcza. Magazyn*, pp. 38-44.

Bartoszewicz, D., & Goźliński. (2001, April 12). 4 Drogi Opatrzności. [Interview with Marek Budzyński]. *Gazeta Wyborcza. Magazyn*, pp. 8-14.

Boniecki, A. (2001, February 4). Kopiec Opatrzności. [Interview with Marek Budzyński]. *Tygodnik Powszechny*, pp. 8-9.

Budzyński, M. (1994). *Marek Budzyński architekt*. Warszawa: Pre-press-process.

Budzyński, M. (2000). Sąd Najwyższy. Założenia autorskie. *Architektura – murator*, (1), 28.

Budzyński, M. (2001). Świątynia Opatrzności Bożej - poszukiwanie prawdy. List Marka Budzyńskiego. *Architektura - murator*, 4, 71-74.

Budzyński, M. (2013a). marek budzyński architekt sp. z.o.o. *marek budzyński architekt sp. z.o.o.* Retrieved from http://mbarch.pl/index.html

Budzyński, M. (2013b). Wielkomiejska Piotrkowska w Łodzi. *marek budzyński architekt sp. z.o.o.* Retrieved from http://mbarch.pl/pl/rewitalizacje/wielkomiejska-piotrkowska-w-lodzi.html

Budzyński, M. (2013c). Biblioteka Uniwersytetu Warszawskiego. *marek budzyński architekt sp. z.o.o.* Retrieved from http://mbarch.pl/pl/uzytecznosc-publiczna/biblioteka-uniwersytetu-warszawskiego.html

Budzyński, M. (2013d). Utrzymanie Życia jako podstawowa wartość przestrzeni Miast. Retrieved from http://mbarch.pl/pl/teksty-i-idee/utrzymanie-zycia-jako-podstawowa-wartosc-przestrzeni-miast.html

Crampton, R. & Crampton, B. (1996). *Atlas of eastern Europe in the twentieth century.* London and New York: Routledge.

Czepczyński, M. (2008). *Cultural landscapes of post-socialist cities. representation of powers and needs.* Hampshire: Ashgate.

Janowska, K. & Mucharski. (2007, April 28). Miasto musi być dla ludzi. [Interview with Marek Budzyński]. *Gazeta wyborcza. Gazeta na majówkę,* 20-21.

Jury. (n.d.). Nagroda główna równorzędna – projekt wskazany do realizacji. opinia Jury. *Architektura – Murator,* 7, 12-14.

Kanon czy chaos? - opinie jurorów i laureatów po konkursie na swiątynię swiętej opatrzności bożej. (2000). *Architektura - Murator,* 7, 45-49.

Kucza-Kuczyński, K. (2001). Lekcja katedr. *Tygodnik Powszechny,* 6, 6.

Mikulski, A. (2001). Dwie strony swiątyni. wyznanie. *A&B,* 4, 66-67.

O Bibliotece. Gmach i ogród. (2013). *Biblioteka Uniwersytecka w Warszawie.* retrieved from http://www.buw.uw.edu.pl/index.php?option=com_content&task=view&id=286&Itemid=91

Prace Komitetu Obywatelskiego przy Przewodniczącym NSZZ Solidarność nr 2 Protokół Podzespołu Okrągłego Stołu ds. Ekologii. (1989). Warszawa.

Rozwadowska, E. (1999). Ghery nie potrzebuje konkursu. Rozmowa z dyrektorem Zachęty – And Rottenberg. *Architektura – Murator,* 10, 68-69.

Sarzyński, P. (2012). Arcydzieła i arcymaszkary. *Polityka,* 70–72.

Śmierzchalska, D. (2011) Budować z myślą o człowieku wywiad z profesorem Markiem Budzyńskim. *National Geographic.* Retrieved from http://www.national-geographic.pl/artykuly/pokaz/budowac-z-mysla-o-czlowieku-wywiad-z-prof-markiem-budzynskim

Uchwała Sejmu Rzeczypospolitej Polskiej. (1991). *Monitor Polski,* (18, poz. 118).

Uchwała Sejmu Rzeczypospolitej Polskiej. (1995). *Monitor Polski,* (4, poz. 47).

Uchwała Senatu Rzeczypospolitej Polskiej. (1994). *Monitor Polski,* (59, poz. 510).

CHAPTER EIGHTEEN

THE AESTHETIC AND SUSTAINABLE ARCHITECTURAL PRINCIPLES OF YAZD

Hoda Shahmohammadian & Samaneh Soltanzadeh

Introduction

Reducing climate change crisis, resource depletion, and environmental pollution caused by human activities and lifestyle, have been considered as the most important global challenges in today's world. Poorly considered architectural activities, wasteful construction practices, and consumer lifestyles in vernacular buildings have had a major role in these crises. Hence, adopting innovative and effective strategies to improve the current situation can be considered the apex of architectural development goals, and new sets of ideas and practices associated with this type of architecture are contributing to what is now called sustainable architecture. In this global environment of change it is important to reflect on traditional Iranian architecture as a complete manifestation of sustainable architecture. In Iran, one of the new approaches to architectural design is to deploy the architectural principles of Iranian traditional architecture. This chapter wishes to examine whether traditional buildings' architectural sustainability in the desert regions of Iran have an aesthetic dimension, or whether their appearance is absolutely subordinate to the climate. In this regard, the city of Yazd is examined as a case sample. We will discuss the role of aesthetics from a number of perspectives before identifying and discussing their application in contemporary sustainable architecture.

Aesthetics from different perspectives

Using nature in all the arts, including architecture, has always been important to artists. As the Swiss artist Paul Klee (1923) observed, communicating with nature is the most essential condition for the artist. The artist is human, a part of nature and embedded in the natural environment. In the Persian language the term aesthetic means wellness, goodness, beauty, elegance and delicacy. Leon Battista Alberti (1965) gives a definition of beauty in *On the art of building* in which he says beauty lies in proportion and the coordination of components of a design set, so that if something is added to it, subtracted from it, or if any change occurs, its harmony will be destroyed. A Platonist, he believed that there is truth beyond phenomena and the physical world, and he suggested artists and architects can emulate that underlying truth by following universal laws of mathematics or harmonious proportions. Alberti (1965) cites three main factors in his theory: number, outline and position. By number he means the quantity of things; by outline, form; and by position the placement of parts. He argues that beauty emerges through the consonance of these parts caused by *concinnitas* that composes the parts in a complete and harmonious whole. Alberti (1965) also believed that everything in nature is regulated by concinnitas and that nature's main objective is that whatever is produced should be perfect at the end. He suggested that beauty in nature is an accidental but (inevitable) characteristic, and that beauty is created from the complex union of components.

Alberti (1965) proposes beauty as the outcome of nature. Architects are still discovering these properties and are trying to use them in design. In nature, it could be argued there is no logic of form following function or function following form because the only objective in nature is optimisation and re-creation amidst endless variety in form. These optimising objectives and consequences in natural design make living creatures extremely beautiful, because as a result they have extraordinary variety of form and performance in function. As a result of this process, nature meets unconscious beauty. The challenge that has arisen in design is the contemporary relationship between humankind and nature. It is often confused however by considering natural beauty apart from its other principles, when designers are unaware that the primary goal in nature is not to create beauty but to exist.

In his paper on sustainable vernacular architecture and the cultural context in which they exist, Cyrus Sabri (2012) links the ideas of nature and vernacular architecture. He quotes Frank Lloyd Wright's view that the architect draws from nature whatever is possible (p. 34) and proposes that the designer should follow nature as a part of the design process. Sabri (2012) argues that nature is an indispensable part of the vernacular landscape. Unity between the designer and the landscape (by designing for existence within it) can provide a deep sense of belonging to the natural world (p. 36). This is evident in any traditional vernacular architecture where buildings have rested in a landscape for centuries without need for refinement. By working with natural materials like mud stone and wood (Sabri refers to them as 'humble') (p. 38), respecting the environment and drawing from longstanding social and cultural conventions, Sabri suggests that drawing together nature and commonly understood knowledge of materials and conditions are the base for an architectural sustainability. Thus, vernacular architecture is sustainable because it is rooted in that long cultural dialogue between form and nature (p. 37).

It can be argued that applying Alberti's (1965) synthesising process of concinnitas to Sabri's (2012) position it can reveal two related concepts. Firstly, how important a deep understanding of the functioning of nature is when designing for the world – form, nature and (cultural) purpose need to be balanced harmoniously. Secondly, how readily the infinite variety of form (as made evident in nature itself) becomes focused when solving a problem caused by humankind's relationship to nature.

Design principles governing sustainable buildings in Yazd

The main purposes of examining the indigenous architecture of Yazd are to focus on the structural approach to designing for a hot climate, to understand the design thinking of Iranian architects in the past, and to understand how these ideas might inform contemporary projects in sustainable design. The main architectural and design principles will be discussed, focusing on ways in which the buildings provide internal and external comfort for their residents in such demanding environmental circumstances. Then the points emerging from this review will be matched with a number of traditional Persian architectural design principles.

Yazd is an ancient city situated in the middle of Iran, dating back 3,000 years. It averages five centimeters of rain per year, Yazd falls under group B in the Köpper - Geiger climate classification system; dry, arid or semi -arid climates. The city is in perpetual sunshine, with summers that sometimes reach forty-five degrees centigrade. Yazd is one on the largest cities in the world to be built principally from clay and its traditional architecture is distinguished by features that are designed principally for the function of cooling but which have contributed to a readily identifiable style.

The city has some of the finest examples of Persian traditional desert residential architecture. It is of foremost importance as a centre of Persian architecture. Traditional buildings created under such extreme climactic circumstances have a number of fundamental design principles and tasks to follow in order for them to be inhabitable.

Internal courtyards of varying shapes and sizes cultivate an internalising of the living space creating a way of maintaining an equitable micro-climate. Rooms are built around the courtyard, with different roles for different times of the year as temperature and sun height changes. A courtyard cools rooms that open on to it during the day, and at night acts as heat storage. Some courtyards are designed with distinct winter and summer aspects, to be respectively both warmer and cooler than the seasonal weather. Materials of differing density are used to reflect or retain heat (Hossein Ayatollahi, 2012).

There is a direct relationship between the internal volume and external surface of buildings, and building structures avoid being too big to limit passive heating. Spaces are open, and modest in size to reduce the need for cooling during the summer. Atriums were used to disperse hot air and provide light in internal spaces. Domes both reduce heat gain and assist in passive cooling (Mahdavinejad, 2013).

Figure 1: Courtyard, Khuneh Lari, Yazd. Photo, Fabien Dany.

The facades of buildings were constructed with a rough finish to reduce heat absorption, increase contact with air, and also to reduce the effect of the sun on surfaces. These strategies contribute to cooling the whole structure. Walls are thick to keep heat out in the summer and in during the winter. In Yazd, few windows are used, and in order to reduce direct sunlight are set deep into the walls so they are in shadow. Windows on the western facades are set low (Hardenberg, 1982). Wind is used as a passive cooler. Windows face the cooling winds and wind towers catch and direct wind to subterranean passages that then distribute cool air throughout the buildings (Bahadori, 1978).

Significant aesthetic approaches to traditional sustainable architecture in Yazd

The most important approach to understanding the sustainable architecture of Iran is to consider the five traditional principles of Iranian architecture. *Mardomvari, darongarayi, khodbasandegi, parhiz az bihodegi, niyaresh* and *peymon.*

Mardomvari (or 'human oriented') relates to the idea of human scale and architecture. A Western parallel may be drawn with Le Corbusier's (2004) idea of the modular. In a traditional Iranian environment the concept means that human scale should be respected within the house's design, both functionally and socially. The entrance to a traditional house in Yazd is through the entrance hall usually linked by a corridor that leads to the courtyard. The house is then divided into two parts, spaces for the family and spaces for guests. The parts of the house reserved for guests are closer to the entrance whilst the family rooms are spread throughout the space. Rooms are identified by their size and seasonal function rather than their use. So a room may have three doors or five doors and be identified as a summer or winter room (Nabavi et al, 2012; Hosseini & Karimi, 2012). The concept of human orientation extends beyond the functioning of the individual home into the relationship between houses. A structure that does not acknowledge its neighbors, psychologically or functionally does not possess the quality of Mardomvari. There must be a balance between privacy and neighbourliness. Ritual and communal spaces, meeting places, mosques and palaces may vary in scale but should still retain this human oriented quality.

The key to Mardomvari is the principal that architecture and quotidian existence are inextricably linked. Human scale also means an acknowledgement of social as well as practical function, and that emotional and spiritual wellbeing is as important as physical efficiency.

The second design principle is darongaray (or 'introverted architecture'). Generally, the world's buildings can be characterized as two types depending on the layout of indoor and outdoor spaces: extrovert and introvert. An 'introverted' building concentrates the attention to the inside and leaves the façade functional but free of architectural symbols. In Iran most of the buildings are introvert, built around a courtyard. This brings privacy and creates a social space that responds to the passage of the sun and seasonal changes, creating a space in which the relationship of the family to the environment is profoundly experienced (Nazidizaji & Safari, 2013).

Architectural introversion arises from the climate of Iran, which is mostly hot and dry. It has dry air, harsh winds, flowing sand, and burning sun. The architect has to create a built environment in order to also create a green and pleasant landscape. Introversion is also derived from Persian culture. Three distinctive features of Iranian culture have emerged in introverted architecture: mystical introversion, veiling, and privacy (Karimi, 2013, p. 158). These social qualities of introversion lead not to isolation, but to a sustainable and manageable set of social relationships that are harmonious with ways of living that are in turn synchronous with the environment.

A third principle of Iranian architecture is khodbasandegi (or self sufficiency). From ancient times Iranian architects tried to procure building materials from the nearest place to the site of construction. They tried to be self-sufficient, believing that building materials should be *bomavard,* or vernacular, and in order to construct the building local facilities were be utilized as much as possible. This is because it increased the speed of construction, was more compatible with the natural surroundings, and should there be the need to repair buildings in the future then materials would be always available. This is further demonstration of the physical and cultural stability of traditional Iranian architecture (Jamshidi et al, 2011).

The fourth principle of Iranian sustainable architecture examined in this chapter is parhiz az bihodegi, the avoidance of idleness. This principle demands the functional relationship of parts to the whole, where nothing about the structure is redundant or useless. In other cultures the decoration of forms through sculpture and painting is an important principle in providing an aesthetic quality to structures. However, in Iranian architecture, what might be thought of as decoration has at its centre a functional necessity. For example, if a dome was tiled it was because the tile worked as *penam* (thermal and humidity insulation) for the dome. Mosaic tiles are multiply coloured because the life of tiles was short, and when repairs were needed small areas could be replaced without spoiling the overall quality of the surface. Geometric forms were used as geometry was seen to express the idea of unity in multiplicity. In other words, geometry is a visual language that stems from the worldview of the artist or architect, and it leads to the production of a work of art that expresses cultural perspectives in addition to their visual qualities (Mahdzar et al, 2013). The decorated inner surface and lining of a building acted as insulation against the cold and heat. In these examples and other cases, the architect has performed what was functionally necessary in the best way artistically.

Principles of building statistics and modular form (niyaresh and peymon) are the knowledge needed when conceiving, siting and creating a building and are the fifth and sixth principles of Iranian traditional architecture. In order for there to be harmony in structural and architectural design, an architectural plan should be created within the bounds of structural feasibility and a synergy should be created between them. The convergence of structure, architecture and decoration in traditional Iranian architecture is based on systematic harmony rooted in complying with technical principles and applying geometrical and mathematical concepts (Golabchi & Khorramirouz, 2009). This is achieved through an understanding of structure, material types and building technology. Principles of building statistics were very important to Iranian architects. The attention to the structural and functional logic of a building gives it consistency and thus its beauty. Beauty in Iranian architecture is therefore based on reasonableness, appropriateness, and the innate sense of everything in its own place. In traditional Iranian architecture, structure and architecture embellishment are not separated from each other, but co-mingled. Peymon determines the proportion between widths of the corridor, thickness of pillars, gradient of arcs, and their relationship to spatial dimensions using a system based on the geometry of the rectangle inside a hexagon.

The best architecture of Yazd conforms to the principles discussed above and at its best provides an urban environment that is both functional and in possession of beauty. It is an architecture that is optimal in its capabilities and logical in its appearance. It comes not from desire but from the needs of people. It reflects the culture of a people formed through a close engagement with climatic extremes, a culture that is bound to the environment but which engages with it in a sophisticated and elegant way.

Conclusion

In the traditional desert architecture of Iran, exemplified in the best of Yazd's architecture, attention to the natural environment as a model to design has been always been considered. Beauty in nature is a kind of beauty that is not planned. As a result of an inevitably correct answer to performance, natural beauty is an unconscious feature. In this way natural structures have evolved to reach stable compounds and forms.

Natural structures are much lighter, more delicate and robust compared to current human construction. Natural forms also have the quality of consistency and continuity, the result of an organic compositional logic, that when observed have an aesthetic elegance. This phenomena of natural systems can be considered as a research methodology for design. The idea of a building's design informed by nature can be revealed through sustainable and appropriate design behaviour. Paying attention to natural phenomena can lead architecture towards sustainability and a beauty that features self-organising and self-regulating features.

Nature reveals that design solutions can be ingenious and economical. In this regard, revealing the geometry of nature is also a solution in discovering the secrets of stability in nature and to be able to use them in art and science. Whether through the writings of Alberti (1965) or through the examination of traditional Iranian architecture what can be uncovered is a human sense of delight in composing in harmony with nature. The architecture of Yazd is deeply functional and its aesthetic qualities come from an understanding of its compositional logic, and how well that composition is made. It suggests that aesthetics and function are related and that the principles of traditional architecture of any nationality can have a significant impact on contemporary sustainable architectural aesthetics.

Hoda Shahmohammadian graduated in MA Architecture from Qazvin University, Iran in 2011. She is an architectural tutor at Karaj technical University. She practises professionally in the field of house design with a special focus on peoples' culture and societies' needs.

Samaneh Soltanzadeh graduated in MA Architecture from Qazvin University, Iran in 2011. She is an architectural tutor at the Islamic Azad University of Qazvin .

References

Alberti, L. B. (1965), *Ten books on architecture*. London: Alec Tiranti.

Bahadori, M. N. (1978). Passive cooling in Iranian architecture. *Scientific American, 238*(1), 144-150.

Golabchi, M., & Khorrramirouz, M. (2009). Assessment of structural components of Iranian heritage building: Persepolis. In C. A. Brebbia, (Ed.), *Structural studies, repairs and maintenance of heritage architecture XI*. Exeter: W.I.T. Press.

Hossein Ayatollahi, S. M. (2012). The passive solar of Yazd: reflections and performance after 10 years use. *American Transactions on Engineering & Applied Sciences, 1*(4), 379-392.

Jamshidi, M., Yazdanfar, N., & Nasri, M. (2011). Increasing of energy efficiency based on Persian ancient architectural patterns in desert regions (Case study of traditional houses in Kashan), *World Academy of Science, Engineering and Technology, 5*.

Karimi, P. (2013). *Domesticity and consumer culture in Iran: interior revolutions of the modern era*. London: Routledge.

Klee, P. (1923). Wege des Naturstudiums (Ways of Studying Nature). *Paul Klee Notebooks, 1-4*.

Le Corbusier, (2004). *The Modulor*. Basle: Birkhauser.

Mahdavinejad, M., Badri, N., Fakari, M., & Haqshenas, M. (2013). The role of domed shaped roofs in energy loss at night in hot and dry climate (Case study: Isfahan historical mosques' domes in Iran). *American Journal of Civil Engineering and Architecture, 1*(1), 117-121.

Mahdzar, S. S. S., Safari, H., & Nazidizaji, S. (2013). Similarity between geometric patterns in Persian-Islamic architecture and carpet design and the expression of concepts. *Journal of Basic Applied Science Research, 3*(9), 336-344.

Nabavi, F., Ahmad, Y., & Goh, A.T. (2012). Daylight and opening in traditional houses in Yazd, Iran. In *PLEA2012 - 28th Conference, Opportunities, Limits & Needs Towards an environmentally responsible architecture*. Lima, Peru.

Nazidizaji, S., & Safari, H. (2011). The social logic of Persian houses, in search of the introverted houses genotype. *World Applied Sciences Journal. 26*(6), 817-825.

Von Hardenberg, J. (1982). Considerations of houses adapted to local climate. A case study of Iranian houses in Yazd and Esfahan. *Energy and Building, 1*(2), 155-160.

CHAPTER NINETEEN

READING FOR SUSTAINABILITY THROUGH BOTANICAL AESTHETICS: EMBODIED PERCEPTIONS OF PERTH'S FLORA, 1829 TO 1929

John Charles Ryan

There's a shrubby plant in blossom just now that lends a great deal of beauty and variety to our bush un-dergrowth. It is especially beautiful when long shafts of morning sunshine filter through trees and bushes, diversifying the monotony of flower-gemmed green with charming light and shade effects of golden sun-light and purple shadow patches.

In reference to Blueboy (*Stirlingia latifolia*) (The West Australian, 1924, September 19, p. 6)

Sustainability—indeed a contested term (Thompson, 2010, pp. 196-214)—can be defined as the meaningful and dynamic long-term equilibrium between environmental and social, human and non-human, sentient and non-sentient "things" co-existing in a physical space. Plant life and human relationships to the botanical world are crucial dimensions of sustainable communities and ethical socio-ecological practices. However, the role of plant life in the theory and practice of sustainability is problematically limited to the utilitarian discourses of sustainable agriculture (Tuteja, 2012), food security (Wright, 2012), organic farming (Burnett, 2008), urban gardening (Reid, 2012), sustainable forestry management (Kitayama, 2012), and ideological debates over invasive plants and their impacts on ecosystems and indigenous species (Coates, 2006). Such discourses exemplify a profoundly limited anthropocentric perspective on the botanical world that largely disregards its other values, most importantly a plant's intrinsic right-to-exist (Hall, 2009) and the metaphysics of the plant world (Marder, 2013).

Despite the utilitarian emphasis, plants figure in multiple ways to the community-based, social, emotional and spiritual facets of sustainability, for example, by supporting diverse dimensions of human wellbeing (Cotton, 1996), contributing to the formation of cultural, regional or place-based identity (Trigger & Mulcock, 2005) and defining the aesthetic characteristics of a region, city, town, place or site (Ryan, 2012). While current research into sustainability acknowledges the functional role of plants, few studies foreground the interrelationships between aesthetics, sustainability and flora. Even fewer foreground the ways in which respectful interactions with plants, founded on human aesthetic values, can sustain social systems. The biogeographical context of the South-West Botanical Province of Western Australia—a biodiversity "hotspot" of international renown, with more than 8,500 species of plants and a 35% rate of floristic endemism (Hopper, 2004)—offers an exceptional case study for exploring the connections between aesthetics, sustainability and flora. By virtue of its physical location in the larger South-West region, Perth can be considered one of the world's most ecologically diverse cities. The late writer and ecologist George Seddon advocated the cultural, social and historic significance of WA plants in the seminal publications *Sense of place* (1972) and *The old country* (2005). However, cultural inflections of the South-West's botanical diversity appear sporadically in historical writings during the first one-hundred years following the founding of the Swan River Colony (1829).

Inspired both by Seddon's writings and Perth's unique yet fragile flora, I began in 2013 initial work on an ambitious long-term project titled "FloraCultures: Conserving Perth's Botanical Heritage through a Digital Repository", with seed funding from Edith Cowan University (www.FloraCultures.org.au). FloraCultures combines "design thinking" (Plattner, 2012) and digital heritage conservation techniques (MacDonald, 2012) in developing an online, open-access repository of WA plant-based heritage content. The project is working towards a broad-based, user-friendly, multi-cultural and multimedia framework for botanical heritage conservation. In collaboration with Botanical Gardens and Parks Authority (BPGA), FloraCultures entails a small pilot study of approximately 50 plants found naturally in the bushland of Kings Park in Perth. Once the pilot project is released in 2014, the online repository will promote the overlays between cultural heritage and indigenous plants through a spectrum of content: Aboriginal Australian uses and beliefs, explorer journals, settler diaries, visitor accounts, poetry, literary works, paintings, photography, music and oral histories. This chapter analyses one component of the heritage archive: a cross-section of written material retrieved from the Battye Library, the digitised newspaper archives of the National Library of Australia (NLA) and other historical collections. These writings (mostly from newspaper and journal articles) point to a sophisticated awareness of Perth's bushland flora amongst the city's burgeoning human population. In order to contextualise these excerpts, references will be made to published, non-fiction accounts of settlers (Moore, 1978) and visitors (Armstrong, 1979) to the South-West region, 1829 and 1929.

An embodied aesthetics of plants: Sensation and the allure of the "lower" senses

Aesthetics has been historically associated with the visual appreciation of artworks (for example, see Berleant, 2005). However, the aesthetics of art and nature share a common preoccupation with the appearance of objects, with vision as the principal sense, with distance as the habitus of interaction and with analytical reflection as the mode of judgement (Ryan, 2012, Chapter 4). Accordingly, in order for a plant (tree, shrub, grass, wildflower or herb) to become a proper object of aesthetics (i.e., to be judged in aesthetic terms), the visible qualities of form (symmetry, harmony, gracefulness, vastness, magnitude) and colour (brightness, tone, contrast, homogeneity) must be manifest in the plant. The species otherwise falls partly or wholly outside of the conventions of aesthetics as conceptualised in Western thought.

In *Aesthetic theory*, Theodor Adorno (1984, p. 91) propounds that aesthetics, particularly since the work of the German philosopher Friedrich Wilhelm Schelling (1775–1854), has been concerned with art rather than nature. Adorno, reflecting a Kantian orientation, maintains that the aesthetics of art and the aesthetics of nature are interrelated; both are concerned with appearances, images and the assessment of beauty. Nature, in terms of aesthetics, is "perceived as [the] appearance of the beautiful and not as an object to be acted upon" (Adorno, 1984, p. 97). As with an object of art, beauty in nature instigates analytical reflection, scientific rationality and objective distance. Echoing Kantian disinterestedness, Adorno asserts that "the beautiful in nature is that which appears greater when seen from a distance, both temporally and spatially" (1984, p. 104). Nature can be an object of aesthetics, but only if conflated with art, that is, only on art's terms.

Immanuel Kant's cognitive model of the senses has played a fundamental part in the Western notion of aesthetics and our regard for plants as beautiful and aesthetically worthy of consideration and, in some instances, worthy of conservation. Kant's model centres on "empirical perception", otherwise known as object cognition—the process of objectification in which information about objects in the world (i.e., those things external to our bodies) is acquired as cognitive data. The senses that can deliver the most information about objects, subsequently, form the basis for a taxonomy, ranked from the lower (smell and taste) to the higher senses (touch, hearing and vision). In *Anthropology from a pragmatic point of view*, Kant splits the "vital" from the "organic" senses. For Kant, changes in temperature, pressure or emotional states engage the vital senses and "penetrate the body to the centre of life" (Kant, 1978, p. 41). For example, proprioception, as a vital sense, is the perception of one's muscles and joints as one moves through space. The five organic senses are either objective or subjective. For Kant, the objective senses are touch (*tactus*), sight (*visus*) and hearing (*auditus*); the subjective senses, taste (*gustus*) and smell (*olfactus*). The objective senses are empirical, leading to knowledge of an object (e.g., its shape and size); the subjective senses register impressions directly on or near the mediating organ (e.g., the tongue, stomach, nose and lungs) and are associated with pleasure rather than cognition. Subjective sense involves variable responses between individuals; objective sense underpins the science of the senses because it results in perceptual consistency between individuals (i.e., form and colour can be measured empirically and communicated). Kant explicitly links sensation to objectification: "all together they [the five senses] are senses of organic sensation which correspond in number to the inlets [nose, tongue, ears, eyes and skin] from the outside, provided by nature so that the creature is able to distinguish between objects" (1978, p. 41).

The Kantian model of sensation requires the cleavage between the objective (higher) and subjective (lower) senses. The difference between the higher and lower senses corresponds to the difference between surface perception and inner sensation. As such, sensation becomes an intellectualised process of acquiring knowledge about objects in an environment. Although a limited faculty in Kant's view, touch produces knowledge of an object's form through physical contact with its surfaces and, hence, is "the most important and the most reliably instructive of all senses" (Kant, 1978, p. 41). In association with sight and hearing, touch leads to empirical understanding; touch is an extension of the human subject towards the object. This non-dialogic concept of sense involves touching the world rather than a being touched by; hearing the world rather than being heard; seeing rather than being seen. It is predicated on control of the external world as a collection of objects. Furthermore, Kant links sight to light, transcendence, the sublime and intellection: "The sense of sight, while not more indispensable than the sense of hearing, is, nevertheless, the noblest, since, among all the senses, it is farthest removed from the sense of touch, which is the most limited condition of perception" (Kant, 1978, p. 43). In contrast to the higher senses, taste and smell do not result in cognition of an object because the concept of the object (i.e., its form and colour) is obfuscated during the sensing process (e.g., the plant is consumed or its volatile oil penetrates the olfactory glands). For Kant, smell is the lowest sense, associated with stench, filth and decay. For example, a nauseating smell penetrates the body against one's conscious will; the uncanniness of stench confounds the Kantian sensory order.

This results in the privileging of the "higher" senses and the denigration of the "lower" senses, and underlies our limited conceptualisation of aesthetics. Far from confined to the canons of Continental philosophy, the Kantian hierarchy has produced sweeping effects in a number of disciplines. For example, developmental psychologist Ernest Schachtel's *Metamorphosis: on the development of affect, perception, attention and memory* (originally published in 1959), although not referring to aesthetics *per se*, defines objectification in comparable language to Kant as the process of perceiving objects that exist outside of the human subject (Schachtel, 1984, p. 85). For Schachtel (as for Kant), the higher sense of vision is object-oriented and, therefore, makes possible the cognition of exterior things. Taste, smell, proprioception and thermal recognition (i.e., touch) are lower, primitive and "objectless". Schachtel distinguishes between the allocentric (vision and hearing) and the autocentric (gustatory, olfactory, thermal and proprioceptive) senses. The allocentric senses exhibit a capacity for objectification and are intellectual and spiritual; the autocentric senses lack the powers of objectification and are physical (Schachtel, 1984, p. 89). Whereas the allocentric senses can be projected at objects over distances through space, autocentric sensations are localised in or near the mediating sense organs. Autocentric and allocentric sense experiences diverge in terms of how they are remembered and communicated in language.

The geographer J.D. Porteous takes up Schachtel's allocentric-autocentric dichotomy in the context of environmental aesthetics (Porteous, 1989, 1996). Autocentric (subject-centred) perception is concerned with pleasure and feeling; allocentric (object-oriented) perception relates to objectification, cognition and knowledge-production, in the Kantian mode (Porteous, 1996, p. 31). In sum, the autocentric senses are physical, "primitive", effective at close-range and acute in children; the allocentric senses are chiefly visual, intellectual, "sophisticated", detached, distanced, easier to recall and more developed in adults. These sorts of taxonomies limit the importance of the lower senses and have serious implications for the design of urban environments today and, more generally, for coming to terms with our relationship to the natural world in the era of climate change.

The FloraCultures framework encompasses the traditional conceptualisation of aesthetics as beauty (based predominantly or entirely in sight) and aesthesis as immanence and sensation. I propose the term *floraesthesis* as a place-based model of aesthetics drawing upon the concept of *aesthesis* as experience through the multiple senses. However, most theoretical accounts of aesthetics, perception and the senses—Adorno, Kant and Schachtel's included—neglect aesthesis, the etymological and conceptual root of the Western formulation of aesthetics as visual appreciation. In Kant's example, sensation (aesthesis through touch) merely serves object cognition. However, as the derivation of Alexander Baumgarten's 18th-century neologism *aesthetics*, aesthesis connotes sensation and embodiment—modes of experience cultivated through touch, taste and smell in dynamic interplay with hearing and vision (Mules, 2008). An investigation of aesthesis entails the concerted exploration of the senses independently of hierarchies (lower vs. higher, autocentric vs. allocentric, cognitive vs. non-cognitive). The oppositions promulgated by such aesthetic models do not lead to well-rounded understandings of human embodiment in a place—as if autocentric and allocentric perception can be divided; as if taste and smell can operate disconnected from vision, hearing and touch; as if the activities of the brain (cognition) can be cleaved from the sensations of the body (aesthesis). Aesthesis is the foundation for exploring the integration of the senses.

Interpreting botanical heritage through floraesthesis: Some examples from Perth, WA

Floraesthesis is an embodied aesthetics of plants—one summoning the five senses while also inviting the vital senses that exist outside of the five-sense regime, including proprioception (bodily awareness in space) and topaesthesia (sense of place) (Ryan, 2012, Chapter 13). It is also the critical perspective I use to analyse the writings from 1829–1929 collected during FloraCultures. Through the intensive exploration of multi-sensoriality and sensation, we can appreciate the extent of colonial-era interactions with Perth's plants. Thinking plants, aesthetics and sustainability together, I note that the historical examples that follow are not single-mindedly attuned to visual appreciation, but also to embodied aesthesis through a variety of activities: the harvesting of plant material for housing, the making of preserves from native fruits, and the appreciation of the endemic perfumes of the bush. Also embedded within the writings are statements about the increasing need to conserve Perth's endemic plant life.

An embodied aesthetics of Marri (*Corymbia callophylla*) is apparent in the accounts of its dark-red resin or kino and the use of its flowers for a beverage. Yet, the tree's scientific name reflects a purely visual aesthetics; the genus *Corymbia* refers to the flower structure while the species name *callophylla* is for "beautiful leaf". In the 1880s, colonist and lawyer George Fletcher Moore recorded "Kardan" as the Whadjuck (metropolitan area) Nyoongar name for "Eucalyptus resinifera; red gum-tree, so called from the quantity of gum-resin of a deep congealed blood colour, which exudes during particular months in the year, through the bark" (A Descriptive Vocabulary, 1978, p. 28). To the Menang (South Coast) Nyoongar, "Marri" defined as "flesh or meat" (Moore, 1978, p. 51) connotes the sensation of eating. Moore lists "Numbrid" as "the flower or blossom of the red gum-tree, from which the natives make a favourite beverage by soaking the flowers in water" (1978. p. 62). For the English novelist D.H. Lawrence, who visited Perth briefly in the 1920s, kino symbolised the melancholy of the bush in physical terms: "This tree seems to sweat blood. A hard dark blood of agony. It frightens me—all the bush out beyond stretching away over these hills frightens me, as if dark gods possessed the place" (cited in Skinner, 1972, p. 112). Despite Lawrence's horror, kino has an extensive history of medicinal use, some of which was of practical interest to colonists. In 1836, the missionary Francis Armstrong (1979, p. 199) recorded the use of kino amongst the Nyoongar as an antiseptic for wounds, whereas in the 1880s the homesteader Ethel Hassell (1975, p. 24) wrote of its use in treating diarrhoea amongst settlers. As for the commercial viability of the kino, Moore (2006) observed that:

> much gum might be collected from the red gum tree. It is said to be a powerful astringent and might be useful in that way or would make a good varnish. I shall try to send you some specimens of it and the white gum from the zanthorrea [*sic*] which here is familiarly called 'black boy'. (p. 14)

During the time period, there was a proliferation of written information about Balga, known by the common names Grasstree and—formerly— Blackboy. Although not related to the Gramineae family, the moniker "Grasstree" comes from the frond-like appearance of its foliage. The name "Blackboy" reflects the colonial-era perception of its trunk, thought to resemble the distant appearance of a Nyoongar person in the bush. The genus *Xanthorrhoea* derives from the Greek words *xanthos* (yellow) and *rheo* (flow) in reference to its sap. Numerous parts of Balga have been consumed traditionally by Aboriginal peoples, making the species the "refrigerator and one-stop shop of the bush". Its leaves (mindarie) have been used for thatching huts (mia-mias) or making torches, dead flower stems for fire and spear-making, living flower stalks soaked in water to produce a fermented drink, and its aromatic sap combined with kangaroo dung and ash to make an early epoxy. The dark black trunk of Balga contains nourishing Bardi grubs. In the 1880s, George Fletcher Moore recorded the traditional uses of the small but long-lived tree, reflecting an embodied aesthetics of touch and taste in particular:

> This is a useful tree to the natives where it abounds. The frame of their huts is constructed from the tall flowering stems, and the leaves serve for thatch and for a bed. The resinous trunk forms a cheerful blazing fire. The flower-stem yields a gum used for food. The trunk gives a resin for cement, and also, when beginning to decay, furnishes large quantities of marrow-like grubs, which are considered a delicacy. Fire is readily kindled by friction of the dry flower- stems, and the withered leaves furnish a torch. (A Descriptive Vocabulary, 1978, p. 3)

An embodied aesthetics or floraesthesis of Balga was also at play during the colonial era, in which some of its Noongar uses were adopted. In 1927, Mrs Edward Shenton published her recollections of her mother's account of arriving in Perth in 1830. Shenton begins with a description of the city's flora, as related by her mother in the aesthetic language of scenery, beauty and pleasing colouration. The natural attractiveness of the soon-to-be-urbanised landscape persisted in Mrs. F. Lochee's memory:

> My mother [nee Emma Purkis] said she could never forget the beauty of the scenery when they arrived in Perth. From Point Lewis to Mill-street, she said, there was a high hill running right down to the river and the bank as far back as Hay-street was very beautiful in colours of green, yellow, white and pink, with small streams running at intervals into the river. From Mill-street commenced another long hill, which ran as far as Bennett-street, and was clothed in beautiful verdure and broken by gaps and running streams. Where Government House ballroom now stands was a ravine and a running stream. (cited in Shenton, 1927, pp. 1-2)

Shenton's recorded oral history speaks of the effects of colonisation on the bushland in an area now quite close to Perth's Central Business District where the Purkis family accepted a land grant: "When they arrived the bush had been cut to make St. George's Terrace the same width as now from Milligan-street to Lord-street (now Victoria-avenue), and there was a narrower cutting (Adelaide-terrace) to a decline in the roadway" (Shenton, 1927, p. 2). Although they arrived in Perth without their belongings, the family soon had accommodation comprising "one large tent with a fly, which was divided into three rooms for sleeping, lined with blankets and carpeted with blackboy rushes over which mats were placed" (p. 2). The first part of the quoted text from Shenton perfectly exhibits a visual aesthetics of flora, with its Kantian emphasis on "the beauty of the scenery", "colours of green, yellow, white and pink" and the Perth landscape "clothed in beautiful verdure". However, Shenton's description of the living arrangements of her mother's family suggests a different kind of perception: a floraesthesis of Balga, its "rushes" or mindarie foliage supplying physical comfort, the sensation of warmth and the pleasure of its organic fragrance in their new home.

Like Balga, Zamia provided more than visual aesthetics to Swan River colonists. Zamia (*Macrozamia riedlei*) is a member of the Zamiaceae family of cycads distributed throughout Australia and prominent throughout Kings Park. Zamia fruits were detoxified by Nyoongar people through a variety of fermentation processes, roasted, ground and baked into a nutritious damper. Moore (1978, p. 17) recorded the fruits as "By-yu" and observed: "This in its natural state is poisonous; but the natives, who are very fond if it, deprive it of its injurious qualities by soaking it in water for a few days, and then burying it in sand, where it is left until nearly dry, and is then fit to eat." Its "wool" was used for clothing, bedding and children's diapers in the early years of the colony, as the following remark in *The Western Mail* indicates: "The wool which surrounds the bases of the leaves has uses for stuffing pillows, cushions, etc." (1922, March 2, p. 30).

The consumption of Zamia fruits or the soaking of Balga flowers to produce a fermented drink are examples of floraesthesis in which a plant substance is taken into the body. Nevertheless, Perth's flowering shrubs have often been constructed in the exclusively aesthetic language of form and colour. For example, an article in *The West Australian* lists the popular names of the endemic *Hypocalymma robustum* as Swan River Myrtle, Pink Myrtle, Pink-all-the-way-up, Monkey Blossom, Wild Peach and Pink Heath and goes on to say: "Its slender branches are erect and rigid, giving the effect in springtime of thick clumps of graceful spikes, closely set with vivid pink blossom fully opened and with innumerable yellow stamens at the base of the stems" (The West Australian, 1928, September 7, p. 7). A plea for conservation follows its aesthetic depiction: "All who remember how plentiful this lovely plant once was around Perth regret its rapid disappearance in recent years from the open spaces in the vicinity of the metropolis" (p. 7).

Stinkwood (*Jacksonia sternbergiana*), however, evokes noxious smell rather than visual pleasure, "so called because the wood when burned gives off evil-smelling gases" (The Western Mail, 1929, February 7, p. 38). Moore (1978, p. 40) described the species as "one of the dullest and most melancholy foliaged trees in Australia. It has an unpleasant smell in burning, from which it is frequently called stinkwood." Whereas Swan River Myrtle impressed the eyes and Stinkwood repulsed the nose, Broom Ballart (*Exocarpus sparteus*) pleased the taste buds, but only somewhat for Moore (p. 24) who described the berries as having "no particularly good flavour".

Like the Marri, Balga and Zamia, many of the herbaceous plants in the bushland of Kings Park bear cultural histories involving the human appreciation of plants through the "lower" senses of taste, touch and smell. For example, Bloodroot (*Haemodorum spicatum* or Bohn in Nyoongar) derives from *haima* for "blood" and *doron* for "gift". Moore recorded the flavour of the root as resembling "a very mild onion. It is found at all periods of the year in sandy soils, and forms a principal article of food among the natives. They eat it either raw or roasted" (Moore, 1978, p. 12, A Descriptive Vocabulary). Accounts of Milkmaids (*Burchardia congesta*) evoke the visual and haptic senses and, specifically, the sensation of touching wax. Perth children were known to collect the flowers: "The flowers of Burchardia are very beautiful individually. The yellow stamens stand upright on the points of an inner white star with a dark-coloured, reddish-green, conical seed-capsule… it is commonly called 'wax' by children, who love to gather the snowy blooms" (The West Australian, 1924, September 26, p. 6). Another herb, *Stirlingia latifolia*, is known as Blueboy or Rust Flower. The name Blueboy refers to the fact that wall plaster—made with sand from where the species grows—turns blue. In 1918, essential oil of the species was examined at the Imperial Institute in the U.K. was found to consist almost entirely of acetophenone, which has soporific properties and was explored medicinally during the period.

Towards aesthesis

Approached from the perspectives of sustainability and aesthetics, these examples collectively suggest the importance of Perth's indigenous plant life for its early European inhabitants. In addition to providing insights from the period following settlement, the writings also reveal aesthetic and conservation attitudes towards flora. The perceptions represented in the written materials neither reflect sustainable practices adopted by the settlers towards the Perth environment nor show an ethical regard for flora beyond the use-value paradigm. They do, however, indicate a wider non-scientific, cultural appreciation of and concern for Perth's environment that I maintain has been largely diluted in the public population of the metropolitan region today. While some aesthetic perceptions are exclusively visual, others reveal embodied interactions with an abundant, diverse and threatened flora. The greater physical distribution of New World plants in the fledgling city and the lack in the availability of essential goods (e.g., food, medicine, fibre, ornamentation and building materials) in the early years of the State necessitated a gamut of embodied interactions with flora. Such human-plant transactions engaged the "lower", intimate senses of touch, taste and smell—which have been atrophied in the Western model of nature aesthetics but which are essential to engendering long-term sustainable relationships with the non-cultivated botanical world.

In developing an analytical approach to FloraCultures, I have found it necessary to rethink the origins and applications of environmental aesthetics and the role of the senses. I have set out to re-read the cultural heritage of plants with attention to aesthesis—not constrained by visual or cognitive bias. A phenomenological aesthetics co-constitutes subjects and objects in a world in which "objects" (here, plants) are regarded as sentient, sensuous, autonomous and agentic. There are lessons in such philosophy and history for today's design practitioners. Sustainability research should be aware of the history of place and should consider the autocentric and allocentric senses as two sides of a coin. Sensuous readings of human-plant histories can help the designers, planners, conservationists, ecologists, architects and educators of today create the pleasurable metropolitan landscapes of tomorrow. These designed places would not only call attention to the beauty of wildflowers, but would simultaneously encourage physical interaction with plants as co-inhabitants of our suburban neighbourhoods and with associated benefits to animals, fungi, insects and other living beings. A radical and subversive form of metropolitan gardening would put edible native plants amongst ornamentals— food and beverage at the peripheries of lawns and playing fields—while specifically protecting endemic species that are endangered or threatened. Our sense of place and plants is an embodied one.

John Charles Ryan is Postdoctoral Research Fellow in Communications and Arts at Edith Cowan University in Perth, Western Australia. He is the author of the books Green Sense (TrueHeart Press, 2012), Two With Nature (Fremantle Press, 2012), Unbraided Lines (CG Publishers, 2013), Digital Arts (Bloomsbury, 2014, with Cat Hope) and Being With (CG Publishers, 2014). His interests include the environmental humanities, human-plant studies, ecocriticism, ecopoetics and practice-led research.

References

Adorno, T. (1984). *Aesthetic theory* (C. Lenhardt, Trans.). London: Routledge & Kegan Paul.

Armstrong, F. (1979). Manners and habits of the Aborigines of Western Australia, from information collected by Mr F. Armstrong, Interpreter, 1836. In N. Green (Ed.), *Nyungar - the people: Aboriginal customs in the southwest of Australia* (pp. 186-206). North Perth: Creative Research.

Berleant, A. (2005). *Aesthetics and environment: Variations on a theme.* Burlington, VT: Ashgate Publishing.

Burnett, V. (2008). *Establishing perennial pastures: The foundation for sustainable organic farming systems.* Barton: RIRDC.

Coates, P. (2006). *American perceptions of immigrant and invasive species: strangers on the land.* Berkeley: University of California Press.

Cotton, C. M. (1996). *Ethnobotany: principles and applications.* Chichester, England: John Wiley & Sons.

Hall, M. (2009). Plant autonomy and human-plant ethics. *Environmental Ethics, 31,* 169-181.

Hassell, E. (1975). *My dusky friends.* Dalkeith, Australia: C.W. Hassell.

Hopper, S. (2004). Southwestern Australia, cinderella of the world's temperate floristic regions. *Curtis's Botanical Magazine, 21*(2), 132-180.

Kant, I. (1978). *Anthropology from a pragmatic point of view* (V. L. Dowdell, Trans.). Carbondale, IL: Southern Illinois University Press.

Kitayama, K. (2012). *Co-benefits of sustainable forestry: ecological studies of a certified Bornean rain forest.* Dordrecht: Springer.

MacDonald, L. (2012). *Digital heritage.* Hoboken: Taylor & Francis.

Marder, M. (2013). *Plant-thinking: a philosophy of vegetal life.* New York: Columbia University Press.

Moore, G. F. (1978). *Diary of ten years eventful life of an early settler in Western Australia, and also a descriptive vocabulary of the language of the Aborigines.* Nedlands: University of Western Australia Press.

Moore, G. F. (2006). *The Millendon memoirs: George Fletcher Moore's Western Australian diaries and letters, 1830-1841.* J. Cameron (Ed.). Carlisle: Hesperian Press.

Mules, W. (2008). Open country: towards a material environmental aesthetics. *Continuum, 22*(2), 201-212.

Plattner, H. (2012). *Design thinking research: measuring performance in context.* Dordrecht: Springer.

Porteous, J. D. (1989). *Planned to death: the annihilation of a place called Howdendyke.* Manchester, England: Manchester University Press.

Porteous, J. D. (1996). *Environmental aesthetics: ideas, politics and planning.* London, England: Routledge.

Reid, N. (2012). *Local food systems in old industrial regions: concepts, spatial context, and local practices.* Farnham: Ashgate Publishing.

Ryan, J. (2012). *Green sense: the aesthetics of plants, place and language.* Oxford: TrueHeart Press.

Schachtel, E. (1984). *Metamorphosis: on the development of affect, perception, attention, and memory.* New York: Da Capo Press.

Seddon, G. (1972). *Sense of place: a response to an environment.* Perth: University of Western Australia Press.

Seddon, G. (2005). *The old country: Australian landscapes, plants and people.* Cambridge: Cambridge University Press.

Shenton, M. E. (1927). Reminiscences of Perth, 1830-1840. *The Western Australian Historical Society Journal and Proceedings, 1*(1), 1-4.

Skinner, M. L. (1972). *The fifth sparrow: an autobiography.* Sydney, Australia: Sydney University Press.

The West Australian. (1924, September 19). Our wildflowers. *The West Australian,* p. 6.

The West Australian. (1924, September 26). Our wildflowers. *The West Australian,* p. 6.

The West Australian. (1928, September 7). Our wildflowers: Swan River Myrtle. *The West Australian,* p. 7.

The Western Mail. (1922, March 2). Western Australian trees. *The Western Mail,* p. 30.

The Western Mail. (1929, February 7). Stinkwood and Swish-Bush. *The Western Mail*, p. 38.

Thompson, P. (2010). *The agrarian vision: sustainability and environmental ethics*. Lexington: The University Press of Kentucky.

Trigger, D., & Mulcock, J. (2005). Forests as spiritually significant places: nature, culture and "belonging" in Australia. *The Australian Journal of Anthropology, 16*(3), 306-320.

Tuteja, N. (2012). *Improving crop productivity in sustainable agriculture*. Weinheim: Wiley.

Wright, J. (2012). *Sustainable agriculture and food security in an era of oil scarcity: lessons from Cuba*. Hoboken: Earthscan.

CHAPTER TWENTY

IDENTIFYING AN AESTHETIC DIMENSION OF SUSTAINABILITY IN THE BANGLADESHI CONTEXT

Amzad Hossain & Dora Marinova

Introduction

Representing a branch of philosophy, the existence of aesthetics is described as search for knowledge rather than a guide to practice (Bosanquet, 2005). In this meaning, its origins can be traced back only to the 18th century. The aesthetic consciousness or sense of beauty however is as old as our species' existence, with aesthetics judgements being a profound part of who we are (Arweck & Keenan, 2006). Aesthetics is pervasive in our everyday life and a profound part of our experience (Schulkin, 2004, p. 58). Our perception of beauty guides our actions, but what we value and where we find inspiration for splendour, wonder and magnificence can vastly differ. Natural miracles, objects of art and pieces of music as well as technological inventions trigger our perceptions of beauty. Our reactions however are strongly influenced by economic and socio-cultural dynamics. In the industrialised Western world, the sources of aesthetics and pleasure are often rooted in consumption and consequently, unchecked use of natural resources. In spiritual Bangladesh, nature remains the main source of beauty and this is implicitly linked to the practicing of sustainability as manifested in the country's light ecological footprint.

This chapter analyses the tangible and impalpable aspects of aesthetics prevailing in Bangladeshi society, arguing that when nature is at the centre of beauty, people live more sustainably. The authors first describe Bangladesh as a country where aesthetics is a living practical philosophy linked to every-day actions and then explore the role of its spiritual leaders, the Baul philosophers, in maintaining the connection and providing the inspiration for sustainable living in harmony with nature.

Nature as a teacher of aesthetics

Bangladesh's diverse topographies with innumerable bodies of water, beaches, charlands (shoals, river islands), mangrove forests, flora and fauna are unique and its aesthetics tangible. Geographically the country occupies an area of 147,570 km^2 with 230 rivers, innumerable natural lakes and canals and millions of artificial ponds (Brammer, 1997). Topographically, Bangladesh is largely a land of flood-plains (80% of its area) – riverine (55%) and coastal (25%). While the landmass under the river flood-plains is covered in water for weeks and months in the monsoon, the coastal floodplains sink twice a day when high tides occur. The country has also terraces (8%) and tracts (12%). Within this varying natural setting, there exists a diversity of aesthetic experiences drawn from the natural world.

Bangladesh also enjoys six seasons. These seasons change the physical appearance of, and cause changes to, the environment. The rainy season (borsha kal) inherently changes the local landscape aesthetics when the Ganges and the Brahmaputra rivers tend to change their courses by breaking the obstructions on their pathway to the Bay of Bengal (Brammer, 1997). In course of changing seasons and normal sliding of the riverbanks, the rivers carry about 2 billion tonnes of silts annually through to the Bay. The silts is spread on the floodplain raising its landscape gradually higher, building up river shoals, and deposited in the Bay, building the mangrove islands.

The other five seasons; spring, summer, autumn, dewy and winter, play diverse aesthetic–roles. The spring unfolds a variety of colours, the summer burns long and hot prior to heavy rains of the monsoon season. The sky clears up in autumn with bright moonlit nights. Just before winter sets in and the start of the winter harvest, Bangladesh enjoys a season known as "the dewy season" *Hemanta Kal*. This constant changing of seasons and variation has contributed to the enrichment of people's emotional aesthetic diversity (Hossain, 1995).

According to Berleant (2005, p. 13) this environmentally driven aesthetic helps "the activating forces of mind, eye and hand, together with the perceptual features that engage these forces and elicit their reactions. We live, then, in dynamic nexus of interpreting forces to which we contribute and respond". The elemental geographical synergies of Bangladesh such as the monsoonal rainfall, floods, riverbank erosion and renewable energy sources (tides, sun, wind and biomass) are inter-related with, and affect its socio-economic dynamics, including poverty.

In rural areas where about 80% of the country's formally uneducated people live, aesthetic judgments are practiced in mundane decision-making. For example, external bodily appearances are first considered for matchmaking in Bangladesh, where most marriages are arranged. Aesthetic judgment is also applied in buying and generating commodities as most goods are sold without any written label and "the visual appearance of food is important" (Stecker, 2005, p. 3).

Traditionally, formally uneducated people receive their aesthetic education in terms of fulfilment and contentment from their respective family, society, spiritual guide and from nature around them. This aesthetic education is assumed to result in enabling a person to judge the lavish green of paddy fields as a source of inspiration for farmers and poets alike. The aesthetic beauty of those fields proves their ability to produce abundant harvests.

Folksongs emphasising geo-environmental synergy describe these phenomena. The Baul philosopher, M. A. Gafur of Pabna district writes:

> Hills, forests, and water bodies,
> Low land, high land and shoals,
> All are dependent on wind, rains and sun.
> They are the keys to people's happiness and misery (Gafur, circa 1962).

Women as guardians of the aesthetic

Bangladesh has been a cultural melting pot of many religions, ethnicities, cultures and dynasties. According to Indian cultural historians such as Bhattacarya (1383 BE), Basham (1975) and Haq (1975), the Tantric Bengalis had their own culture and religion that had mystical elements, as does Sufi Islam. Sufi Islam further mixed Tantrism and Islamic culture through religious syncretism. The Tantrics of medieval India linked the study of perception, cognition, aesthetics and spirituality (Becker, 1993).

When separated for farm work married people wonder about the ultimate meaning of life, and seek answers to metaphysical questions about the inner aesthetic reality of heterosexual love. This spiritual search is linked to an awareness of longevity (sustainability) (Hossain, 2001). Men's passion of maya (attachment) towards women is perceptible in Bangladesh culture. Dasgupta (1976, p. 178) observes that as the tree is fixed to the earth by its roots and the black-bee is attached to the lotus, so is a man bound to the woman – and all in love. A popular Baul song that vibrates in rural Bangladesh day and night reveals insights into men's maya towards women, children and the world in which they live:

> I have willingly bounded myself with the chain of maya.
> A chain of steel can be broken open, but not the chain of maya.

I was born as a complete entity.
I have liberated my half entity in marrying,
a quarter to my offspring, and
a quarter for sustaining Samsara (socio-economic activities)
(Hossain and Hossain-Rhaman, 2007, p. 91).

The contemporary and traditional cultural traits of Bangladesh value women both as a tangible and as an aesthetic partner for nurturing human sustainability. Women are at the heart of achieving and maintaining household sustainability. The home environment plays a formative role for the development of values and practices that can facilitate the establishment of a sustainable culture. Women's multiple roles in mothering, on one hand, and harvest processing, food preparation, hospitality and housekeeping, on the other, are not only significant, but also irreplaceable. Men's role is mostly associated with that of a provider, while women engage more actively with the holistic upbringing of the future generations. The unity of diversified pluralistic religious culture in Bangladesh have created a woman centric aesthetics that recognises women in a way that is qualitatively different from Western culture, and that allows Bangladesh to retain its conjugal sustainability culture even in a very difficult economic situation.

"Women's attributes generate family happiness" – this popular wisdom is religiously believed, promoted, facilitated and observed in the Islam-influenced pluralistic culture of the country. The Bangladeshi culture acknowledges that the female population contributes to individual, social, economic and ecological sustainability more than its male counterparts; for women have, as Shiva (1989) observes, holistic knowledge about conserving natural resources and using them for long-term survival. Women of Majority World countries, such as Bangladesh, have maintained ecological thought and action that make survival, justice and peace possible (Shiva, 1989).

Ruether (1996) explains the women's roles in managing ecological sustainability from a spiritual perspective: women's spirituality is basically earth-based. The relationship between women and the earth is a reciprocal one – women take care of the earth while the earth in return provides for the needs of women. Shiva (1989) points out that productivity is a measure of producing life and sustenance and although this kind of productivity has been rendered invisible, it does not reduce its centrality to survival. In Indian cosmology (that the Baul philosophers share) person and nature (purusha-prakriti) are a duality in unity. They are inseparable complements of one another. Women's knowledge is ecological and pluralistic, reflecting both the diversity of natural ecosystems and the diversity in cultures that nature-based ecological living gives rise to (Shiva, 1989). The Hindu Sahajya cult (a pre-Baul mystic tradition of Bengal) claims that all women manifest the aesthetics of Radha, whom the god Krishna venerated; thus, no harm should be done to them, nor should any female animal be sacrificed (Dimock, 1966).

In Bangladeshi culture, women's most important aesthetic manifestation is in motherhood – the starting point towards achieving completeness in the purpose of being on earth. Women's spirituality expressed in nurturing their offspring and the environment is profound in Bangladeshi culture. The relationship between women and the earth is aesthetic. The women take care of beautifying the earth while the earth in return beautifies women.

Duley and Edwards (1986: p. 406) in particular point out that historically Islam has adapted to, and interacted with, a wide variety of women/ecology relationships that are expressed in a Baul song:

Say to me, who can understand
woman in this world?
 She gives birth to the three worlds.
As a mother she brings up (her children).

In ignorance, do not neglect her.
Think once, by whose energy keeps you working? (Hossain, 2001, p. 103)

Through the synergies generating from the confluence of all these female driven cultural aesthetics, the people of Bangladesh are inspired to lead a lifestyle which is in general feministic service-centric in sociability, naturalistic in consumption habits and mystical in spirituality (Joshi, 1992; Hossain et al., 2007). The evolution of the unique mystical Baul tradition in Bangladesh also places the status of women at the centre of society and directs the way people relate to their ecological aesthetics.

Bauls as inspiration for aesthetics

The ecstasy intense, mystical songs of the Baul philosophers incorporate the aesthetics of spontaneous and eternal sustainability. The Bauls – from both Muslim and Hindu background – are mostly unlettered, yet full of spontaneous poetic, musical, and philosophical talent. They are seen as being at the root of Bengali culture. As an aesthetic tradition in the Bengali cultural context, the Bauls are unique in aestheticising socio-religious syncretism. The Bauls roam from one shrine to another in the country's villages and cities, showing a full measure of poetic, musical, and philosophical talents. They usually accompany a female associate. In many ways their philosophy and multiple messages conveyed through their songs are feministic as they put a very high value on the role of women in society (Hossain, 1995).

Writers understand aesthetics diversely. For instance, Kant "aligns himself with the tradition that conceives aesthetic phenomena in light of the formula 'Unity within the manifold'" (cited in Henrich, 1992, p. 55). According to Hughes (2010, p. 84), aesthetics "presents a standard for judgment not simply derivative from our experience of other things". Baul Guru Aziz Shah Fakir (104) understands 'aesthetics' simply as wisdom of nature – the supra-natural sustainer. He also perceives aesthetics as a supra-logical source of contentment as well as the basis for assessing and practicing sustainability.

Within the Baul philosophy, humans inherently live with the sense of (the beauty of) place, conjugality and sociality. Most people of Bangladesh are yet to be literally familiar with the concept of sustainability as a matter of formal educational study. Yet this literal unfamiliarity does not indicate that they miss sustainability perspectives. This is because the Bangladeshi people's cultural understanding of spirituality can capture their dynamic, transformative quality of spirituality as lived experience. This experience is linked to self, society and nature (King, 2008, p. 4). Spirituality for sustainability awareness being the inherent driving force for all living things for their co-existence, it is inherent in people so they are inclined to want to understand, assess and practice sustainability.

Culturally, Bangladesh is abundantly affluent with aesthetical sustainability indicatives as stated in the national aesthetical icons of sustainability:

Water in river,
field full of crops,
pond full of fish,
cow in the cowshed,
homestead with trees,
melodious tune of the birds,
uproar of children,
songs of Bauls and boatmen,
fear of wild animals and ghosts at night.

This aesthetic intensive blue-print is widely referred to by media, school texts books, Baul songs and folk discourses and proverbs (Hossain & Marinova, 2005).

In Bangladesh, life is aesthetics and aesthetics is life. Bengalis are fond of poetry. Many write poems but nearly all love listening for hours of recitations and singing. This is a very popular practice that involves the people of all strata – Muslims and Hindus, youngsters and grown-ups alike. Baul songs, composed and performed by usually well-reputed religious men or women, belong to a particular musical and poetic genre liked by everybody (Hossain, 2001).

On the one hand, the songs inspire the listeners to understand the aesthetics of the universe; and on the other, they help to understand the aesthetics of the place – one of the key values for sustainability management. Lamarque and Olsen (2004, p. 446) also assert that music's ability to express emotions is what gives it its enduring value – and indeed might account for its profundity.

The Bauls are environmentalist by their beliefs and practices. They are simple, natural, unembellished and rooted in the soil. They do not believe in writing down their spontaneously composed songs. They sing as they go along, and as the feeling comes to them. The messages conveyed through their songs and music are of great relevance to what the authors mean and understand by aesthetics of sustainability.

Conclusion

The aesthetic experience as perceived by the people of Bangladesh can be academically conceived as the mixture of tangible and intangible aesthetics that can generate contentment (for the eye and hope for the heart) underpinning their sustainable co-existence with nature. These aesthetics have been the basis for assessing sustainability in the past, are current at present, and will remain crucial in the future. Amongst the tangible aesthetics there exists a natural manifestation of the country's diverse topographies with ecological riches. This is why while judging Bangladesh on the scale of aesthetics of sustainability, it appears that life there is conditioned externally with its geo-environmental and socio-cultural aesthetics, and internally with the country's diverse spiritual aesthetics.

While the role of aesthetics in sustainability has been neglected in the West, the culture of aesthetic judgment relating to sustainability traditionally exists in Bangladesh. It is reinforced day and night by way of the Baul songs and folk stories. The Bangladeshis are culturally educated as to how to acquire the spiritual skill (spirituality) for developing the faculty of aesthetic judgment from tradition, society, spiritual gurus and nature. From a practical point of view, people understand spirituality as 'wisdom for living', and spiritual practice means a particular discipline to follow the guidance of a mystic teacher who has a set of rules for educating about aesthetics mystically (King, 2008, p. 31).

The mystically perceived aesthetics of the natural, socio-cultural Bangladesh has made the country's people highly spiritual in terms of cultural features such as simplicity, neighbourhood, sociability, endurance, resilience and happiness that exist as a syncretistic set of aesthetic values. Aesthetics in terms of 'heart contenting beauty' that people of Bangladesh like, love, adore, and value appears crucial to them in their sustainability optimism.

The people of rural Bangladesh recognise 'aesthetics' as the tangible and indescribable features that emanate from a supra-natural source, and an aesthetic judgment can help determine the state of the productive richness of all entities of a country. Thus, Bangladeshi people's mundane and spiritual contentment are complemented in terms of longevity, sustainability, spirituality and naturalism.

Dr Amzad Hossain is an action researcher and sustainability scholar whose interests cover simple lifestyle, appropriate technology and values with relevance to sustainability. Amzad is a Research Fellow at Curtin University and a Visiting Professor at Rajshahi University in Bangladesh. He is widely published academically and has also authored popular articles on the Baul philosophy and its popularity in Bangladesh.

Dora Marinova is Professor of Sustainability and Associate Director of the Curtin University Sustainability Policy (CUSP) Institute. Her research interests cover innovation models, including the evolving global green system of innovation, self-reliance and the newly emerging area of sustainometrics related to the modelling and measuring of sustainability. Dora has conducted research for the Australian Research Council, Western Australian, Commonwealth Government departments and industry. She has more than 400 refereed publications and has supervised to successful completion 45 PhD students.

References

Arweck, E., & Keenan, W. (Eds). (2006). *Materializing religion: Expression, performance and ritual.* Aldershot, UK: Ashgate.

Basham, A. L. (1975). *A cultural history of India.* London: Clarendon Press.

Becker, J. (1993). *Gamelan stories: Tantrism, Islam, and aesthetics in Central Java.* Tempe, AZ: Arizona State University.

Berleant, A. (2005). *Aesthetics and environment: variations on a theme.* London: Ashgate.

Bhattacarya, U. N. (1383 BE). *Banglar Baul o Baul Gaan.* Calcutta: Oriental Book Company.

Bosanquet, B. (1892). *A history of aesthetic.* London: George Allen & Unwin.

Brammer, H. (1997). *Agricultural development possibilities in Bangladesh.* Dhaka: University Press.

Dasgupta, S. (1932). *A history of Indian culture.* Vol. 2. Cambridge: Cambridge University Press.

Dimock, E. C., Jr. (1966). *The place of the hidden moon.* Chicago & London: The University of Chicago Press.

Duley, M. I., & Edwards, M. I. (1986). *The cross-cultural study of women: a comprehensive guide.* New York: The Feminist Press.

Gafur, M. A. (circa 1962). *Collection of folk songs.* Unpublished hand-written manuscript.

Haq, E. (1975). *A history of Sufi-ism in Bengal.* Dhaka: Asiatic Book Society of Bangladesh.

Henrich, D. (1992). *Aesthetic judgment and the moral image of the world: studies in Kant.* Stanford, CA: Stanford University Press.

Hossain, A. (1995). *Mazar culture in Bangladesh.* (Doctoral dissertation). Murdoch University Perth, Australia.

Hossain, A. (2001). *Renewing self-reliance for rural Bangladesh through renewable energy technology system.* (Doctoral dissertation). Murdoch University Perth, Australia.

Hossain, A. & Hossain-Rhaman, P. (2007). Men's spirituality and women in Bangladesh culture. In *Education, Employment, and Everything: The triple layers of a woman's life.* In *Proceedings of the International Women's Conference* (pp. 90–94). Queensland, Australia: University of Southern Queensland. Retrieved from http://eprints.usq.edu.au/3321/2/Albion_Collins_eds_IWC_Proceedings_2007.pdf.

Hossain, A., Hossain Rhaman, P., Islam, R. & Marinova, D. (2007). Women at the heart of sustainability: Bangladesh perspective. In *Proceedings of the International Women's Conference* (pp. 95–99). Queensland, Australia: University of Southern Queensland. Retrieved from http://eprints.usq.edu.au/3321/2/Albion_Collins_eds_IWC_Proceedings_2007.pdf.

Hossain, A. & Marinova, D. (2005). Poverty alleviation – a push towards unsustainability in Bangladesh? *In Proceedings of the International Conference on Engaging Communities.* Brisbane, Queensland, Australia: Queensland Department of Main Roads. Retrieved from www.engagingcommunities2005.org/abstracts/Hossain-Amzad-final.pdf

Hughes, F. (2010). *Kant's critique of aesthetic judgment.* London: Continuum.

Joshi, N. (1992). *Economics of the spinning wheel.* Ahmedabad, India: Navajiban Mudranalaya.

King, U. (2008). *The search for spirituality: Our global quest for a spiritual life.* New York: Blue Bridge.

Lamarque, P. & Olsen, S. H. (Eds). (2004). *Aesthetics and the philosophy of art: the analytic tradition*. Oxford: Blackwell.

Ruether, R. (Ed.) (1996). *Women healing earth: third world women on ecology, feminism and religion*. New York: Orbis Books.

Schulkin, J. (2004). *Bodily sensibility: intelligent action*. New York: Oxford University Press.

Shiva, V. (1989). *Staying alive: women, ecology and development*. New Delhi: Zed Books.

Stecker, R. (2005). *Aesthetics and the philosophy of art: an introduction*. New York: Rowman & Littlefield.

John Thackara

Scientists at Harvard have reported, with great fanfare, that the human mind runs on less energy than a household light bulb. Given its 86 billion neurones and phenomenal computing power, this is an impressive technical performance. The only shame is that our brain has not proved itself to be as wise as it is energy efficient. The opposite is in fact the case. Our cool-running brains perceive it as normal to gorge on non-renewable resources, at an accelerating rate, in a finite world. They barely flinch when told that these energy and material flows have increased by a staggering 1,500 times in just fifty years. When informed of the grave environmental and social costs of this epic binge, our brains are barely perturbed. It's not that our brains lack processing capacity - more, that they're preoccupied by the wrong inputs. If you put it to someone (as I have done) that, without soil, humanity will quickly starve, she will probably agree, nod sagely - and wait for me to change the subject. Few of the city people I know ever touch, feel, taste or smell soils, healthy or otherwise. Soil health is rarely in the news. Their children are not taught about it at school. It's the same with climate change, the loss of biodiversity, deforestation; or dying seas: Out of sight, out of mind. Why *would* we care?

Even people who care about consequences reason in curious ways. Many intelligent business and money people, for example, believe passionately that growth is a good thing in and of itself. So what if it's a finite world: growth, like motherhood, is good. Most people in the financial system never actually think about the implications of exponential resource growth on a finite physical planet. It's not just that they're predisposed by ideology to know that growth is good; they also don't need to think through the consequences because their time horizons, and nature's, are so different. Money people are also sanguine about the possibility of rapid, unpredictable, non-linear change; such events happen sometime else, so they don't think about them. At one level, this account is reassuring: There's no evil plot by banksters to crash the economy and turn us all into serfs. At another level, our position is even more alarming: At a push, one can imagine sticking a pitchfork into a despot - but blinkered perceptual frameworks are much harder to pin down.

Our brains have not lacked for prompts, either, as the biosphere burns. Scientists, designers and artists have created a dazzling array of maps, images, data sets, videos and visualisations that are available for the most part free to the environmental movement. Water footprinters have rendered complex data into clear and affective stories. Media artists have used lasers to reveal the toxic emissions of power stations. Land artists have turned whole hills into informative stories about degraded soil. The only problem: making harmful activity visible has proved less effective than we hoped; at worst, it has proved counter-productive. A simple example is the campaign against plastic shopping bags. The plastic bag was successfully turned into an emblem of waste, only for word to get out that the environmental impact of the bag is responsible for about *one-thousandth* of the footprint of the industrially-grown food it contains. The shopping bag campaign influenced our actions as consumers - but it left untouched the underlying system that does the real damage.

All of which poses two tough questions: Why is it that, even when we are exposed to shocking stories and images, nothing seems to change? And, what are we to do as artists and designers if we create a powerful piece of communication – and it has no impact?

I've discovered that these are not new questions. Saint Augustine, in *The City of God* (2012), attacked 'scenic games' as being responsible for the death of the soul - and that was fifteen hundred years ago. More recently, but still in 1908, the American philosopher John Dewey decried the emergence of what he called a 'Kodak fixation' - a photographic attitude that reduces the citizen's role to that of a spectator, detached from that which is experienced (1977, p 129). Another social critic, Ivan Illich, decided that our troubles back in 1120 when monks stopped reading texts aloud to each other and became solitary scholars. For Illich, the reading-to-oneself revolution paved the way for a symbolic culture that placed language, art, and number above more direct ways of knowing and acting in the world (1993). John Berger developed this critique in his essay *Photographs of agony*: the picture exists to prick our consciences and provoke action, but if no action related to its origin in a specific political situation occurs, then the picture is depoliticised. "The picture becomes evidence of the general human condition. It accuses nobody and everybody" (1980, pp. 37 -40). Susan Sontag raised similar issues - about our capacity to ignore inconvenient information - in her classic text about war photography, *Regarding the pain of others* (2003). The problem, Sontag concluded, is that that photographs— and by implication all visualisations—have a tendency to "shrivel sympathy ... image-glut keeps attention light, mobile, relatively indifferent to content" (p. 106). Compassion, Sontag concluded, is an unstable emotion. It needs to be translated into action, or it withers. It is *passivity* that dulls feeling. This persuasive insight raises a new question: What sort of activity best suited to make environmental communication effective? If emitting messages or designing visualisations is ineffective without some kind of follow-up action - what kinds of action do we need to take?

New ways of knowing

This is where cultural and aesthetic practices come in - and with them, the essays in this book. Although they draw on diverse perspectives - from plants, architecture, and garden design, to music, dance and poetry - the writers in this book are united in their passion for re-connection with the living world. In different ways, they explore what it might take to grow a culture that values nurture, more than extraction. Without agreeing on the means to get there, they imagine a world in which 'the economy' is a subset of the environment - and not the other way round. They ask: What it would take for the public interest to be defined as the wellbeing of all living systems, and just human ones? They explore how different art forms might help foster attentiveness to living system, or a sense of obligation towards future generations.

Taken together, these chapters here do not add up to a unified theory of ecological aesthetics. There is no agreed to-do list. For some writers here, aesthetic practice is the communication tool we've been waiting for to tell a new story in a frazzled world. For others, ecological aesthetics are better thought of as a way of being, than a narrative form. For many of the voices here - and eyes, and hands - the natural world should be cherished for what it is, on its own terms - not for its contribution to the wellbeing of humans. Both approaches agree on one proposition: Change doesn't happen just because you tell people things. Change is more likely to happen when people share meaningful experiences in rich, real-world, contexts.

This last insight is important in a special respect: The issue of trust. As we develop new ways to govern our ecosystems and communities, a diversity of different actors and stakeholders will need to learn how to work together - often, for the first time. Think about the food systems of a city; the restoration of a river; or the management of waste: Working with people unlike ourselves, in such contexts, is not an option. Few rules or laws are in place, so this cooperation must necessarily depends a lot on trust - and trust grows best when we to talk to each other, ideally, face to face. In his book *I and Thou* in 1923, the theologian Martin Buber counselled that "all knowledge is dialogic" - but he did not just advocate talk. Community and connection are not just about words, he said; they're about encounter, and presence. Buber taught us that that literally "vital" conversations need to be embodied, and situated - and his teachings apply strongly in ecological contexts, too (1958). Nature is extremely complex, and constantly evolving. Effective stewardship depends on living in close conversation with nature; it cannot be done remotely.

For several writers in this book, the importance of embodied and situated knowledge is a reminder that many indigenous peoples have a closer connection with their lands than we do. Their ceremonies, arts, participatory ritual, and performance, maintain harmony between nature and culture in ways that we can only envy. And perhaps most pertinently of all, indigenous people do not aspire to protect nature in some imagined, perfect and unchanging form; for people who live among dynamically changing systems on a daily basis, perpetual co-evolution is - well, second nature.

A tendency to binary thinking - an either/or mindset - is an additional obstacle to ecological literacy among educated people. We are too easily inclined to perceive scientific and indigenous knowledge, or top-down, or bottom-up, as alternatives. This book is a valuable reminder that the Western scientific tradition is just one among myriad knowledge systems in the world. We need to learn how to navigate freely among a diverse ecology of information actors and resources. We need to foster connections between them. We should look for ways in which radically different kinds of expertise can complement each other. The curious but respectful open mindedness evidenced in this book is a model for the rest of us to emulate.

Even without the encouragement of artists, old and new forms of knowledge are already reconnecting. Neuroscientists have discovered that the boundary between mind, body, and world far are more permeable than modern man, at least, had earlier thought. The mind is hormonal, as well as neural, it appears. The boundary between our bodies, and the environment, is porous. Two-way chemical communications - not just verbal or pictorial ones - shape the ways we experience the world. Mental processes are not neatly contained within the drawn nor even by the skin. On the contrary: in Teed Rockwell's explanation, mental phenomena emerge not merely from isolated brain activity but from a single unified system embracing the nervous system, body, and environment (2005). In a similar vein, so to speak, the neuroscientist Andy Clarke, concludes that the environment does not just influence cognition: The human organism, and the external world, are a coupled and unified cognitive system (1997).

The importance of this new perspective is profound. If it turns out that our minds are shaped by our physical environments - and not just by synapses clicking away inside our box-like skulls - then the division between the thinking self, and the natural world - a division which underpins the whole of modern thought - begins to dissolve. This understanding is startling for us - but its old news in other traditions than the western scientific one. In Buddhist thought, for example, it's been taken for granted for 2,600 years that the organism and its environment are as one. The insights of modern science provoke a renewed respect for indigenous peoples whose cognitive and aesthetic relations to the biosphere have evolved over many thousands of years. Because they do not break things down into parts, indigenous people understand life more holistically than we do. Their everyday experience, being *polyphasic*, enriches their lived experience that people and nature are interconnected. Their holistic understanding and experience of the world makes them better stewards of their environments, too.

Conclusion

We've worked hard throughout the modern era, to lift ourselves 'above' nature - only to be reminded by modern science that man and nature are one, after all. The human mind is hormonal, as well as neural. Our thoughts and experiences are not limited to brain activity in the skull, nor are they enclosed by the skin. Our metabolism, and nature's, are inter-connected on a molecular, atomic and viral level. Our nervous systems and our bodies co-exist within the same, life-filled, environment. As embodied creatures - and like all other organisms - we interact continuously with living systems that surround us.

Various fields of inquiry have explored complex, non-linear and multi-scale interactions between culture and nature in recent years. Gaia theory had captured the public imagination; systems thinking, and resilience science, have gained serious traction in the worlds of research, and even policy. All this is heady stuff - but it is also worth remembering that 'savage' people have known much of this all along. We, too, are born with an inherited aesthetic tendency to appreciate our intimate connection with the world, but our education and culture disconnect us from the earth. If it is true we have a genetically inherited affiliation with the natural world, and that we are, by nature, sensitive to patterns that connect, then those of us advocating for ecological literacy are pushing at an open door.

John Thackara is director of Doors of Perception. A writer, philosopher, and event producer, he leads workshops, and organises festivals, at the intersection between ecological, social and societal change. He is the author of a widely-read blog and of the best-selling book 'In the bubble: Designing In a complex world.'

References

Berger, J. (1980). *About Looking.* London: Readers and Writers Publishing Cooperative.

Buber, M. (1958). *I and thou.* New York: Charles Scribner's Sons.

Clarke, A. (1997*). Being there: Putting brain, body and world together again.* Cambridge, MA: MIT Press.

Dewey, J. (1977). *Early works.* Carbondale: Southern Illinois University Press.

Illich, I. (1993). *In the vineyard of the text: A commentary to Hugh's Didascalicon.* Chicago: Chicago University Press.

Rockwell, T. (2005). *Neither brain nor ghost.* Cambridge, MA: MIT Press.

Saint Augustine. (2012). *The city of god.* New York: New City Press.

Sontag, S. (2003). *Regarding the pain of others.* New York: Picador.

INDEX

A

Adorno, Theodor, 81-83, 85, 87, 89, 194, 196, 200
aesthesis, 196, 199
aesthetic, 9-11, 13-20, 25-28, 31, 33, 35, 36-38, 55-56, 58-59, 61-62, 65, 67, 69-70, 79, 81-87, 89-98, 108-109, 111, 116-119, 123-124, 128-133, 136-139, 141-148, 162-164, 166, 169-172, 176, 180, 184, 187, 190-194, 196-199, 203-208, 212-214
aesthetics, 1, 3-4, 9-10, 16-20, 25-27, 29-31, 36--39, 55-56, 59-61, 64-67, 89, 91, 93-94, 98-100, 103-106, 108-109, 111-112, 116-119, 123-125, 127-129, 131, 133, 136, 138, 141-147, 161, 167, 170, 172, 175, 187, 192-200, 203-209, 212
Alberti, Leon Battista, 187-188, 191-192
anaesthesis, 30
anthropocene, 25, 31, 55
architecture, 18-19, 37-39, 85, 106, 108, 109, 112, 116, 124-125, 139, 141-146, 152-153, 157, 162-167, 169-170, 172, 175-176, 178-181, 183-184, 187-188, 190-192, 212
Aristotle, 93
art, 9-10, 15-17, 19, 23, 25-33, 38, 41, 43-46, 53, 55-63, 65-67, 69-71, 73, 76-79, 81-85, 89-91, 99, 106, 109, 112, 116, 119, 124-125, 131,138, 141, 155-156, 162, 167, 172, 180, 184-185, 187, 191, 194, 203, 209, 212
art and creativity, 43
art and nature, 10, 16, 194
art and popular culture, 64
art practice, 16, 30, 55, 85
artistic, 15-16, 28, 41, 43-44, 51-52, 69, 71, 76-77, 83, 111, 134, 164, 166, 169, 183
artistic practice, 28, 69, 76-77
Arts and Crafts Movement, 11, 84

B

Bachelard, Gaston, 149, 153
Barthes, Roland, 92, 99, 128-129, 132, 143, 145
Bauman, Zygmunt, 18-19
Baumgarten, Alexander, 15, 196
beauty, 9, 11, 15-18, 35-39, 56, 59-61, 65-67, 72-73, 77, 79, 83, 85, 91, 93, 94, 112, 116-117, 121, 139, 141-142, 145, 162, 187, 191, 193-194, 196-199, 203-204, 206-207
Bildung, 69, 77, 79
Bing, Xu, 76, 79
Blake William, 9, 91
Bonsiepe, Guy, 143
botanical, 193-194, 196, 199
Bourdieu, Pierre, 10, 19
Brundtland Report, 13, 55, 134
Buber, Martin, 212, 214

built environment, 33, 35, 39, 116-117, 119, 122, 124, 169, 171-172, 190

C

Chinese aesthetics, 18
Chinese gardens, 103, 106, 108-110
Christian, 15, 18, 29, 103, 111, 180
Christianity, 180
Chuang-tzu, 16
climate change, 9, 20, 35, 41, 43, 47, 52-53, 63, 187, 196, 211
climate crisis, 143
co-design, 134, 137-138
communist, 18, 175
complexity, 25-29, 32-34, 37, 56, 58, 60, 65, 66, 85, 93, 133-137, 178
complexity theory, 65
conceptual art, 69-70
conspicuous consumption, 61-62
consumer culture, 10, 14, 15, 127, 136, 192
consumer economy, 13, 128
consumer lifestyle, 187
craft, 64, 81-82, 84-85, 89, 112-113, 156, 162
Crane, Walter, 11-12
creative expression, 41, 43-44, 52
creativity, 18, 29, 43-44, 52, 66, 84, 125, 137
Cullen, Gordon, 169
cultural crisis, 85
cyclonic change, 67

D

Darwin, Charles, 71, 79
décroissance, 14
design, 17-19, 33-39, 45, 87, 103, 105-106, 108, 111-112, 115-116, 118-119, 124-125, 127-129, 131, 133-139, 141-146, 151-152, 155-159, 161-162, 165-166, 169-173, 175-176, 178, 180-183, 187-188, 190-192, 194, 196, 199, 212
designing, 33, 35, 87, 119, 132, 137, 144, 188, 212
development, 11, 13-14, 16-17, 20, 33-35, 42, 44, 45, 51-52, 55-56, 62, 66-67, 69, 82-83, 85, 89, 92, 103, 115, 117, 128-129, 134, 149, 151, 162, 169-170, 173, 175, 178, 180, 184, 187, 195, 200, 205, 208-209
Dewey, John, 25, 31, 124, 211, 214
Disneyland, 149, 150, 152, 153

E

eco-aesthetics, 60
ecoart, 29-31
ecocriticism, 60, 91, 98, 199
ecofeminism, 26, 29

ecological, 11, 14, 26, 28-39, 42, 44, 46, 55-59, 62, 66, 67, 72, 81, 115-116, 118-119, 123, 125, 133, 135, 156, 163, 169-170, 176-177, 179, 182, 184, 193, 200, 203, 205, 206-207, 212, 213-214
ecological aesthetics, 26, 36-37, 206, 212
ecological art, 28-30, 32, 38
ecological crisis, 11
ecological design, 37, 116, 156
ecological literacy, 213-214
ecological sustainability, 115, 170, 205
ecological systems, 29, 33, 35, 38, 46, 57-58, 67
ecology, 9, 19, 28, 29, 31, 33-34, 55-56, 60, 65, 67, 82, 85, 116, 124, 138-139, 145, 162, 170, 172, 205, 209, 213
ecomodernist, 115
economy, 9, 13-17, 42, 46, 84, 89-90, 127-128, 130-132, 135, 211-212
embodied aesthetics, 194, 196-197
environment, 9-11, 13, 17, 19-20, 25-26, 29, 31-32, 35-37-39, 41, 46, 57, 60, 66-67, 69, 74, 77, 81-82, 91-92, 94-95, 98, 111-112, 115-121, 124, 130-132, 136, 138, 141, 143, 147-148, 152, 155, 157, 161, 163-164, 166, 169, 170-172, 175, 180, 184, 187-188, 190-191, 195, 199-200, 203, 205, 208, 212-213
environmental art, 55-60, 65
environmental change, 31
environmental crisis, 9, 19, 115
environmentalism, 11, 29, 55, 58-59, 62, 65, 67, 73, 112, 136
ethics, 21, 31, 91, 98, 116, 119, 131-132, 138-139, 143, 200-201

F

fashion, 18, 143-144, 155, 157-158, 161-162, 165, 184
fauna, 91, 94, 203
flora, 18, 91, 94, 193, 197-199, 203
FloraCultures, 193, 196, 199
floraesthesis, 196-198
forest, 14, 20, 58, 110, 118, 120, 200
Friends of the Earth, 13
Fuller, Peter, 85, 89, 172

G

gardening, 9, 28, 103, 108, 110-111, 193, 199
gardens, 18, 28, 46-47, 103-106, 108, 111-113, 130, 169
Giddens, Anthony, 81-82, 89
Gramsci, Antonio, 10, 19
graphic design, 18, 45, 133-138
greenwashing, 55, 136, 143
Guattari, Felix, 55, 66

H

Habermas, Jürgen, 10, 20, 81-83, 85, 90
habitus, 10, 16-18, 194
happiness, 9, 62-63, 84, 116, 204-205, 207
Hara, Kenya, 117

hegemony, 10, 83
Hosey, Lance, 115-118, 123-124, 134, 136, 138, 142, 144-146
human nature, 85, 91-93, 106

I

Illich, Ivan, 164, 212, 214
industrial development, 16, 175
industrial revolution, 25, 33
innovation, 39, 89, 157, 161, 208
interior design, 141, 145
Islam, 204-205, 208
Islamic, 18, 192, 204

J

Jolley, Elizabeth, 69-70, 76-77, 79

K

Kant, Immanuel, 15-16, 19-20, 194-196, 200, 206, 208
Keats, John, 91

L

landscape, 13, 16-18, 20, 35-39, 47, 70, 75-76, 105-106, 109, 117, 155, 164, 169, 170-173, 175-176, 180, 188, 190, 197-198, 203
landscape architecture, 37
Latouche, Serge, 14, 16, 20
Le Corbusier, 141, 190, 192
Lefebvre, Henri, 16, 20
lifeworld, 10, 18, 81, 82-83, 85, 90

M

Merleau-Ponty, Maurice, 149, 150, 151, 153
modernity, 11, 13, 14, 26, 28, 62, 69, 77, 175, 180
Modernity, 16, 19, 89
Monsanto, 150-151
Morris, William, 84, 87, 89, 103, 108, 112
Morton, Timothy, 62-64, 66, 115, 117-118, 125
musical, 56, 118, 178, 206-207

N

Naess, Arne, 14
natural elements, the, 38, 87, 106, 108, 170
natural forms, 106, 156
Natural Resources Defence Council, 148
natural world, the, 10, 13-16, 20, 33, 36, 41, 44, 59, 73, 76, 93, 95, 115, 117-119, 123-124, 156, 172, 188, 196, 203, 212-214
nature, 9-11, 13-19, 25-26, 28-29, 31-38, 42, 45, 51, 55, 57-59, 61, 65-66, 67, 69- 79, 82, 84-, 87, 89, 91- 93, 95-97, 103, 106, 108, 109-111, 117-118, 124-125, 128-129,

133, 135, 137-138, 155-158, 161-163, 165-167, 169, 171-172, 175-176, 178, 180, 183-184, 187-188, 191, 194-195, 199, 201, 203-207, 211-213
nature and culture, 10, 14, 25, 175-176, 213
nature, harmony with, 13, 106, 108, 156, 192, 203
Naturphilosophie, 71

O

ocean ecology, 9
organic, 71, 87, 129-130, 132, 155-159, 161, 166, 169, 191, 193-194, 198, 200

P

painting, 45, 76, 106, 112, 116-117, 190
Plato, 15, 20, 178, 187
poetry, 69, 71-73, 75-78, 116, 194, 207, 212
pollution, 41, 59, 62, 103, 119, 175, 178, 187
Post-Christian, 111
praxis, 19, 92
Pye, David, 116-118, 125

Q

queer ecology, 28-29
queer theory, 98

R

recycling, 115, 146
regeneration, 33-37, 39, 76, 89
Rio Declaration, 17, 20
Romantics, the, 69-71, 73-75, 77-78
Ruskin, John, 61, 81, 84-86, 89-90

S

Schelling, Friedrich Wilhelm, 194
Seddon, George, 104, 109, 112, 193, 200
serendipity, 27-28, 32, 38
spiritual, 18, 30, 44, 61, 136, 166, 190, 193, 195, 203-205, 207-208

spirituality, 42, 204-208
sublime, the, 14, 28, 91, 93-95, 98, 195
sustainability, 9-11, 13-15, 17-18, 25-27, 29-33, 35-39, 41-47, 49, 51-53, 55-56, 58-63, 65-68, 81-82, 84-85, 91-94, 100, 103, 108, 111, 115, 116-119, 124, 127, 131-139, 141-148, 152, 163, 166, 169, 170, 173, 187-188, 191, 193, 196, 199, 201, 203-208
sustainable design, 36, 46, 116, 133-134, 136-139, 141-146, 161-162, 166, 175, 188
sustainable development, 13-14, 52, 55-56, 66-67, 128-129, 134, 173, 175, 180, 184

T

Taoist, 16, 18
townscape, 169-170, 172-173
transcendence, 61, 77, 89, 195
transect, 171-172

U

United Nations, 13, 20, 32, 42, 54, 127, 132, 134, 141
United Nations World Commission on Environment and Development, 13, 17, 20, 21, 55, 67, 103, 113, 134
urban design, 35, 38, 112, 170, 172-173
urban ecology, 170

V

Verbeek, Peter-Paul, 117, 125
visioning, 41-44, 53
Von Schlegel, Freidrich, 69-71, 75-79

W

walking, 9, 27-28, 30-31, 33, 38, 47, 59, 65, 110, 117
Winton, Tim, 18, 91-98, 100
Wordsworth, William, 75
World Wide Fund for Nature, 13, 115

X

Xun, Lu, 16, 19, 21

CPSIA information can be obtained at www.ICGtesting.com
Printed in the USA
BVOW09s2359070915

416814BV00004B/78/P

9 781627 345255